WRITINGS BY WESTERN ICELANDIC WOMEN

Edited and translated by Kirsten Wolf

WRITINGS BY
WESTERN ICELANDIC WOMEN

The University of Manitoba Press

The University of Manitoba Press
Winnipeg, Manitoba R3T 5V6

Printed in Canada
Printed on acid-free paper

Design: Norman Schmidt

The poems by Helen Sveinbjörnsson are reprinted with the kind permission of her daughter, Eleanor Oltean; the stories by Laura Goodman Salverson are reprinted with the kind permission of her son, George Salverson. The photographs of Margrjet Benedictsson and Jacobína Johnson courtesy of the Icelandic Collection, University of Manitoba Libraries; of Laura Goodman Salverson courtesy of the University of Manitoba Archives; of Helen Sveinbjörnsson courtesy of Eleanor Oltean. Cover photograph: Steina Vidal rowing out to a big rock (courtesy Provincial Archives of Manitoba, Icelandic Coll. 6, N17235).

This book has been published with assistance from the Icelandic Language and Literature Fund at the University of Manitoba, the Grettir Eggertson Fund, the Páll Gudmundsson Memorial Fund, and from the Manitoba Arts Council.

Canadian Cataloguing in Publication Data

Main entry under title:
Writings by western Icelandic women

Includes bibliographical references.
ISBN 0-88755-641-8

1. Canadian literature (English) - Women authors.*
2. Canadian literature (Icelandic) - Women authors - Translations into English.* 3. Canadian literature (English) - Icelandic Canadian authors.* I. Wolf, Kirsten, 1959-

PS8255.W4W75 1996   C810.8'09287   C96-920159-1
PR9198.2.W42W75 1996

CONTENTS

ACKNOWLEDGEMENTS

For patient and imaginative help, especially with the poems in this translation, I am grateful to Julian Meldon D'Arcy of the University of Iceland, who also read through the entire manuscript and made many improvements, and to Árný Hjaltadóttir for her comments on a previous version of a number of the translations. I am indebted, too, to Phillip Pulsiano of Villanova University for his correction of my initial efforts and critical comments on the introduction, and to Anna Sigurðardóttir, head of the Library for Women's History in Iceland, for her expansion of my initial list of Western Icelandic women writers. I am grateful also to Helga Kress of the University of Iceland for her encouragement and to Christine Stuart Smith and Eleanor Oltean, both of Calgary, Alberta, and Nelson Gerrard, of Arborg, Manitoba, for their help with a number of biographical details. Finally, I wish to thank the Icelandic Language and Literature Fund at the University of Manitoba for financial assistance for this project; and David Carr, Director of the University of Manitoba Press, and the staff, for a pleasant collaboration.

Torfhildur Þorsteinsdóttir Holm

Undína
(pen name of Helga
Steinvör Baldvinsdóttir)

Guðrún H. Finnsdóttir

Margrjet J. Benedictsson and family
(husband Sigfús and children Ingi and Helen)

Júlíana Jónsdóttir

Jakobína Johnson

Helen Sveinbjörnsson

Laura Goodman Salverson

WRITINGS BY WESTERN ICELANDIC WOMEN

INTRODUCTION

This collection of short stories and poems by Western Icelandic women writers spans almost a century of writing, from the emigration and settlement of Icelanders in the early 1870s to their assimilation into a North American culture in the 1950s and 1960s, and includes works by both Icelandic-writing (in translation) and English-writing authors. As a cross-section of representative works, the stories and poems demonstrate a wide variety of styles, from the romantic to the realist and symbolic. Whether the narrator is a male or a female, the contributions are with only few exceptions about women: in childhood, adolescence, maturity and old age, and in relationships as daughters, lovers, wives and mothers. Although the authors are all of Icelandic descent and most of them North American citizens by birth or by choice, their cultural heritage, their nationality, and their gender have different meanings for each of them. Some write as Icelandic nationalists, some write as feminists, and others avoid these issues entirely. But, whatever the particular stance of the writer may be, and however individual readers may assess the quality of the works as literature, taken collectively, the works stand in their own right as socio-historical documents that play against a background of the development of women as legitimate voices in the early history of Western Icelandic settlement and Western Icelandic literary history. From the modest poetry of Undína to the more mature short stories of Laura Goodman Salverson, specific stages can be traced in the development of Western Icelandic women's literature.

Emigration and Settlement

In 1870, four Icelanders responded to favourable reports of North America by a Danish store clerk named William Weckmann and set out for Washington Island on Lake Michigan, Wisconsin.[1] The event marked the beginning of a more general emigration of Icelanders to North America that continued well into the first decades of the twentieth century and grew to such proportions as to cause concern in Iceland that the island would be depopulated. The national sentiment subsequently aroused against the emigration undoubtedly worked to keep the exodus within bounds, and the migration was gradually brought to an end by the return to prosperity in the 1890s and the economic expansion after the turn of the century.

Letters from the Wisconsin settlers to Iceland led more people to escape political dissatisfaction and poverty and seek their fortune in the New World. In 1872, twenty-two Icelanders left for North America, including two young men, Páll Þorláksson (1849-1882), who headed a group that settled in Milwaukee, Wisconsin, and Sigtryggur Jónasson (1852-1942), who left Iceland alone and went to Ontario. Both became instrumental in the emigration movement.

The early settlers fared reasonably well; indeed, in 1873 approximately 165 Icelanders arrived in North America, followed in the next year by another group of roughly 365. In the new country, they spread from one coast to the other, although Wisconsin (Washington Island and Milwaukee), North Dakota, Ontario (Rosseau in the Muskoka area and Kinmount), and Nova Scotia (the Mooseland Heights) attracted most of the settlers. A number of these initial settlements proved unsuitable, however, and were later largely abandoned.

An active search for a colony site within which all the Icelandic immigrants could settle began in 1874. Ontario was considered a suitable place for settlement, but by 1875 it had become apparent that there was no territory in the Free Grant area appropriate for a large Icelandic colony. It was then decided to explore the West, especially the Red River Valley. A party of six, including Sigtryggur Jónasson, undertook an expedition to investigate the area and were favourably impressed. The territory selected for the colony site extended thirty-six miles along the west shore of Lake Winnipeg and about ten miles inland, commencing in the south at Boundary Creek (at Winnipeg

Beach) and extending north of the White Mud River (later the Icelandic River) including Big Island. They named the territory New Iceland, and the order-in-council setting out the reserve was issued that same year, 1875. The region comprised an entirely Icelandic state founded upon a separate constitution that existed for ten years (1877-1887).

Government aid to finance the movement from the scattered settlements in eastern Canada and the midwestern United States to New Iceland was secured, and a group of approximately 280 Icelanders arrived in Winnipeg in October 1875 and proceeded by flatboats to Willow Point, where they settled and established themselves in what is now Gimli. Some 1,200 to 1,400 Icelanders, primarily from the north and east of the island, which had been covered with volcanic ash from the great eruption of Dyngjufjöll, arrived in Canada in 1876, and, apart from a few who went to Nova Scotia, they all went to New Iceland.

The first years in the New World were full of hardship for the Icelandic immigrants. Not only did large areas of the settlement consist of woods choked with underbrush, which made transportation, clearing and cultivating the land difficult, but, also, grain-farming, inland fishing methods, industrial life and lumbering were new to the settlers. Moreover, the sudden change in climate and diet, crowded living quarters (often with cattle and pigs for close companions), and lack of proper sanitation took their toll. In Kinmount, there was, for example, an incidence of serious stomach disorder, and about twenty people died, the majority of them infants. In New Iceland, the newcomers were greeted by mud and pestilential swarms of flies, and in 1876-1877 a smallpox epidemic killed over 100 Icelandic settlers, leaving only eleven or twelve households out of over 100 on the mainland unaffected, and causing the Health Board in Winnipeg to place New Iceland in quarantine for 228 days.[2] In the autumn of 1879, a great flood accompanied by strong winds drove the water of Lake Winnipeg inland and brought disaster to the crops and left the settlers with a severe shortage of hay. At a farmhouse two miles north of Gimli, water rose almost to the level of the bed of a woman who lay in childbirth! Employment, too, was scarce, although, when the large group arrived in Winnipeg in the summer of 1876, a considerable number of the immigrants obtained work. Icelandic women in particular were in demand as domestic servants in Winnipeg and on farms in Manitoba, although at alarmingly low rates of pay. Salaries for those who had some command of English were eight dollars a month, and, for those without, four to six dollars. While most of these women were single, a number were married and had to leave their husbands in New Iceland to mind the home front. The employment that Icelandic men could obtain was usually of a more casual nature and seasonal. Many worked in the sawmills or on the construction of the railroad, while others found work digging the sewers in Winnipeg and spent the spring and summer away from home, while the women remained in New Iceland to look after the farms and the children.[3]

The disasters of the first years in the New World had dealt the Icelanders a severe blow, and the rise of religious factionalism further exacerbated their situation. Two factions emerged, and this caused many immigrants, especially the adherents of the fundamentalist preacher Páll Þorláksson, to leave for North Dakota, while others left for "the Argyle settlement" in Manitoba and for Winnipeg. By the end of 1881, three-quarters of the population of New Iceland had gone, leaving only 250. Immigration into the colony was resumed in 1883, but by then New Iceland had lost its status and influence as the leading Icelandic settlement to Winnipeg; indeed, by 1893 one out of eight inhabitants in Winnipeg was an Icelander, and even today the city has the largest concentration of Icelanders in North America.

For many later immigrants, however, Winnipeg was no more than a stopover. By the last decade of the nineteenth century, many smaller settlements had been formed in the United States, especially the midwestern states, and in Canada. Icelandic settlement in Saskatchewan (the districts of Þingvalla, Lögberg, Hólar and Foam Lake) thus began in 1885, chiefly by new immigrants who only just paused in Winnipeg. However, in the second period of settlement, the so-called Lakes Settlement, which began around 1900, the settlers who moved in had resided for some years in other Icelandic settlements. Similarly, the Tindastóll settlement in Alberta was formed not by new immigrants but by a group of Icelanders who in 1888-1889 left North Dakota. Other Icelandic settlers later left for Calgary, and after the turn of the century some moved to Victoria, British Columbia. The move westward began in the mid-1880s, and, although many continued on to Point Roberts, Washington, in 1894, there has always been a fairly large settlement of Icelanders in Victoria. Settlement in

Vancouver began somewhat later and was slow and irregular since most of the settlers came singly or in single families.

Cultural Life among the Icelandic Settlers

Despite the trials facing the Icelandic settlers and their initial struggle for material progress, intellectual pursuits and civic responsibilities were kept alive with remarkable vigour. Poor, even destitute, though most of them were, they had brought books with them from the old country. By the end of its first year, the New Iceland population had managed to organize its own local government, a village council, whose chief responsibilities were the equitable distribution of government supplies, supervision of sanitation and fire protection. They also established a school in Gimli, for although Iceland did not have an organized school system when these people left, almost every person could read and write, and home education or tutoring by a local church minister was the general practice. The settlers had also managed to procure a printing press and launch their first printed newspaper, *Framfari* (1877-1880). This was soon to be followed by a host of other papers and magazines, including *Leifur* (1883-1886), *Heimskringla* (1886>) and *Lögberg* (1888>); the "church-journals" *Sameiningin* (1886-1964), *Aldamót* (1891-1903) and *Áramót* (1905-1909); and *Svava* (1895-1904), *Vínland* (1902-1908), *Breiðablik* (1906-1914), *Syrpa* (1911-1922), *Tímarit Þjóðræknisfélags Íslendinga* (1919-1969) and *Saga* (1925-1931). These newspapers and magazines were needed to accommodate the enormous literary production that followed in the wake of the emigration. A community library was established in Gimli in 1887, a large community hall was built at Icelandic River in 1886 and one in Gimli in 1893, an Independent Order of the Good Templars lodge was formed at Icelandic River in 1892. As well, numerous literary and cultural societies were established in the various Icelandic settlements, including The Icelandic Cultural Society, founded by Stephan G. Stephansson (1853-1927) in North Dakota in 1888, and The Verse Makers' Club, founded by Sigurður Júl. Jóhannesson (1868-1956) in Winnipeg in 1903.

A number of the local societies were established at the instigation of women. In general, the Icelandic immigrant women were extraordinarily active in community life, playing an integral part in the congregation, in the Sunday school, and in The Icelandic Society, which was founded in Winnipeg in 1877. In addition to sponsoring a Sunday school, the Society worked to help new immigrants and the poor in the Icelandic community. It is clear that the women's contribution to the activities of the organization was substantial, for when The Icelandic Progressive Society, a reorganization of The Icelandic Society, was formed in 1881, its constitution formally accorded equal rights to men and women. In the same year, the first Icelandic Women's Society in Winnipeg was founded, the general purpose of which was to aid people in difficult circumstances and to support undertakings that would assist young and old alike in becoming responsible citizens. Thus, the proceeds from raffles and banquets sponsored by the Society were given to people in strained circumstances, especially newly arrived immigrants; scholarships were awarded to young Icelandic women for educational purposes; and one of the members was appointed to give guidance to Icelandic girls in selecting suitable places of employment. In 1884, the Society inaugurated the traditional Icelandic custom of holding a midwinter celebration (Þorrablót), which at this first gathering featured speeches by Baldwin Lárus Baldwinson (1856-1936) on equal rights for men and women, and by Kristrún Sveinungadóttir (1835-1917) on the cultural position of Icelandic women.

That Icelandic women should be among the first in Manitoba to voice the issue of granting women the right to vote, thus, hardly comes as a surprise. They had received the right to vote in church matters, and the establishment of women's clubs or societies followed quickly whenever an Icelandic religious organization was founded. Early in 1890, *Heimskringla* published a column entitled "Women's Affairs," sponsored by The Icelandic Ladies Aid of Winnipeg. Written by a member of the Ladies Aid, it discussed the affairs of women's organizations and the right of free speech to temperance and emancipation of women. Although the column was short-lived — the women were discouraged by the mocking remarks of Einar H. Kvaran (1859-1938) in *Lögberg* and ceased publishing the column — it nevertheless attested to the marked advance that women had made in securing a public forum in which their voices could be heard.

In many respects, the concern for women's rights among Western Icelanders was a direct continuation of the women's movement in Iceland, which was well under way at this time. Women in Iceland had been granted the right to vote in municipal and congregational elections in 1881, and, during the last two decades of the nineteenth century, the issue of women's rights was hotly debated. In 1885, Valdimar Ásmundarson (1852-1902), editor of *Fjallkonan*, wrote and published an article entitled "Women's Liberation" (1 [1885]:1-2, 2 [1885]:5-7), and in subsequent issues of the paper (11 [1885]:42-43; 12 [1885]:45-47) Bríet Bjarnhéðinsdóttir (1856-1924) followed up on the discussion with articles about the education and rights of women. In the same year, Páll Briem (1856-1904) delivered his lecture, "On the Liberation and Education of Women," and in 1887 Bríet delivered her "Lecture on the Conditions and Rights of Women," the first public lecture by a woman in Iceland. In 1894, the Icelandic Women's Society was established; it was the first women's society with equal rights for women on its agenda, and its establishment marks the beginning of an organized women's movement in Iceland. Finally, in 1895, two women's magazines were established: *Framsókn* in Seyðisfjörður and *Kvennablaðið* in Reykjavík.

Sigfús B. Benedictsson (1865-1951; 1941:3), a well-known poet and printer in the Icelandic community in Manitoba, mentions that before he emigrated in 1888, he had read John Stuart Mill's work on the liberty of women, which Jón Ólafsson had translated into Icelandic, and Bríet Bjarnhéðinsdóttir's lectures. In 1889-1890, Sigfús B. Benedictsson presented public lectures in Winnipeg and Icelandic River on the issue of the emancipation of women. However, it was not until 1893, when he married Margrjet Jónsdóttir, that the two began an organized and sustained campaign that eventually resulted in women being granted the provincial suffrage in 1916 — for the first time in Canadian history.[4]

The Benedictssons' contribution to the cause finds its most concrete expression in the founding of an Icelandic women's suffrage society in Winnipeg in 1908 and in the publication of *Freyja* (1898-1910), the only women's suffrage paper published in Canada at the time.[5]

Whether seen as precursors to the women's movement in Manitoba or as continuations and extensions of its influence, women's societies constituted a rich part of the fabric of the Icelandic communities and were as diverse in their activities as they were numerous. Two women's societies, for example, were organized at Gimli just before the turn of the century: "Framsókn," which was Lutheran, and "Tilraun," which was Unitarian. Another society, The Senior Ladies Aid, was founded in Winnipeg in 1884 and has a long record of service, including charitable work in the Lutheran congregation, support of the temperance movement, contributions to the missionary funds, the Red Cross, the YWCA, Lutheran World Relief, and other relief causes. Yet another society, The Ladies Aid Society of the Winnipeg Church, was organized in 1904 with Margrjet J. Benedictsson as its first president. In 1905, the Society became affiliated with the General Alliance of Unitarian and other Liberal Christian women, and in 1926 the Society took the lead in the formation of a central association of the ladies aids of the Federated Churches in Manitoba, and in Wynyard, Saskatchewan. Later, the Society was affiliated with The Winnipeg Council of Women and The Women's International Council for Peace. Somewhat later, in 1916, The Jón Sigurðsson Chapter, Imperial Order Daughters of the Empire, was founded in Winnipeg to supply comforts to the soldiers of Icelandic origin overseas and to aid soldiers' families in a time of need. It also maintained a hospital ward in Winnipeg and provided entertainment for the enlisted men from rural parts stationed in the city. The membership soon rose from the original twenty to nearly 200, and it is still in existence. Finally, in 1925, The Lutheran Women's League of the Icelandic synod was formed as an association of some twenty local women's societies in the synod. Its major achievement has been the founding of a young people's summer camp at Husavick on the shores of Lake Winnipeg. The members of the League also sponsored their own publication, *Árdís* (1933-1966), featuring material of a religious, literary and biographical nature.

Whether involved in issues of equal rights, in church organizations, in relief agencies or as editors and writers, Western Icelandic women commanded an important role in the development of the early settlement and beyond, displaying a strong, indomitable spirit that matched well the pioneer ethos that helped shape the foundations of their communities. As Wilhelm Kristjanson (1965:177) writes, "Well may the descendants of these pioneer Icelandic women look back with pride on their achievement, and find it a source of inspiration." Yet, while the efforts of the Western Icelandic women have been acknowledged on many fronts, their work as literary artists has remained in the shadows, despite their surprisingly voluminous output in all genres and in both Icelandic and English.

The Western Icelandic Literary Canon

The Western Icelandic literary canon[6] is commonly associated with the works of those writers included in Einar H. Kvaran and Guðmundur Finnbogason's anthology entitled *Vestan um haf*, published as a gesture of friendship to North American-Icelandic visitors at the millennial celebration of the Althing in 1930. Although the book has done much to attract attention to Western Icelandic literature, the editors' selection is somewhat unfortunate, because it gives the impression that there were few women writers among first- and second-generation Icelandic immigrants. Of the thirty-six writers included in *Vestan um haf*, only three are women: Jakobína Johnson, Guðrún H. Finnsdóttir and Laura Goodman Salverson. Other surveys of Western Icelandic literature also tend to overlook the presence of women writers. Stefán Einarsson's (1948:233-255) survey of Western Icelandic prose writers adds to these just Rannveig K.G. Sigbjörnsson and Arnrún from Fell (the pen name of Guðrún Tómasdóttir), and makes brief mention of Torfhildur Þorsteinsdóttir Holm and Hólmfríður G.C. Sharpe (1858-1898). Richard Beck (1950:199-242), in a similar survey of Western Icelandic poets, mentions only Jakobína Johnson, Laura Goodman Salverson and, briefly, Undína (the pen name of Helga Steinvör Baldvinsdóttir) and Helen Sveinbjörnsson (*alias* Helen Swinburne Lloyd).

A quick perusal of the numerous newspapers, magazines, and journals published by the Icelandic immigrants shows how misleading a picture these surveys give of the involvement of women in the literary life of the Icelandic settlements. For instance, Ólafur F. Hjartar's *Vesturheimsprent* (1986), a bibliography of publications by or relating to the Icelandic settlers in the West, lists a fair number of works, both fiction and non-fiction, by Western Icelandic women. The silence surrounding the women writers in these earlier critical works may, therefore, at first glance seem surprising. A clarification, at least in part, is inadvertently given by the journalist and poet Jón Ólafsson (1850-1916), editor of *Lögberg* (1891-1892) and *Heimskringla* (1892-1894), insofar as his words very clearly express what appears to have been the general attitude toward literature written by women. When,

11

in 1893, he established the magazine *Öldin*, he introduced the first issue with a poem by Undína prefaced by the following remark:

So far, women folk have made only a small contribution to Icelandic literature, and least of all a contribution that is of any worth. Why this is so we will not examine here; we only mention this as a fact which is clear to anyone acquainted with literature and who investigates the matter. Probably no other nation has produced as much *verse* as the Icelanders, but of that relatively little is *true poetry*. In *Heimskringla*, we have earlier had the privilege of being able to publish some poems by an Icelandic woman; her poems are an exception to the rule insofar as they are *true poetry*. She calls herself Undína, and we do not hesitate to say that no Icelandic poet should be ashamed of her poems. They will live longer than the papers in which they are published; they will have a future place in Icelandic literature. They give evidence of a strong natural talent and a taste for beauty. In short: they show that Undína is a *poet*. We owe her a debt of gratitude for her poems, and for the sake of Icelandic literature we urge her to cultivate her talent. (1893:15-16)

Jón Ólafsson's words about the literary productivity of women before the turn of the century are on the whole accurate, for there was no real tradition of women's writing in Iceland, and it was not until late in the eighteenth century that women began to make their appearance on the Icelandic literary scene. Among the better known writers are Látra-Björg Einarsdóttir (1716-1784), Katrín Jónsdóttir (1761-1820), the Ljósavatn-sisters Rut (1758-1813) and Júdit Sigurðardóttir (1761-1843), and Vatnsenda-Rósa Guðmundsdóttir (1795-1855). Common to these women, however, is that their poetry never appeared in print. Indeed, as Guðrún P. Helgadóttir (1961-1963: 2, 15) notes, around 1800, writing by women was evidently viewed merely as a hobby for which most women had little time. She also sees this as an explanation of why so few of these women composed long poems and resorted instead to quatrains. From Guðrún P. Helgadóttir's study, it is clear that the origins of Icelandic women's literature are to be sought in poetry and that their form as well as their topics (nursery rhymes, folk poetry and lullabies) are shaped by their traditional activities as housewives and mothers. No sources have been preserved from earlier times about prose by women; one must assume, however, that the women played a central role in the preservation and transmission of, for instance, folk and fairy tales, although they were recorded by men. Guðrún P. Helgadóttir (2, 17-18) draws attention to the fact that *Brjáns saga*, one of the oldest fairy tales committed to writing, was recorded around 1700 from a female informant. It is no doubt telling that the first book printed by a woman in Iceland is a cookery book: Marta Stephensen's (1770-1805) *Einfalt matreiðsluvasakver fyrir heldri manna húsfreyjur* (Leirá, 1800), a work that some critics have asserted was not written by her, but by her husband or brother-in-law (Helga Kress 1977:22).

While Jón Ólafsson's comments on the quality of works produced by women necessarily bear revision in view of contemporary debates on what constitutes literature and a literary canon, that women contributed less than men is a fact, and although Jón Ólafsson does not wish to explore the reasons, it is apparent that they were as clear to him as to anyone else: the traditional roles of housewife and mother placed practical restrictions on the amount of time that could be devoted to literary interests. More significantly, there was little expectation, on the part of men and women alike, that women could fully participate in literary activity. Indeed, it is worth noting that two of the women writers included in this volume, both women who have secured for themselves a prominent place in Icelandic literary history, were single; Júlíana Jónsdóttir never married, while Torfhildur Þorsteinsdóttir Holm was widowed after only one year of marriage, and neither had any children. Margrjet J. Benedictsson's comments in her letter of 6 June 1901 to Stephan G. Stephansson is in many ways quite telling:

> If *I* had been a poet, you would have seen from my hands a poem with a title like "The Poet with a Spade for a Pen." I understood so well what you meant when you said that it was difficult to compose with a spade in one hand. But that's how it goes. The common man — the labourer with the spade in his hand — the woman and the mother never has a minute to herself. (ed. Finnbogi Guðmundsson 1971-1975: 2, 29-30)

Common to many of the women writers who did marry is that they began writing fairly late in life. It is notable that the bulk of the literary output from the hands of Guðrún Finnsdóttir and Rannveig K.G. Sigbjörnsson, both of whom had large households, dates from when they were in their fifties, that is, after they had raised their families. Undína's poetry, on the other hand, was composed primarily between the time of her arrival in Canada in 1873 and the turn of the century; the reason may be, in part, that she became a widow early in life and had to raise three children alone, but perhaps also that she lost contact with the Icelandic community.[7] In fact, only Arnrún from Fell and Jakobína Johnson show an even flow of publications, yet the latter's working conditions, as described by Friðrik A. Friðriksson in his introduction to her *Kertaljós: Ljóðasafn*, were not ideal:

> It is known that she early set for herself a specific working schedule. In the morning and evening she cut off time from her sleep. She also had a different view of free time.... It became a useful habit of hers to have ready on the edge of the stove a book, a piece of paper, and a pencil. If she had a minute or two — while the food was cooking or she had to wait for something — she could read a short poem or a page in a scholarly book or write down a word she had found or a line of verse which had occurred to her. (xxiv)

The acclaimed Laura Goodman Salverson, too, had to train herself to write under restricted circumstances. She remarks, "All those years of bondage to stupid duties had taught me to regiment and perfect mechanical labours to an extent that left my mind free to pursue more fascinating speculations" (*Confessions of an Immigrant's Daughter*, 501) and decribes this training as follows:

> I kept scribbling away, jotting down scenes and dialogues that ran through my head as I went about the household chores.... I could carry on pages of conversation as I flew about, dusting, sweeping, ironing, and baking, and never lose a word of it! I could visualize, without any particular effort, scenes that I had thought long since forgotten. I had only to recall some quaint turn of speech heard in the drug store, on the street corner, or in the theatre, and all of it was there in my mind's eye. Without this ability I should never have been able to write as much as I did write in the next few years. (501)

The privilege of having free time or, to use Virginia Woolf's words, "a room of one's own," seems to have been unavailable to most of the early Western Icelandic women writers. Many of them, in addition to their duties within the home, had to hold down a job to supplement their husbands' income. And yet it may very well have been the pioneer experience, forcing many women to redefine their feminine role within the family unit and within the society around them, that in certain instances gave women a sense of greater personal freedom from constricting societal rules and that, by extension, gave them confidence to write and prompted literary productivity. It is difficult to consider it a mere coincidence that the first Icelandic woman to publish a book of poetry (Júlíana Jónsdóttir), the first Icelandic woman novelist (Torfhildur Þorsteinsdóttir Holm), and the first Icelandic woman to publish a play (Hólmfríður G.C. Sharpe) were all Western Icelanders.

A contributing factor that shaped both the literary production of Western Icelandic women writers and subsequent views of their place within literary history was the difficulties that many women writers faced in having their work published. Guðrún Þórðardóttir (1817-1896), for example, managed to have only two of her poems published, and then only in newspapers. The reason is no doubt twofold: the publishers had little confidence in women writers, and women writers had little confidence in themselves. Undína's poetry, for example, was not published in book form until after her death, although she did make attempts to find a publisher during her life; in a letter written in 1931 to the author Jóhann Magnús Bjarnason she writes: "I have not decided what to do with my poems. I simply was not certain if they were worth the publication costs, and then I have always been so poor — and still am — that I cannot cover the costs myself. Perhaps someone at home would be interested in publishing them" (Jóhann Magnús Bjarnason 1942:275-276). Accordingly, he offered to type her poems, but, even with a typed manuscript in hand, her attempts to secure a publisher failed, and it was not until 1952 that the manuscript was published. Another telling example is Kristín Hansdóttir's (1857-1938) apologetic and humble preface to her collection *Fró*, published in Winnipeg in 1927, in which she writes:

> This little collection is by an entirely uneducated woman, who has no other background than difficulties on the path of life, and it is therefore only to be expected that the poems may contain many mistakes. But I hope that the reader will show mercy in his judgment and consider the fact that the author is an uneducated and old shepherd from the fosterland from around the mid-nineteenth century. . . . All things considered, it is quite daring to let these childish poems appear in public. (7-8)

In fact, almost every author in this collection has spoken of the problem — for the woman writer — of self-confidence, of finding the courage to believe in herself as a writer, and of resisting instinctive self-censorship. Even Salverson comments on the problem:

> Without the encouragement of Mr. Bothwell and his dear wife, Jessie, I should never have dared to attempt a serious piece of work, or come to recapture the hope which had always lain at the back of my mind since that long-gone day in the West Duluth Library, when my heart quickened with the determination to write a book. But to dream and to act are not quite the same. I had yet to conquer my self-mistrust, my fear of ridicule upon the ultimate discovery that I was just what papa would call another miscreant of letters; and I was sorely depressed. (500)

Certain writers, however, were more fortunate in publishing their works. Margrjet J. Benedictsson and Guðrún H. Finnsdóttir both had husbands who were printers and editors. Margrjet published primarily in her and her husband's journal *Freyja*, and Guðrún primarily in *Tímarit Þjóðræknisfélags Íslendinga*, which was edited first by a friend (the Unitarian minister Rögnvaldur Pétursson [1877-1940]) and later by her husband, who, as Stefán Einarsson (1947:17) notes, was the one who encouraged her to write. Stefán Einarsson also points out that in her earlier years Guðrún kept her writing a secret and later made little of her short stories and referred to her writing merely as a hobby. Surprisingly, considering her financial situation, Júlíana Jónsdóttir managed to have two volumes of poetry published, but on both occasions the necessary funds were secured by friends. While it is known that Ólafur S. Thorgeirsson (1864-1937) sponsored the publication of her *Hagalagðar* in 1916, it is generally believed that Árni Thorlacius (1802-1891), a well-to-do merchant in Stykkishólmur, assisted her with the publication of *Stúlka* in 1876.[8]

Women Writers

Undína's poem "Á burtsigling frá Íslandi 1873" ("Departure from Iceland 1873"; *Kvæði*, 5-6) may conveniently be regarded as the beginning of Western Icelandic women's literature. As its title announces, the poem was written in 1873 when Undína, then a young woman, emigrated from Iceland with her family and settled first in Rosseau in the Muskoka district in Ontario and later in Pembina County in North Dakota. She had composed poetry before she left Iceland, but it was not until she came to Canada that her poems were published, first in *Heimskringla* and later also in *Öldin* and *Freyja*. Simple in composition yet rich in beauty, they evidently enjoyed much popularity; Jóhann Magnús Bjarnason (1942:274), for example, mentions that he knew people who could recite stanzas of some of her poems by heart.[9]

Undína's poetry deals mostly with the psychological costs of emigrating: the uprooting, the losses and insecurity, and the departure from family, friends, and everything familiar. Many of her poems, especially her earlier ones, reveal her deep-rooted love for Iceland, such as "Íslandsminning" ("Memory of Iceland"; *Kvæði*, 3-4), composed only a few months after her arrival in Canada, "Eykonan" ("Island-woman"; *Kvæði*, 7), and "Vor í Vesturheimi" ("Spring in the

West"; *Kvæði*, 7-8). Her profound attachment to her native land lasted throughout her life and is still evident from her last poem, "Í Lincoln Park" ("In Lincoln Park"; *Kvæði*, 159-160), read at a festival of Icelanders in Blaine, Washington, in 1937, in which she says:

> Great fortune has led us far to the west,
> Till we finally reached the Pacific shore.
> Of all earthly healers, time is the best;
> It eased our grief, but broke no bonds of yore;
> For though we're here on home our minds are set,
> For who ever learns one's first love to forget?

Most of her poems are highly personal, clearly the outburst of an inner urge, and they mirror her experiences, often bitter, sorrowful and melancholic. With the exception of a number of love poems (e.g., "Ástin til þín" ["My Love for You"], "Þú og jeg" ["You and Me"], and "Ástin er alt" ["Love Is All"] in *Kvæði*, 44, 107-108, 124-126), a few occasional poems and some rhymed letters, her poems are pervaded by feelings of sadness and loneliness. Some, such as "Barnið mitt" ("My Child"; *Kvæði*, 79), "Við gröfina" ("By the Grave"; *Kvæði*, 80) and "Sorgin" ("The Sorrow"; *Kvæði*, 81-82), describe the grief of losing one child after another,[10] whereas others, such as "Helför" ("Journey to Hel"; *Kvæði*, 144-146) and "Undína á hafsbotni" ("Undína at the Bottom of the Sea"; *Kvæði*, 153-154), seem to have been inspired by her unhappy marriage to, and subsequent divorce from, Jakob Jónatansson Líndal. The general sentiment of a number of the poems in this category may be said to be crystallized in the poem "Gamla árið og jeg" ("The Old Year and I"; *Kvæði*, 148-150), an imaginary dialogue between the personified old year (1892) and Undína, in which the old year says:

> The ugliest thing in this world I have seen
> Is the life with men some women maintain.
> All of life's joys are made putrid and mean,
> Each moment of time is turned into pain.
> But as far as public opinion's concerned,
> The rights of women are always spurned.

Six years after Undína wrote "Á burtsigling frá Íslandi 1873," another woman, Kristín Hansdóttir, commemorated her own leave-taking of Iceland in a poem;[11] this is "Kveðja til Íslands" ("Farewell to Iceland"; *Fró*, 19-22), written on her voyage across the sea in 1879. Strong moral and religious feeling characterize most of her poems, revealing her deep faith, as in "Svarið" ("The Answer"; *Fró*, 23), written during her first week in the new country:

> When on the ocean I sailed away
> With no one to care for me,
> To the God of goodness I did pray
> To protect me on land and sea.
>
> Since then the one true Lord so stern
> Has sent me His strength from above
> And taught me how real riches are earned
> From His blessings and His love.

Her interests were clearly wide-ranging, and many of her poems are inspired by current events. Her abhorrence of war is expressed in a large number of poems published as a subsection of her collection under the title "Ýms kvæði á stríðstímunum" ("Various Poems during the War-times"; *Fró*, 53-73). But her collection also includes many rhymed letters, wedding and obituary poems, some written under the names of kinsmen and friends, and epigrams, through which she throws light on a number of aspects of the life and culture of Icelanders in North America. In many respects Kristín's poetry resembles that of Karítas Þorsteinsdóttir Sverrisson (1852-1928), who five years previously, in 1922, had published a collection of nine poems under the title *Draumaljóð og vers*.[12] Apart from "Draumaljóð, ár 1917" ("Dream Verse 1917"; 5-6), "Annar draumur, ár 1918" ("Another Dream 1918"; 6), and the curious "Kveðið um Kanada í Ameríku" ("Composed about Canada in America"; 7-8), all the poems are of a religious nature.

Among women poets of this generation we also find Guðrún Þórðardóttir and Júlíana Jónsdóttir, both from the Breiðafjörður region of Iceland. Guðrún Þórðardóttir emigrated with her husband Brynjólfur Jónsson, a farmer in Valshamar in Barðastrandarsýsla, in 1883 and settled in North Dakota. Apart from two obituary poems, "Anna Einarsdóttir" and "Jón Ormsson," published in *Norðri* (31 December 1860, 140) and *Norðanfari* (March 1863, 23), respectively, her poetry, which includes as well a number of *rímur*, remains unpublished, however, and is housed in the National Library in

Iceland.[13] The other, Júlíana Jónsdóttir, came to North America in 1880. She had originally made arrangements to emigrate in 1874,[14] but for financial reasons her plans were disrupted, and instead she spent the next six years in Stykkishólmur.[15] It was during this time, in 1876, that Júlíana Jónsdóttir published the first of her two collections of poetry, *Stúlka*, which occupies a special place in Icelandic litera-ture in that it was the first book of poetry by a woman to be printed in Iceland. Among the many personal poems, the opening one, addressed to her prospective readers, is significant, not least because it may be said to be symbolic of women and women's literature at the time:[16]

A little maid greets
her countrymen,
young and unlearned,
but not shy;
she seeks acceptance
of kind men,
a fatherless child
of a poor mother.

Her second book of poetry, *Hagalagðar*, appeared forty years later, and, like *Stúlka*, it seems to have attracted little attention, if any at all. Except for the two first poems, all the poetry contained in *Hagalagðar* was composed in North America and gives a fairly clear picture of the harsh fate that met Júlíana Jónsdóttir in the West: after brief sojourns in Garðar, North Dakota, and Winnipeg, she moved to Interbay near Seattle, where she made her home in a little log cabin, but due to financial difficulties and ill health she was moved to a poorhouse. Finally she was taken into the home of Icelandic friends in Blaine, Washington, where she died. Some of her poems, such as "Andvöku nætur" ("Wakeful Nights"; 6-7), "Heilræði til hjartans" ("Counsel for the Heart"; 8-9), "Dauf jól" ("Sad Christmas"; 10-11), and "Eintal mitt fyrir jólin 1914" ("My Monologue before Christmas 1914"; 30-32), reveal an immense sadness and loneliness with undertones of vehement bitterness bordering at times on misanthropy. Her only friend is her "little goddess of poetry" ("Litla ljóða-dísin mín"; 12-13), who "brought out laughter when in secret the heart was crying." Yet, Júlíana Jónsdóttir was not longing to return to Iceland; charac-teristic of both *Stúlka* and *Hagalagðar* is the unusually small number of patriotic poems and the at-times unfavourable picture she paints of

Iceland (cf. her poem "Ísland" ["Iceland"; *Stúlka*, 8-9], which begins: "You ancient land of ice, / infertile is your soil, / windblown and barren").[17]

Like her fellow women writers, Júlíana Jónsdóttir rests firmly in the tradition of the unschooled poet. Her *Hagalagðar* is characteristically Icelandic in containing many rhymed letters, occasional poems and quatrains, in which she is often at her best. Among these, her "Staka" ("Epigram"; 73) on her verse-making abilities is noteworthy because in it is crystallized her sense of cultural and social inferiority, which pervades many of her poems:

> My poetry and writing alone are mine,
> Though to create new roses I cannot aspire,
> For in my youth I had no time
> To learn ought but to muck out the byre.

To be sure, Júlíana Jónsdóttir is no great artist, yet some of her poems, such as "Sléttubönd" (literally "level verse"; 39), an Icelandic term for a quatrain that can be read backwards as well as forwards, reveal fine craftwork.[18]

The group of early women authors also includes two prose writers, Torfhildur Þorsteinsdóttir Holm and Margrjet J. Benedictsson.[19] Torfhildur Þorsteinsdóttir Holm occupies a significant place in the history of Icelandic women's literature for being the first woman novelist, and in Icelandic literature in general for being the first Icelander to make a living as an author. She came to Canada in 1876, where she settled in New Iceland and Winnipeg, until, in 1889 she returned to Iceland. Because she returned to Iceland, and considering the fact that the immigrant experience is not the topic of her fiction, she is not commonly grouped among Western Icelandic writers, although it was in Canada that she commenced her literary career in earnest. Her first two years were spent collecting and recording a large number of oral tales by Icelandic immigrants, which were later edited and published by Finnur Sigmundsson (1962),[20] and in the third year her first short story, "Tárablómið" ("The Flower of Tears"; *Framfari* 14 August 1879, 116-117), was published. In 1882, her first novel, *Brynjólfur Sveinsson biskup*, appeared, a historical novel of seventeenth-century Iceland. Although Jónas Jónasson (1856-1918) in his review calls the book "rather long-winded and boring" (*Þjóðólfur* 24 July 1882, 65), it was on the whole well received and was followed, in 1884, by *Sögur og æfintýri*, and, in 1886, by *Smásögur handa börnum* and the novel *Kjartan og Guðrún*, based on the dramatic and tragic love story of the two noted characters in *Laxdœla saga*. Torfhildur Þorsteinsdóttir Holm's career as a writer coincided with that of the realists, and, although romanticism runs strong in her works, realist strains can be found in some of her writings, especially her short stories. While many of these are fables and allegories, others portray real life and often have as their theme the education of women, which she sees as a basis for their liberation; this view is strongly expressed especially in "Týndu hringarnir" ("The Lost Rings"; *Sögur og æfintýri*, 36-51), which is an account of Jósef Hermannsson's development from youth to manhood as well as a depiction of his gradual change from being a suppressor of women to an advocate for their emancipation.

No further books were published during Torfhildur Þorsteinsdóttir Holm's stay in Canada. In fact, it is clear that during her last four years in the West, when she was on her own and earning her livelihood by teaching in Winnipeg, she had fewer opportunities to dedicate herself to her writing than during the first years when she had been living with her sister-in-law, Rannveig Ólafsdóttir Briem (1853-1916), and her husband, Sigtryggur Jónasson.[21] In a letter to Sigríður Einarsdóttir of 11 August 1885, she describes her working conditions as follows:[22]

This summer I have been and still am in Winnipeg, where I teach a few young girls book-learning and practical skills. The teaching brings in rather little, especially since there is much unemployment here, but I manage. What bothers me most is that I am unable to work on my stories, but the two cannot be combined. I am a painter in oil, but I cannot sell my paintings for a profit. Never have I heard of a piece of needlework that pays. I am good at such kind of work. Perhaps you could give me some advice in this matter? — It is not out of indifference to my people and my fatherland that I am here in the West, but out of poverty. I had no one at home to support me, and I owned nothing myself, that is to say, I had no money. And for every opportunity there was to make some money, there were many competitors. Here there are many more possibilities, and it is easier to make a living. For that reason I came here, and in many respects I have liked it well. Nonetheless, I would not raise my hand against going back to the fatherland if my fortunes would improve over there, even though most of my kinsmen have passed away or are scattered here and there. (Finnur Sigmundsson 1962:xii)

Soon after her return, Torfhildur Þorsteinsdóttir Holm was awarded a state pension because of the quality of her works and also because she was the first established woman author. The award gave rise to much debate, both in the Althing and in the press, and consequently the amount originally awarded was reduced and later included under the widow's pension fund (Finnur Sigmundsson 1962:ixx-xx). In a letter from around the turn of the century, Torfhildur Þorsteinsdóttir Holm herself comments: "I was the first whom nature condemned to harvest the bitter fruit of old, deep-rooted prejudice against literary ladies" (Vilhjálmur Þ. Gíslason 1949:viii).

As Helga Kress notes (1977:28), such attitudes toward women's literature had a considerable effect on the Icelandic women writers about to appear on the literary scene at the time and caused many of them to publish under various pseudonyms. Whether these attitudes are the reason that a large portion of Margrjet J. Benedictsson's literary work, most of which was published in her and her husband's journal *Freyja*, appears under pen names, or whether she considered it inappropriate to publish her own material in her own journal and so concealed her identity as author, cannot be ascertained. It is a fact, however, that Margrjet J. Benedictsson is known primarily for her editorial work and for her pioneer suffrage work in Manitoba and less, if at all, for her literary contributions.[23] Yet, her stories, sketches, poems and translations, which appear under pen names such as "Brynhildur," "Herold" and "Myrrah," are quite numerous.[24] Some of these are satirical in the realist vein, others are profoundly symbolic, yet others are light impressions of the surroundings or of the writer's mood. Written in a crisp and elegant style, they are for the most part inspired by current events; as may be expected, the condition of women is a common theme as in, for example, the poem "Litlu stúlkurnar" ("The Little Girls"; *Freyja* 2:4 [1899]:1) and the short stories "Þau: Æfisaga í fám orðum" ("They: A Biography in Few Words"; *Freyja* 4:8-9 [1901]:154-156) and "Hann og hún" ("He and She"; *Freyja* 9:2 [1906]:29-32).

Margrjet J. Benedictsson emigrated to North America in 1887, residing first in North Dakota and later in Manitoba, and it is probable that before she emigrated she was to some extent involved in the women's-rights movement. However, *Freyja* is to be rated not only as a women's suffrage journal, but also as a literary magazine.[25] Featured were serial stories, original as well as translated, biographical sketches of prominent people, poetry, book reviews and a children's section. It began as an eight-page monthly with 300 subscribers, and at its height it reached forty pages in size and had 1,200 subscribers. *Freyja* ceased publication in 1910, when domestic relations between the Benedictssons had become so strained as to cause Sigfús to put a hold on all mail addressed to the journal and refuse his wife access to the printing press, which he owned. Nevertheless, the magazine played a significant role in the women's movement in featuring material about and of interest to women. Although male authors are predominant in its literary sections — Margrjet J. Benedictsson, Undína, Karólína Dalmann (1845-1921)[26] and Jakobína Sigurbjörnsdóttir (later Johnson) are the only women whose names appear on a regular basis — it seems probable that *Freyja* and, by extension, the women's movement encouraged women writers to make their début on the literary scene.[27] With one exception, Hólmfríður G.C. Sharpe,[28] who wrote the play *Sálin hans Jóns míns* (*My Jón's Soul*; 1897), most of these women writers appear in the first and second decades of the twentieth century, which, incidentally, also saw the publication of Júlíana Jónsdóttir's *Hagalagðar*, Karítas Þorsteinsdóttir Sverrisson's *Draumaljóð og vers*, and Kristín Hansdóttir's *Fró*.

Foremost among these later writers is Guðrún H. Finnsdóttir, who as a woman of twenty emigrated to Winnipeg in 1903 with her husband, the poet and printer Gísli Jónsson. Both as a young girl and during her first years in Canada, she wrote stories, but her duties as a mother and a wife made her abandon her literary activities, and it was not until the 1920s that these activities were resumed.[29] Encouraged by the minister Rögnvaldur Pétursson, editor of *Tímarit Þjóðræknisfélags Íslendinga*, she began publishing her short stories in newspapers and magazines; many of her stories were later reprinted in *Hillingalönd* (1938) and in *Dagshríðar spor* (1946), and some of her essays and talks in *Ferðalok* (1950), a memorial volume published after her death.

Moreso than any of the later writers, Guðrún H. Finnsdóttir writes from the point of view of the immigrant still rooted in the old country. This does not mean, however, that she is unjustly critical of the new land and its ways. On the contrary, she is loyal to her new home, and this sense of loyalty informs her first published short story,

"Landskuld" ("Duty to One's Country"; *Tímarit* 2 [1920]:114-119), in which she describes how bitterly divided her compatriots were in the face of World War I. Yet she cannot help seeing the uneven bargain of the immigrant; as she says in "Fýkur í sporin I" ("Lost Tracks I"; *Tímarit* 3 [1921]:89-93): "The wages of the immigrant are often meagre and always the same. To be sure, he is given land, but in return he gives his life, his health, and all his abilities. Yes, the land absorbs him, body and soul, and his children for a thousand generations" (93). This inexorable fate of the immigrant is always at the back of her mind, and the conflicts of his torn soul are the main theme of, for example, "Jólagjöfin" ("The Christmas Gift"; *Heimskringla* 17 December 1924, 4-5) and, not least, "Utangarðs" ("Beyond the Pale"; *Hillingalönd*, 9-36). Although published late in Guðrún H. Finnsdóttir's career, the latter story probably records her earliest impressions of the new land. It is also one of the stories in which the immigrant duality between the old and the new, between loss and gain, is most clearly and sincerely expressed — through old Una in her response to whether she has disliked it in the West:

> "Disliked it," Una repeated, "I wouldn't say that, but so much of me stayed behind which I always wish I could have assembled into one piece instead of dividing. Our entire past is in Iceland, and the roots run deep in the country where our race has developed for more than a thousand years. Here we cannot teach our children their ancestors' history in place names or show them any physical traces except in words. . . . Then there's the other side, which pertains to life here. The American dream was an incentive to make us work our fingers to the bone. Sveinn's back was bent and his hands were rough when he died, but he paved the way for our children's future and gained confidence in his own abilities. I'm not ashamed and I'm not being ostentatious when I say that I've often felt proud of being able to manage on my own, of owning my own home, and of knowing that my children and I will never be treated as paupers." (22-23)

As such, Guðrún H. Finnsdóttir's fiction forms a transition from that of the older generation of Western Icelandic women writers, represented by poets such as Undína and Júlíana Jónsdóttir, to that of the younger generation of writers like Jakobína Johnson and Laura Goodman Salverson, who are thoroughly North American.

Unlike most of the earlier writers, Guðrún H. Finnsdóttir is optimistic, for she firmly believes in the reunion of the polarized selves through love and understanding and through faith in the future.

This positive outlook is clearly expressed in "Fýkur í sporin II" ("Lost Tracks II"; *Dagshríðar spor*, 207-230). Ragnhildur, a second-generation Western Icelander, has married into an Anglo-Canadian family against her father's will, but her in-laws treat her with contempt, and in their home she finds snobbery, materialism and spiritual poverty, those aspects of North American society that many of the older Icelandic immigrants feared. Ragnhildur is torn between her loyalties to her husband and to her father, between the Canadian and the Icelander in herself, and after a confrontation with her father-in-law, who reproaches her for bringing up her daughter bilingually and biculturally, she returns to her father and to the Icelandic community, where she finds the rich spiritual values and the human sympathy her new life is lacking. In these surroundings, she contemplates her dilemma and eventually manages to come to terms with her situation and herself through her belief in love and the future:

> Ragnhildur still loved her Icelandic heritage and the Icelandic language, but she had acquired the broadness of mind and tolerance only years and experience can provide. And she admitted to herself that the course of events had completely changed her outlook. The young, upcoming Canada was on its way to absorb her nationality, herself, and her child, but she and her husband had managed in time to save from shipwrecking what was most precious to them — their love and their marriage. Like so many others, they had been stranded on the skerries of different temperaments and different backgrounds, but their good fortune had carried them on the highest wave up onto the beach. (229)

It is not without regrets that Ragnhildur sees her Icelandic heritage being subsumed by an Anglo-Canadian culture, but, as she concludes:

> Generations continue to come and go — like the wind that whistles around one's ears — like the leaves that flow on the currents of a river. They continue, century after century, and rarely take the time to look back. And time is like a bird that comes from the direction of sunrise and flies towards the sea until it disappears from sight — or like a cloud of dust that follows a cavalry regiment. The hoof-beats are heard for a while — the tracks, deep or shallow, are imprinted in the sand. The wind blows — the dust of the ages covers the tracks — and before one knows it no traces of them are seen. But the dreams of humankind continue to appear and disappear — and appear anew — and with each new dream a new hope is raised — and with the hope new life. (230)

Yet, Guðrún H. Finnsdóttir firmly believes in the heritage of the race and the survival of its values, a belief that is voiced in stories such as

"Rödd hrópandans" ("The Voice of the Caller"; *Tímarit* 17 [1935]: 65-72), "Dyr hjartans" ("The Door of the Heart"; *Heimskringla* 16 December 1942, 1-3), and "Frá kynslóð til kynslóðar" ("From Generation to Generation"; *Tímarit* 26 [1944]:99-112). In her two last stories, "Ekki er allt sem sýnist" ("Not Everything Is As It Seems"; *Heimskringla* 19 December 1945, 4) and "Sárfættir menn" ("Footsore People"; *Tímarit* 27 [1945]:85-98), she gives examples of how the Icelandic-Nordic heritage can still assert itself in people who would not have regretted abandoning it long before.

While these themes overshadow all others in Guðrún H. Finnsdóttir's short stories, there is no lack of secondary issues and side interests. Her scorn for the hypocrisy of public opinion as well as her admiration of self-sacrifice are expressed in "Kveðjur" ("Greetings"; *Saga* 6 [1930]:21-30) and "Enginn lifir sjálfum sér" ("No One Lives for Himself Alone"; *Hillingalönd*, 55-84), both about a divorced woman.[30] In "Stríðsskuldir" ("War Debts"; *Tímarit* 13 [1931]: 43-47) she describes the sad lot of a returning veteran, and in "Úr þokunni" ("Out of the Fog"; *Tímarit* 22 [1940]:75-84), she shows her antipathy against Hitler's totalitarianism during World War II. Other stories, like "Traustir máttarviðir" ("Sturdy Timbers"; *Tímarit* 20 [1938]:85-91) and "Salt jarðar" ("Salt of the Earth"; *Tímarit* 21 [1939]:40-52), depict everyday heroes, weathering hard years and exasperating companionship with courage and kind hearts. In these two stories, as indeed in many others, tribute is paid to the strong, independent and loyal women upon whose unfailing support the settlers were wholly dependent.[31] "Traustir máttarviðir," for example, describes an old couple watching a thunderstorm destroying their hard-earned crop, which was supposed to pay off their debts and give them financial security for the year to come. On the verge of giving up, the farmer grabs his wife's hand and says:

> "You've a strong hand, Þórhildur; there's a life force in it, I have known that
> for a long time. Once I almost passed away, but your warm hand would not
> let me go. . . . I grabbed that straw which was your hand, and the strength
> which called me back to life was you." (90-91)

As Helga Kress ("Women Writers") notes, the character of Þórhildur is interesting in the context of women's literature. Þórhildur is described as an elderly woman who had a long time before "dreamt childish dreams of composing poetry" (87). However, she had emigrated and married, and her duties as a mother and wife had demanded all her energy, time and attention. "But sometimes when she was alone, the young Icelandic girl appeared in her mind; she looked at Þórhildur with reproachful eyes which said: 'You have deceived me, buried me at the bottom of the chest with yellowed scraps of paper'" (87). In times of distress, the young girl appears more frequently, but eventually Þórhildur manages to arrive at a kind of compromise between the hopes of the past and the reality of the present, between the Icelander and the Canadian in her:

> As she sat there looking over the land, she understood that it was with the bright eyes of the little girl, who tried to compose a long time ago, she saw the beauty around her. . . . She saw lands and seas, towns and farms, parishes and provinces seething with life and activity; she saw her children disappear into the crowds and make their contributions to life and continuity. They were her poems, equipped with life and soul. (87-88)

Rannveig K.B. Sigbjörnsson, Arnrún from Fell and Bína Björns (the pen name of Jakobína B. Fáfnis; 1874-1941) all emigrated from Iceland as adults, as had Guðrún H. Finnsdóttir. Rannveig K.B. Sigbjörnsson came to Canada in 1902 at the age of twenty-two, settling first in Winnipeg, where she worked as a maid, and later in Leslie, Saskatchewan, as a farmer's wife. She is, however, thoroughly Icelandic, and the matter of emigration is not addressed in her writings. Common to those of her stories that can be located geographically is that they are all set in Iceland, primarily, it seems, in Bolungarvík and Ísafjörður, and take place toward the end of the nineteenth century. Rannveig K.B. Sigbjörnsson began writing articles, mostly of a religious nature, and short stories, which appeared in *Lögberg* in the second decade of the twentieth century, but it was not until 1936 that her *Pebbles on the Beach*, a collection of three short stories, appeared. The book was followed in 1937 by *Þráðarspottar* and in 1956 by *In Days Gone By*, which consists of translations by herself and others of her previously published short stories. *Pebbles on the Beach* and *In Days Gone By*, both of which are marred by stylistic defects and linguistic flaws related to her inadequate command of English, were ignored by both the press and later literary historians; *Þráðarspottar*, containing six short stories, attracted a fair amount of attention and received favourable reviews. As Sigurbjörn Á. Gíslason in his review in *Morgunblaðið* (1 October

1937, 5) points out, her stories are not romances in which characters eventually find each other and live happily ever after; instead, they depict ordinary, middle- to lower-class people in a rural fishing community, and with an often almost-disturbing realism she explores the details of domesticity and everyday problems. In her foreword to *In Days Gone By*, the author herself offers a few words about writing and literature in general:

> Writing is a complicated business and has many sides to it. Most people write, I imagine, about what impresses them most. . . . But it is not always the beautiful verses of poetry that settle in one's mind. Sometimes sounds from the world, from one's own life and from the lives of others, come forward instead, and one does not know what to do with them but to write them down. If you doubt this, please look into the newspapers of the world. What do you see? You see news about churches, social life, work and commerce. Fine. Then you also see heartbreaking stories which no sound-minded person could possibly enjoy writing. But it must be done. If a child or an adult falls into a well, his screams call for help. And after you have succeeded in saving the person in danger, you think fervently about how such a thing can be prevented from happening again. And in many cases you do something — yes — a tremendous lot of things about it. Calling people's attention to a need is a very important item for those who write. Especially those who can write effectively. Then there is the reminder of what happened and what helped. That is possibly the most important item to write about. (7-8)

Hjálmar Gíslason and Richard Beck in their reviews in *Lögberg* (3 November 1938, 3; and November 1940, 4, respectively) as well as Stefán Einarsson (1948:25) single out "Hávamál á Vöðum" ("Hávamál at Vöð"; 188-194) as a particularly fine story. Inspired, it seems, by the laws of hospitality in the eddic poem *Hávamál* (*The Sayings of the High One* [= Odin]), the story describes three fateful days in the home of Vöð and the life of the proud mistress of the house, who keeps her dignity to the bitter end. The story, which concludes with the following almost prophetic words of an old and mentally disturbed woman, "There is no point in playing host to the minister if the door is barred against the Lord" (194),[32] testifies to the author's Christian outlook, which, along with her denunciation of humankind's greed and materialism, is expressed, often somewhat systematically and doctrinally, in almost all of Rannveig K.B. Sigbjörnsson's stories.

Arnrún from Fell (the pen name of Guðrún Tómasdóttir) emigrated to the United States in 1917 at the age of thirty-one, settling in Massachusetts. She had written short stories for *Eimreiðin* and *Iðunn* before she left Iceland, and the ones she composed in the West have appeared mostly in *Tímarit*. A collection of thirteen of her stories was published in 1956 under the title *Margs verða hjúin vís*.

A number of Arnrún's stories, including some written in North America, such as "Á fornum stöðvum" ("In Old Haunts"; *Margs verða hjúin vís*, 7-15), take place in Iceland, while others are set in the West. The latter often have first- and second-generation Icelanders among their personae, yet the matter of emigration and life among Icelandic immigrants is never more than a detail. An example is "Goody" (*Margs verða hjúin vís*, 110-125), in which it is only noted in passing that Goody's father, Jóhannes Goodman, had come from Iceland as an infant, and that her mother, Ísafold, was born in New Iceland.

The protagonists in the majority of Arnrún's stories are teenage women, the setting is commonly domestic, the theme is often (unrequited) young love, and the style is usually light. "Margs verða hjúin vís" ("Much Do Servants Know"; *Margs verða hjúin vís*, 16-25), for example, treats of young Daisy's infatuation with the master of the house in which she works, and the bittersweet "Steina fyrir brauð" ("Stones for Bread"; *Tímarit* 5 [1923]:71-78) describes the regretful yearning of Sveina for her ex-boyfriend Gunnar, who becomes engaged to her former classmate Dúlla.[33] However, Arnrún's stories are more than melodramas, for many of them also deal with generation gaps, and in this respect she is a pioneer, for in her writings the modern woman with her own rights and demands appears, who rejects the previous generation's ideas of the role of women.

Like Arnrún, Jakobína B. Fáfnis was a midwife by profession. She, too, had written poetry before she left Iceland. She emigrated in 1923 at the age of forty-nine and settled in Winnipeg, where her son Egill, who had left in 1921, served as a minister.[34] In the West, however, it was not until the mid-1930s that she resumed her literary activities. Some of her poetry, most of which consists of occasional poems, was published in Western Icelandic newspapers under pen names such as Argylebóndi (Farmer in Argyle) or Fjarlægur vinur (Distant Friend), and a couple of these are included in her nephew Björn Sigfússon's edition, *Hvíli ég væng á hvítum voðum*, published in 1973. However, the book also contains a few more personal poems, such as "Finnast þau spor?" ("Can the Traces Be Found?"; 52) and "Farfuglinn" ("The Bird of Passage"; 41), from the first line of which ("I rest my wing on white sheets") the title of the book is derived, symbolizing her immigrant feelings of rootlessness. Like Guðrún H. Finnsdóttir, Jakobína B. Fáfnis writes from the point of view of the immigrant still rooted in the old country, but her poems are highly personal and are not concerned with the issues of adaptation and assimilation.

The phase of what may be called Western Icelandic literature draws to an end with Jakobína Johnson. She emigrated to Canada with her family in 1889 at the age of six, settling in the Argyle district in Manitoba. She later married Ísak Jónsson (Johnson), brother of the poets Einar Páll and Gísli Jónsson. The couple moved to Seattle where they raised a large family and where Jakobína was active in cultural and social affairs.

Inspired no doubt by her father, the poet Sigurbjörn Jóhannsson (1839-1903), and encouraged by Rögnvaldur Pétursson and her brother- and sister-in-law Gísli Jónsson and Guðrún H. Finnsdóttir, Jakobína Johnson began publishing her poems in 1913 in Western Icelandic newspapers and magazines, but it was not until 1938 that her collection of poetry *Kertaljós* appeared, which in 1942 was followed by *Sá ég svani*, containing poems for children. In addition, she translated into English a large number of poems by leading Icelandic poets; most of these appear in her *Northern Lights*.[35]

Jakobína Johnson's poems, whether original or translated, soon won acclaim for their lyric quality and pure beauty, and, apart from the English-writing Laura Goodman Salverson, she is no doubt the Western Icelandic woman writer who has received most attention both in the West and the East.[36]

Jakobína Johnson's collections testify to her versatility as a poet; she wrote personal poems, nature descriptions, historical poems, patriotic poems and children's verses with equal facility. Yet, critics have often drawn attention especially to those poems that, light in tone and mellow in mood, portray the role of the mother, such as "Gestur í vöggu" ("A Guest in the Cradle"; *Kertaljós*, 52-53), "Jú, ég hef áður unnað" ("Yes, I Have Loved Before"; *Kertaljós*, 54-55), and "Vögguljóð" ("Cradle Poem"; *Kertaljós*, 57), and to her nature poems, many of which are rich in pictorial quality and reveal her deep attachment to her home, such as "Hugsað á heimleið" ("Thoughts when Homeward Bound"; *Kertaljós*, 60-62). All her poems speak of contentment and happiness in her adopted country; she is American (cf. her use of "amerísk" [American] in her description of her daughter in "Hún elskaða Sylvia" ["Beloved Sylvia"; *Sá ég svani*, 9-10]) and does not ponder the immigrant's lot as did Guðrún H. Finnsdóttir (Stefán Einarsson 1957:353). Yet, her collections also contain a number of poems, including her longest, in which she expresses her deep-rooted love of Iceland and the Icelandic cultural heritage. In addition to the poems composed during her visit to Iceland in 1935 can be mentioned "Íslenzk örnefni" ("Icelandic Place Names"; *Kertaljós*, 15-18), in which the names of places and natural phenomena are skilfully interwoven to create a charming metrical picture of Iceland. Her indebtedness to her literary heritage, the sagas and the poets (although her poetic talents are also inspired by other sources), is expressed in poems such as "Fornmenn" ("Men of Old"; *Kertaljós*, 19-22), "Leifur heppni" ("Leif the Lucky"; *Kertaljós*, 23-25), "Íslendingur sögufróði" ("The Learned Icelander"; *Kertaljós*, 26-28), and not least "Harpan" ("The Harp"; *Kertaljós*, 92-93), for in Old Icelandic literature and in other Icelandic lore she found themes for many of her most powerful and original poems.

The poetry of the English-writing Helen Sveinbjörnsson in many respects resembles that of Jakobína Johnson in that she, too, favours nature descriptions and children's verses and in that Old Icelandic literature serves as a source of inspiration for a number of her poems. The daughter of the Icelandic composer Sveinbjörn Sveinbjörnsson (1847-1926) and a Scottish mother, Eleanor, she was born and raised in Edinburgh, Scotland. In 1919, she emigrated with her family to Canada, settling first in Winnipeg and later near Calgary, Alberta, as a farmer's wife. Although she had written stories as a young girl, it was not until the early 1930s that she began writing short poems. In her autobiographical sketch, she remarks, "As the work on the farm is very constant, my time for writing . . . was very limited, so much so that these hard-earned moments seemed of the greatest possible value" (21). Nonetheless, her literary output is quite substantial, and her poems have from time to time appeared in *Lögberg*, *Heimskringla*, *The Icelandic Canadian*, *The Albertan*, and *The Farm And Ranch Review*. She also had poems accepted for the *Alberta Poetry Yearbook* and the *Nova Scotia Yearbook* sponsored by the Canadian Authors' Association. In 1973, a collection of her poetry was published under the title *Cloth of Gold and Other Poems*.

Laura Goodman Salverson was born of parents who emigrated from Iceland in 1887 and settled in the North American midwest (Minnesota, North Dakota and Manitoba) and for a short while in Mississippi. The epoch of Western Icelandic literature, if not chronologically then at least thematically, must be said to have come to an end with Salverson. She writes from the point of view of the first English-speaking generation, the first Canadian generation, and in her writings the pioneer experience and Icelandic settlement in North America have become history. To be sure, there are works of a later date by Icelandic women who have made their homes in North America. Mention can be made, for example, of Rannveig (Þorvarðardóttir) Schmidt (1893-1952), who wrote a large number of articles in *Heimskringla* and *Lögberg*,[37] and Þóra Marta (Stefánsdóttir) Hirst (1905-1981), who in 1949 chronicled the history of the emigration in her children's book *Lóa litla landnemi*,[38] but since their connections with North America were limited, it is debatable if the two should be grouped among Western Icelandic women writers. Rannveig (Þorvarðardóttir) Schmidt left Iceland after the wave of emigration had ebbed, while Þóra Marta was born in Iceland of parents who had emigrated to Canada but later returned. Similar circumstances apply to Guðrún Guðbjörg Stephensen (1919>), who co-authored a children's book about Iceland entitled *Sigurdur in Iceland* (1942); she was born in Winnipeg of parents who had emigrated from Iceland, but she herself returned in 1937.[39]

Salverson wrote prose and verse even in her youth. In fact, the determination to be a writer came with her first visit to the West Duluth Library, where the world of books opened before her:

> I could see that nothing in the world mattered, except the faculty to see and to feel and to understand what went on in the world of men, so that it might be caught up at a centre, and called a book. And then, in a blinding flash of terrifying impertinence, the wild thought leaped to my mind. "I too, will write a book, to stand on the shelves of a place like this — and I will write it in English, for that is the greatest language in the whole world!" (*Confessions of an Immigrant's Daughter*, 301)

In 1903 she published her first story in a Mississippi newspaper at the age of twelve or thirteen;[40] however, her career was not formally launched until 1922, when her short story "Hidden Fire" won a prize offered by The Women's Canadian Club in Regina, Saskatchewan, and was printed in newspapers throughout western Canada. In the following years, she became a regular contributor of stories, articles and columns to numerous papers and magazines, including *Maclean's*, *The Western Home Monthly*, *Maple Leaf*, *Toronto Star Weekly*, *Chatelaine*, *The Canadian Pictorial Review* and *The Canadian Bookman*. Many of these stories, such as "Hidden Fire" (*Maclean's* 15 February 1923, 14, 50-51) and "When Blind Guides Lead" (*Maclean's* 1 February 1925, 13, 50-52), a continuation of the former, present a rather vigorous defence of women. They also seem to be based on people or episodes later found in Salverson's autobiography, *Confessions of an Immigrant's Daughter*. The character of Tilly shows strong affinities with Salverson's teenage friend, the Norwegian Tilly Rhinertsen, a "timid little mouse" (367), who was "stoop-shouldered" and "bent as a little old woman" (282) from looking after her far too many younger siblings. The Italian pedlar woman Bianca in "The Alabaster Box" (*Maclean's* 15 December 1927, 3-4, 41-42) gets her own chapter as "Mrs. Yes-mam" in *Confessions of an Immigrant's Daughter* ("Treasured Portrait"; 57-61), while "The Greater Gift" (*The Western Home Monthly* December 1924, 11, 63), one of Salverson's most popular stories, is summarized in her description of her mother in the chapter on "Those Child Transgressions" (132-146).[41] Much the same may be said of many of the episodes and characters in her first novel, *The Viking Heart* (1923), which describes the arrival and ultimate assimilation of Icelanders into Canadian life. The novel is romantic in emphasis, but it is given substance by an authentic account of the domestic life and early hardships of the pioneers. In fact, at the time of its appearance it was hailed as the initiator of a new era of realism in Canadian fiction. This "Canadian epic," as some critics rightly called it, was extraordinarily well received by the Anglo-Canadian public, but less so by her critical countrymen, many of whom were too near to the subject matter to appreciate the story. Jakobína Johnson, for example, voices her scepticism in a letter of 27 June 1924 to Stephan G. Stephansson:

> I would . . . be interested to know on what grounds the great honour she has done Icelanders with her book is founded. — I dislike so many things about it that I have avoided lending it to my American friends. But I had better be careful when speaking to Canadian Icelanders considering how proud everyone seems to be of her. — But do not think that I am jealous of all the festivities and all the praise. (ed. Finnbogi Guðmundsson 1971-1975: 3, 30-31)

In her letter of 3 December 1925, she continues:

> — The most enjoyable I have read in a long time is a story by Johan Boyer "the Emigrants". Then I thought of what Mrs. Salverson is lacking, for then I realized better than any other time how little she has of what is required to write the history of the Icelandic immigrants, not least a feeling for what is national, "tradition and values". (ed. Finnbogi Guðmundsson 1971-1975: 3, 35-36)

Stephan G. Stephansson, too, is unenthusiastic and says among other things that the book is not above average and does not compare with what is being written in Iceland (*Bréf og ritgerðir* [1938-1948]:3, 140).[42]

The Viking Heart was followed by a book of poetry, *Wayside Gleams* (1925), making Salverson the first Icelandic-Canadian to publish a collection of original poems in the English language. In the same year she also published her second novel, *When Sparrows Fall*, which deals with a similar theme of pioneer hardship set in the northern United States. This book has little of the charm of its predecessor, however; in fact, few of Salverson's later novels lived up to the promise of *The Viking Heart*. In *Lord of the Silver Dragon* (1927), she turned to her Icelandic heritage, weaving a new romance out of the Vinland sagas, but the book is little more than a historical melodrama. Her *Immortal Rock: The Saga of the Kensington Stone* (1954), which is likewise a historical novel about Norse explorations in North America, and which won the Ryerson Fiction Award, lacks structure and is hardly any superior. Much the same may be said of *The Dove* (1933), recounting the adventures of an Icelandic girl at the hands of the piratical "Turks" of Algeria in 1627, and of *Black Lace* (1938), a pot-boiler about Louis XIV, his mistress and some pirates. Further attempts to depict the lives of Scandinavian settlers were made in *Johann Lind*, which appeared in serial form in *The Western Home Monthly*, and to some extent in *The Dark Weaver* (1937). The latter novel is of much greater scope and also on a higher level of achievement than the former — it won the Governor-General's Award — but, like her other novels, the canvas is too crowded and the language far too verbose, and the book lacks clarity and unity. In *The Dark Weaver*, Salverson follows the fortunes of immigrants not only from Scandinavia, but also from other parts of Europe, and throws them together in a western Canadian settlement. This is, for Salverson, the melting pot from which the new generation emerges as Canadian.

Salverson's finest single achievement is no doubt *Confessions of an Immigrant's Daughter*, which also won the Governor-General's Award. Covering the years between 1890, when Salverson was born, and 1923, when *The Viking Heart* appeared, it is as much an account of a girl's development from childhood to womanhood as it is a depiction of the process of an immigrant community adjusting itself to life in the New World.[43] The title not only mocks popular fears of ethnic inferiority, it also implies emphasis on inner truth rather than the outer truth of historicity that one associates with memoirs. Salverson is not concerned with the documenation of facts but instead with chronicling selective events, impressions and recollections. These recollections deal on one level with her friends, family and environment, and on another with social exploitation, moral injustice and North American materialism in a male-oriented society. Immigration is a sustained social theme in Salverson's writings, although she does not stand as an advocate of ethnic assimilation, particularly into American culture. "It may be," she says, "that, like myself, some child of immigrants longs to justify her race as something more than a hewer of wood; dreams in the starlight of the lonely prairie of some fair burnt offering to lay upon the altar of her New Country, out of love of a small, passionate heart" (521).

In her *Confessions of an Immigrant's Daughter*, Salverson offers a comment that in some respects brings into perspective — and to closure as well — the history and development of writings by Western Icelandic women:

> I have seen what I came to see. I have seen the fulfilment of a dream. That is something, in a world that prides itself on materiality. A small triumph, for so many years; but a small thing can demonstrate a great truth. That I accomplished so little is beside the point. That truth may serve a bolder spirit to better purpose: what you want, you can do, no matter what the odds against you! (521)

With Salverson comes the fulfilment of a dream that had its origins in the efforts of Undína, Kristín Hansdóttir, Júlíana Jónsdóttir and Torfhildur Þorsteinsdóttir Holm as early as the 1870s — to secure an independent voice as legitimate writers. If, as Salverson remarks, she accomplished so little, that accomplishment builds firmly on the work of her predecessors, who, in their struggles, paved the way for Salverson as they shaped their own histories as Western Icelandic writers.

About this Collection

As editor and translator of this volume, I have found it most gratifying and informative to read and collect poems and stories by Western Icelandic women writers and to present the varieties of background and experience upon which they draw. Constraints of space have led me to include those writers who have to their credit a substantial body of work, and, where this is not the case, writers whose work is of historical, sociological or cultural significance.

In rendering the stories into English, I have kept as close as possible to the originals in an attempt to capture their individual styles and modes of expression, though without doing actual violence to English usage. In translating the poems, I have aimed at retaining alliteration and rhyme schemes and, as a consequence, have had on occasion to depart slightly from the original. I have retained Icelandic spelling of proper names throughout and, in order to keep the Icelandic flavour of the stories, have refrained from normalizing the Icelandic characters ð (the *th*-sound as in "bathe") and þ (the *th*-sound as in "bath"), the accented vowels *á* (as in "house"), *é* (roughly as in "yes"), *í* (as in "sleet"), *ó* (as in "those"), *ú* (roughly as in "lose"), *ý* (as in "feet"), and the mutated vowels *æ* (roughly as in "five") and *ö* (roughly as in "burn").

Notes

1. Weckmann had been employed by a merchant in Eyrarbakki on the south coast of Iceland. He emigrated from Iceland to Wisconsin in 1865.

2. In connection with the epidemic, Lindal (1967:133) comments, "There were many instances of almost unbelievable courage and endurance. Aldis, Mrs. Grimur Laxdal (née Bergman), who was serving as a midwife in the district, was permitted, after being vaccinated, to cross the quarantine post at Netley Creek. During the winter there was a desperate need of medical supplies. On three occasions, Aldis walked all the way to Winnipeg, a distance close to sixty miles. She would, at least the first night, have to sleep outside in the heavy bush." See also Kristine Benson Kristofferson's short story "The Tragedy at Sandy River" in *The Icelandic Canadian* 29:4 (1971):11-14.

3. An especially touching tribute to these women is given by Holmfridur Danielson in her short story "Pioneer Mother" in *The Icelandic Canadian* 5:1 (1946):10-13.

4. For a survey of the history of this campaign and the contribution of Western Icelandic women to the cause, see Johnson (1981).

5. It is generally believed that the impetus for the establishment of the magazine was the visit of Ólafía Jóhannsdóttir (1868-1924), president of the Women's Christian Temperance Union, in the winter of 1897-1898, who spent half a year travelling throughout North America, including Manitoba, and lecturing on the subjects of temperance and women's rights. For an account of her visit to North America, see her autobiography, *Frá myrkri til ljóss* (1935:75-86).

6. This section and the next are extracted from my 1994 article.

7. Cf. her letter to Jóhann Magnús Bjarnason, from which he quotes an extract (1942: 276). See also, Snæbjörn Jónsson's introduction to *Kvæði* (1952:xix-xx, xxv).

8. Júlíana was a close friend of the Thorlacius family. Together with Árni's son, Ólafur, she was involved in the theatre in Stykkishólmur, for which Júlíana wrote *Víg Kjartans Ólafssonar*. The play was performed in the winter of 1879 and Júlíana herself played the role of Guðrún Ósvífrsdóttir. The play, which is preserved in a manuscript (Lbs. 1784 4to) in the hand of Ólafur Thorlacius, was the first play written by a woman to be performed in Iceland.

9. See also Jóhann Magnús Bjarnason's letter of 11 November 1897 (ed. Finnbogi Guðmundsson 1971-1975: 1, 128) to the poet Stephan G. Stephansson, in which he speaks very highly of her poetry.

10. Only two of her five or more children lived. See Snæbjörn Jónsson's introduction to *Kvæði* (1952:xiii and xvi).

11. Only a few biographical details are known about Kristín Hansdóttir. It is known that she emigrated from Sauðárkrókur in Skagafjarðarsýsla in 1889 and that she died in Winnipeg in 1938. It appears that she was a single woman and had no children. Most probably she was a *vinnukona* (maid) in Winnipeg.

12. While it is known that Karítas Þorsteinsdóttir Sverrisson came from Krókur in Vestur-Skaftafellssýsla, the details of her life remain obscure.

13. The large number of manuscripts in the National Library testifies to her popularity and to the fact that her poetry was read and enjoyed until the mid-twentieth century (cf. Lbs. 3472 8vo). It also shows that her *rímur* in particular were popular, especially her *Arons rímur Hjörleifssonar* and *Snældustólsríma*. In a letter of 6 May 1896 with news from the Icelandic settlements in North Dakota ("Brjef frá Norður Dakota"), published in *Lögberg*, 14 May 1896, the anonymous writer says in her brief obituary that her verse-making abilities were great but adds that it is doubtful that people "nowadays" appreciate her poetry.

14. It was then that she wrote the poem "Kveðja til Íslands" ("Farewell to Iceland"; *Stúlka*, 4-6).

15. Cf. her poem "Jeg sit kyr" ("I Remain"; *Stúlka*, 7-8).

16. As Helga Kress ("Women Writers") notes, the poem can, of course, be interpreted as an autobiographical description (Júlíana Jónsdóttir was the daughter of a single and poor mother). But it can also be viewed as a personification of the book (*Stúlka* [*Girl*]) itself, the book being a daughter of a single mother, the woman poet with no tradition behind her.

17. Helga Kress ("Women Writers") notes that the opening of the poem is, in fact, a parody of Bjarni Thorarensen's (1786-1841) "Íslands minni," which was for a long time a cherished national song of Iceland; in this poem he sings of his homesickness, contrasting the flat Danish landscape with the magnificent mountains at home.

18. Magnús Gíslason (1946:2) suggests that Júlíana Jónsdóttir learned verse-making from the poet Eyjólfur Jóhannsson (1824-1911), the son of Þorbjörg Þorsteinsdóttir, who was married to Júlíana's grandfather. The two were raised together, and it is likely that Eyjólfur taught Júlíana to read and write.

19. The latter also wrote a fair amount of poetry; see n. 23.

20. Four of these tales were, however, published by Torfhildur Þorsteinsdóttir Holm herself under the title "Nokkrar þjóðsögur" in *Draupnir* 4 (1897): 161-173.

21. For Rannveig Briem's view of why Torfhildur chose to live on her own, see her letter of 5 June 1887 to her brother Eggert Briem (ed. Finnur Sigmundsson 1961:287-289).

22. Sigríður Einarsdóttir was married to Eiríkur Magnússon (1833-1913), an Old Norse scholar, who worked as a librarian in Cambridge, England.

23. Cf. her (ex-)husband Sigfús B. Benedictsson's (1941:7) comment, in which he draws attention to the fact that she also wrote poetry: "There are many poems by her — and many more than is known to the general public, because it was a habit of hers to publish many of her best poems under pen names. She was a good speaker, even eloquent, especially when she spoke of things that were of interest to her. She wrote numerous short stories, but she rarely attached her name to them. Accordingly, I am the one who knows best what she composed and wrote which may be considered poetry and fiction. In addition, she was an excellent translator after she became good at syntax, which was in the beginning her weakest point."

24. Cf. Árný Hjaltadóttir (1994:97).

25. In her first editorial, Margrjet J. Benedictsson describes the policy of the journal: "*Freyja* shall be completely independent in all matters. Its aim is to enlighten and delight. Accordingly, it will not, without cause, become involved in matters such as religion and politics that are likely to cause dissension. There is, however, no topic pertaining to human and moral issues which it considers irrelevant, and it will not be obliged to keep silent about such matters. . . . *Freyja*'s foremost concern will be developments in women's rights. It will support prohibition and anything that leads to the improvement of social conditions."

26. Karólína Dalmann was born in Reykjadalur, the daughter of Jón Þorgrímsson and Elín Halldórsdóttir. She married Gísli Jónsson, and the couple emigrated to Canada in 1873, settling in Alberta, where they adopted the name Dalmann. Karólína died in Winnipeg.

27. Margrjet J. Benedictsson comments on the matter of the predominance of male authors in her letter of 4 January 1902 to Stephan G. Stephansson: "There as elsewhere one has to yield to the wishes of the buyers. The truth is that the strong attractions — or voices must be included" (ed. Finnbogi Guðmundsson [1971-1975]: 2, 32).

28. Hólmfríður G.C. Sharpe was the daughter of Þorvaldur Stephensen and Ragnhildur Einarsdóttir. She emigrated with her family in 1873 to Chicago, Illinois, where she married Dr. G.C. Sharpe.

29. As noted by Gerður Jónasdóttir (1950:172), Guðrún did not scorn the duties of motherhood, and as such there seems to have been no conflict between her creative urge and her daily tasks. In fact, in her story "Enginn lifir sjálfum sér" ("No One Lives for Himself Alone"; *Hillingalönd*, 55-84, esp. 66) her views on this matter are clearly expressed: "Human beings are like flowers, dependent on the same conditions. We need a good soil, light and warmth, in order to obtain beauty of form, rich colours and fragrance in our lives and our conduct, outer and inner."

30. Interestingly, these two stories in particular attracted the attention of reviewers of *Hillingalönd*; see Guðmundur Friðjónsson's review in *Morgunblaðið* 18 October 1938, 5 and 7 (esp. 7), the review by Á.H.B. in the same paper on 21 December 1938, 5 and 7 (esp. 7), Sveinn Sigurðsson's review in *Eimreiðin* 44 (1938):237-238 (esp. 237), and Einar Páll Jónsson's review in *Lögberg* 9 June 1938, 4. As noted by Stefán Einarsson (1947:24-25), these stories as well as a number of Guðrún's earlier stories are presented as a story within a story; the story is typically related by an elderly female narrator, who speaks in the first person.

31. These qualities are much emphasized in Guðrún H. Finnsdóttir's characterization of her female protagonists; the picture of the typical woman that emerges from her writings is of a self-assured, confident woman, one who adapts to adverse circumstances, one who is capable in an emergency, and one who plays a vital role in community life. As such, her characters fit the character type unique to Canadian fiction from the time of the earliest creative writing up to and including the present time, which Thompson (1991) has

labelled "pioneer woman," and which, in her view, has its origins in Catharine Parr Traill's writings. In these, Traill attempted to help other immigrant women develop the skills required in the course of the pioneering experience. As demonstrated by Thompson, the pioneer woman occurs regularly in Canadian writings, and it is tempting to suggest that Traill has influenced the female characters in Western Icelandic writings as well. Nonetheless, it seems more probable that the Western Icelandic writers turned not to Traill's female characters for role models, but to the strong, wilful women of the sagas, who were likewise pioneers having to cope with a real, physical frontier. That Guðrún was inspired by saga women is evident from her speech "Minni Íslands" ("Toast to Iceland"; *Ferðalok*, 9-25, esp. 12) held in Gimli in 1940: "No less admirable are the ancient women, who stood by their husbands' sides, strong and free, holding their children's hands, following the affairs of kinsmen and friends, and governing their households with cleverness and hospitality. The difficulties of the pioneer years had developed their independence, and a free upbringing increased their beauty and abilities. Indeed, the ancient men admired influential women; that is widely made apparent in the sagas."

32. In her preface to *In Days Gone By*, Rannveig K.B. Sigbjörnsson describes the message of the story: "Efficient people anywhere may become so engrossed in the practical things of life, because they are so necessary, so pleasant to handle for those who can do it with success, the competition is so keen, the stride so swift, that regardless of all that is being done for the good of man, the most necessary things of life may be overlooked as it was in the case of little Guest" (9-10).

33. "Steina fyrir brauð" was reviewed by Rannveig K.B. Sigbjörnsson in her article "Á víð og dreif" in *Lögberg* (3 July 1924, 2 and 7). In her review, she criticizes Arnrún for her description of Sveina's feelings for Gunnar, claiming that she is too wordy. Nonetheless, she concludes by expressing her conviction that Arnrún has many more slices of bread to offer the world and that she will not mind if stones are thrown at her in return. That Arnrún was appreciated as a writer by a fellow countryman in the West is also indicated by the poem "Óður útlagans" ("Ode to the Outlaw") by J.S. frá Kaldbak in *Lögberg* (12 May 1938, 1), which is dedicated to her.

34. Jakobína was the daughter of Björn Magnússon and Hólmfríður M. Pétursdóttir. In 1894, she married Hjálmar Stefánsson, with whom she had two sons and one daughter. The couple divorced in 1906. By that time, Jakobína had completed her education as a midwife and received employment in various places in the north of Iceland, where she worked until 1923, when she emigrated to Canada together with her daughter.

35. In his article "Kveðju kastað á gest ("Greetings to a Guest"; *Heimskringla* 13 October 1926, 4-5, esp. 4), Stephan G. Stephansson describes her skills: "Her accomplishments are enviable, and the proof comes when an Icelander sensitive to poetry finds an Icelandic poem equally good in a language other than his own. This is something she has done. We make particular demands for specific reasons: because of a poetic language and its uncompromising vocabulary. Even when the meaning of the words is strictly rendered and the rhyme fully observed, a work has not been translated if the spirit in it does not come through. The tone and mood of the poetry must continue on through the rewording. Jakobína reclothes a poem so skilfully that it is hardly noticeable: she excels in this uneasy task, patched-up as English is compared to the Icelandic outfit. She also understands that a good translation does not adhere rigidly to the sentence structure of the original tongue" (trans. Finnbogi Guðmundsson 1982:11). See also his complimentary comments in his letter to Jakobína of June 1918 (*Bréf og ritgerðir* [1938-1948]:2, 162).

36. See, for example, Guttormur J. Guttormsson's letter to Stephan G. Stephansson of 22 October 1926: "Jakobína was very well received here. People got together and held

a party in her honour in my home and gave her a gift of money 'with many well-chosen words'. The war-clouds were hanging low during that time, because everyone wanted her. Nonetheless, the peace was not broken. Since then there has been an armed peace" (ed. Finnbogi Guðmundsson 1971-1975: 3, 114).

37. Rannveig was born in Iceland and came to North America with her husband Adam Vilhelm Schmidt. The couple lived first in California and later in Montana. While in North America, she gave numerous lectures about Iceland and wrote a great number of articles, some of which were published in *Hugsað heim* (1944) and *Kurteisi* (1945). When in 1944 she returned to Iceland, she was awarded the Order of the Falcon.

38. Þóra Marta was the daughter of Stefán Bjarnason, who had emigrated to Canada in 1887, and Guðný Jóhanna Sigfúsdóttir, who had emigrated in 1875. In 1899 the couple moved to Reykjavík, where Þóra Marta was born. She studied at schools in Iceland, Denmark and Germany and taught in a number of schools. In 1933, she married Karl Hinrik Hirst, an engineer from Germany, with whom she had two sons. In addition to *Lóa litla landnemi*, she published *Niðjatal séra Jóns Benediktssonar og Guðrúnar Kortsdóttur* (Reykjavík, 1971) as well as articles and poems in newspapers and magazines.

39. Guðrún Guðbjörg is the daughter of Stefán Stephensen, who emigrated in 1904, and Friðný Gunnlaugsdóttir. She received her education in Winnipeg and later studied also at Georgia State Women's College, the National College of Education in Chicago and the Teachers' College at Columbia University. Upon her return to Iceland, she married Páll Pálsson and worked as a teacher. She now lives in Reykjavík.

40. Paul Hjartarson (pers. 1993).

41. "She [my loving mother] was always pathetically eager to plan some happiness for us, to join in gaiety, however tired she might be. Those early years of unrelieved privation had concentrated into one unbearable memory. Her small son weeping out his heart because on Christmas Eve, when he had set out so stoutly through the storm to attend the church concert, there was not even so much as a red apple on the tree for him. She had not wanted him to go, but he had argued so defensively out of his child's high faith. He had been so good — and did not God love good children? He had watched little sister while mamma worked and tried his best to wait on papa, who was sick in bed. Oh, there would be something on the Christ Child's lovely tree for him — he would not be forgotten because he was little and shy and so very poor" (138-139).

42. See also *Bréf og ritgerðir* (1938-1948):3, 117, 162, and 230. Salverson makes the following comment: "It is never pleasant to be wounded in one's dearest affections. I loved the brave past of my little country. I thrilled to the courage of a tiny nation that neither poverty nor tyranny could reduce to spiritual bondage. This courage and integrity of purpose, under whatsoever cloud or affliction, were the qualities that I tried to represent as the payment Canada might expect from my people for their place in national life. However, although I and all my works have been tacitly repudiated by my own people, with but few exceptions, it has not changed my own affection, which is all that matters. There are no losses, except they rob the heart" (*Confessions of an Immigrant's Daughter*, 513-514).

43. Cf. Gunnars (1986: 152): "The act of writing her autobiography can be seen as an attempt to heal the divisions within herself. The confession that is lodged therein can similarly be viewed as an effort to dismantle a myth or a conception that she thinks other Icelanders have of her. Insofar as the book is an *autobiography*, it is a New World *comedy;* and to the degree that the work is a *confession*, it is an Old World *tragedy*.

Bibliography

Arnrún frá Felli. *Margs verða hjúin vís*. Reykjavík, 1956.

Árný Hjaltadóttir, trans. Brynhildur, "The Messenger of Peace." *The Icelandic Canadian* 53:2 (1994):95-97.

Beck, Richard. *History of Icelandic Poets, 1800-1940*. Islandica 34. Cornell, 1950.

Bína Björns (Jakobína B. Fáfnis). *Hvíli ég væng á hvítum voðum*, ed. Björn Sigfússon. Reykjavík, 1973.

Einar H. Kvaran, and Guðm. Finnbogason, eds. *Vestan um haf. Ljóð, leikrit, sögur og ritgerðir eftir Íslendinga í Vesturheimi*. Reykjavík, 1930.

Finnbogi Guðmundsson, ed. *Bréf til Stephans G. Stephanssonar. Úrval*. 3 vols. Reykjavík, 1971-1975.

_____. *Stephan G. Stephansson in Retrospect: Seven Essays*. Reykjavík, 1982.

Finnur Sigmundsson, ed. *Sendibréf frá Íslenzkum konum 1884-1900*. Reykjavík, 1952.

_____, ed. *Konur skrifa bréf. Sendibréf 1797-1907*. Reykjavík, 1961.

_____, ed. *Þjóðsögur og sagnir*. Reykjavík, 1962.

Gerður Jónasdóttir. "Guðrún H. Finnsdóttir skáldkona." In Guðrún H. Finnsdóttir, *Ferðalok. Fyrirlestrar, ræður, æviminningar, erfiljóð*, 171-173. Winnipeg, 1950.

Guðrún H. Finnsdóttir. *Hillingalönd*. Reykjavík, 1938.

_____. *Dagshríðar spor*. Akureyri, 1946.

_____. *Ferðalok. Fyrirlestrar, ræður, æviminningar, erfiljóð*. Winnipeg, 1950.

Guðrún P. Helgadóttir. *Skáldkonur fyrri alda*. 2 vols. Akureyri, 1961-1963.

Gunnars, Kristjana. "Laura Goodman Salverson's Confessions of a Divided Self." In *A Mazing Space: Writing Canadian Women Writing*, ed. Shirley Neuman and Smaro Kamboureli, 148-153. Toronto, 1986.

Helga Kress. "Um konur og bókmenntir." In *Draumur um veruleika: Íslenskar sögur um og eftir konur*, ed. Helga Kress, 11-35. Reykjavík, 1977.

_____. "Women Writers." In *A History of Icelandic Literature*, ed. Patricia Conroy. Lincoln and London. Forthcoming.

Hirst, Þóra Marta Stefánsdóttir. *Lóa litla landnemi*. Reykjavík, 1949.

Jóhann Magnús Bjarnason. "Úndína skáldkona." *Eimreiðin* 48 (1942):273-278.

Johnson, Jakobína. *Kertaljós: Úrvalsljóð*. Reykjavík, 1938.

_____. *Sá ég svani: Barnabók*. Reykjavík, 1942.

_____. *Kertaljós: Ljóðasafn*. Reykjavík, 1956.

_____, trans. *Northern Lights*. Reykjavík, 1959.

Johnson, Sigrid. "The Icelandic Women in Manitoba and the Struggle for Women's Suffrage." *Lögberg-Heimskringla*, 19 June 1981, 9-10.

Jón Ólafsson. "Ritstjóra-spjall." *Öldin* 1 (1893):15-16.

Júlíana Jónsdóttir. *Stúlka*. Akureyri, 1876.

_____. *Hagalagðar*. Winnipeg, 1916.

Júníus H. Kristinsson. *Vesturfaraskrá 1870-1914: A Record of Emigrants from Iceland to America, 1870-1914*. Reykjavík, 1983.

Karítas Þorsteinsdóttir Sverrisson. *Draumaljóð og vers*. Reykjavík, 1922.

Klinck, Carl F., ed. *Literary History of Canada: Canadian Literature in English*. 3 vols., 2nd. ed. Toronto and Buffalo, 1976.

Kristín Hansdóttir. *Fró*. Winnipeg, 1927.

Kristjanson, Wilhelm. *The Icelandic People in Manitoba: A Manitoba Saga*. Winnipeg, 1965.

Writings by Western Icelandic Women

Lindal, W.J. *The Icelanders in Canada*. Canada Ethnica 2. Ottawa and Winnipeg, 1967.

Lloyd, Helen M. (Swinburne). "Outline of My Life." *Árdís* 22 (1954):18-22.

Lúðvík Kristjánsson. "'Stúlka' og höfundur hennar." In *Vestræna*, 210-223. Reykjavík, 1981.

Magnús Gíslason. "Skáldkonan Júlíana Jónsdóttir." *Nýtt kvennablað* 7 (November 1946):2-3.

Neijmann, Daisy L. "The Icelandic Voice in Canadian Letters: The Contribution of Icelandic-Canadian Writers to Canadian Literature." Ph.D. dissertation, Free University of Amsterdam, 1994.

_____. "Íslenska röddin í kanadískum bókmenntum." *Skírnir* 170 (1996):145-171.

Ólafía Jóhannsdóttir. *Frá myrkri til ljóss. Æfisaga*. Akureyri, 1935.

Ólafur F. Hjartar. *Vesturheimsprent. Skrá um rit á íslensku prentuð vestan hafs og austan af Vestur-Íslendingum eða varðandi þá. A bibliography of publications in Icelandic printed in North America or elsewhere by or relating to the Icelandic settlers in the West*. Reykjavík, 1986.

Pacey, Desmond. *Creative Writing in Canada*. Toronto, 1952.

Rögnvaldur Pétursson. "Að frægðar-orði: Frú Lára Goodman Salverson." *Tímarit Þjóðræknisfélags Íslendinga* 5 (1923):109-111.

Salverson, Laura Goodman. *The Viking Heart*. Toronto, 1923.

_____. *Wayside Gleams*. Toronto, 1925.

_____. *When Sparrows Fall*. Toronto, 1925.

_____. *Lord of the Silver Dragon*. Toronto, 1927.

_____. *The Dove*. Toronto, 1933.

_____. *The Dark Weaver*. Toronto, 1937.

_____. *Black Lace*. Toronto, 1938.

_____. *Confessions of an Immigrant's Daughter*. Toronto, 1939.

_____. *Immortal Rock: The Saga of the Kensington Stone*. Toronto, 1954.

Schmidt, Rannveig. *Hugsað heim*. Reykjavík, 1944.

_____. *Kurteisi*. Reykjavík, 1945.

Sharpe, Hólmfríður G.C. *Sálin hans Jóns míns. Leikr í þremr þáttum*. Reykjavík, 1897.

Sigbjörnsson, Rannveig K.G. *Pebbles on the Beach*. Treherne, 1936.

_____. *Þráðarspottar*. Reykjavík, 1937.

_____. *In Days Gone By*. Ilfracombe, 1956.

Sigfús B. Benedictsson. "Sögu-ágrip af hluttöku Íslendinga í kvennréttindahreyfingum í Manitoba." *Lögberg,* 13 November 1941, 3-4.

Stefán Einarsson. "Vestur-íslensk skáldkona." *Eimreiðin* 53 (1947):10-26. Rpt. in Guðrún H. Finnsdóttir, *Ferðalok. Fyrirlestrar, ræður, æviminningar, erfiljóð*, 139-158. Winnipeg, 1950.

_____. *History of Icelandic Prose Writers, 1800-1940*. Islandica 32-33. Cornell, 1948.

_____. *A History of Icelandic Literature*. New York, 1957.

Stephansson, Stephan G. *Bréf og ritgerðir*. Ed. Þorkell Jóhannesson. 4 vols. Reykjavík, 1938-1948.

Stephensen, Guðrún Guðbjörg, and Alida Visscher Shinn. *Sigurdur in Iceland*. Philadelphia, 1942.

Stich, K.P. "Introduction." In Laura Goodman Salverson, *Confessions of an Immigrant's Daughter*. Social History of Canada 34. Toronto, 1981.

Sveinbjörnsson, Helen. *Cloth of Gold and Other Poems*. Devon, 1973.

Sveinn Sigurðsson. "Góður gestur." *Eimreiðin* 41 (1935):257-260.

Thompson, Elizabeth. *The Pioneer Woman: A Canadian Character Type*. Montreal and Kingston, London, and Buffalo, 1991.

Torfhildur Þorsteinsdóttir Holm. *Brynjólfur Sveinsson biskup*. Reykjavík, 1882.

_____. *Sögur og æfintýri*. Reykjavík, 1884.

_____. *Kjartan og Guðrún*. Reykjavík, 1886.

_____. *Smásögur handa börnum og unglingum*. Reykjavík, 1886.

_____. *Elding*. Reykjavík, 1889.

_____. *Högni og Ingibjörg*. Reykjavík, 1889.

_____. *Barnasögur*. Reykjavík, 1890.

Undína. *Kvæði*. Reykjavík, 1952.

Vilhjálmur Þ. Gíslason. "Formáli." In Torfhildur Þ. Holm. *Ritsafn*. 3 vols, vol. 1, v-xii. Akureyri, 1949-1950.

Wolf, Kirsten. "Introduction." In *Western Icelandic Short Stories*, trans. Kirsten Wolf and Árný Hjaltadóttir, vii-xvii. Winnipeg, 1992.

_____. "Looking across Generations: Sveinbjörn Sveinbjörnsson, Helen Swinburne Lloyd, and Eleanor Oltean." *Lögberg-Heimskringla*, 26 November 1993, 4-5.

_____. "Western Icelandic Women Writers: Their Contribution to the Literary Canon." *Scandinavian Studies* 66 (1994):154-203.

_____. "The Pioneer Woman in Icelandic-Canadian Women's Literature." *Scandinavica*. Forthcoming.

Undína

Undína (the pen name of Helga Steinvör Baldvinsdóttir) was born in 1858 at Litlu-Ásgeirsá in Víðidalur, Vestur-Húnavatnssýsla, the daugther of Baldvin Helgason and Soffía Jósafatsdóttir. She emigrated to Canada with her family in 1873, settling first in the Muskoka district, Ontario, and later in Pembina County in North Dakota. In Ontario she married Jakob Jónatansson Líndal, whom she divorced in 1892. With her two children, Stephan and Sophia, she lived first with her father in Selkirk, Manitoba, and later with her brother Ásgeir in Campbell River, British Columbia. A few years later she married Skúli Árni Stefánsson Freeman, with whom she had one son, Walter. Skúli died in 1904, and her son Stephan eleven years later; she then raised the remaining two children alone and supported her family primarily with her needlework, for which she won several prizes. She spent the last decade of her life with her daughter, Sophia (Mrs. H.F. Kyle) in Poulsbo, Washington, where she died in 1941.

Helga Steinvör Baldvinsdóttir wrote poetry before she left Iceland, but it was not until she came to Canada that she published her poems, first in *Heimskringla* and later in *Öldin* and *Freyja*. Most of her poetry was written between the time of her arrival and the turn of the century, although one poem, "Í Lincoln Park," was written in 1937. In addition, she translated poetry from English into Icelandic; it is known, for example, that she assisted Magnús J. Skaftason with the poetry in his translation of George Noyes Miller's *The Strike of a Sex (Verkfall kvenna;* Gimli, 1895). She was unable to finance the publication of her poetry in book form, and it was not until 1952 that her poems were published in Reykjavík under the title *Kvæði*.

"Departure from Iceland 1873" is translated from "Á burtsigling frá Íslandi 1873"; "Spring in the West" from "Vor í Vesturheimi"; "My Love for You" from "Ástin til þín"; and "Ode to the Sun" from "Til sólarinnar" in *Kvæði* (5-6, 7-8, 44 and 65-66).

Departure from Iceland 1873

The sturdy vessel will sail,
Bear the snow-maid over the waves
From the isle of ice and hail
Out across the blue sea-trail.

The clear sun descends from the sky
Into the salty waves of the sea—
Like a gentle tear from on high
Falls from a sorrowful eye.

Fade away mountain tops and farms,
Fade away valleys with great speed,
Fade away linden trees crystal-clear,
Fade away delights both far and near.

I bid farewell to kinsmen here,
I bid farewell to the field in flower.
I bid farewell to the land most dear,
I bid farewell to yesteryear.
                    [1873]

Spring in the West

A mild spring day now gives warmth to the soil,
Flowers are blooming, freed from winter's toil;
Forests are now clad in a dark green cloak.
To be under the branches of the oak
Seems to me the greatest delight.

The manifold voices of birds I hear;
I see the land adorned with flowers each year;
But waterfalls tumbling down to the sea
From high mountains are now lost to me
— I see but brooks and gentle slopes.

46

Delightful it is to live on western soil
And in the wood's grove to rest from toil,
When the evening sun bids farewell to the trees,
And the quiet bird, who lives in the leaves,
Begins its soft evening song.

But my mind still drifts to the land far away,
Where my childhood was spent in laughter and play,
For there I smiled the first smile of delight
– The beautiful smile now lost in time's flight
Like the joyful places of youth.

The memory of you, Iceland, will always remain,
Though I pass my days on a far distant plain.
When I took leave for the very last time
Your beautiful flowers gave me a smile sublime
And softly whispered: "Forget-me-not."
[1874]

My Love for You

Why I love you so dearly, do not ask;
My words are simply not up to the task.
Why does the ocean's roar round the world ring?
Why are flowers fragrant? Why do swans sing?

Know you not how the stars twinkle and pose?
See you not how the wind rocks a young rose?
All things of this world have their calling too,
As my heart was created with love for you.

As from mountain tops the brooks will flow
Rushing o'er rocks to the deep sea below,
Past each hindrance the world can beget,
All my thoughts and hopes on you are set.

As the sun gives the earth life, warmth, and light.
So your eyes, my dear friend, my soul makes bright.
The strength of a magnet, nought can subdue,
And no less is the power that draws me to you.

[1882]

Ode to the Sun

Have you glided away, sun, from the sky?
You leave me so early in the day.
No gleam of light appears from on high;
I can no longer see your golden ray.

You used to gaze down with your shining eyes
Upon one who so much love for you felt.
The peace of my heart in your bosom resides;
And your smile the winter's frost will melt.

Oh, how quickly we are parted from things;
Into the silent shadow I was led.
The dark cloud was borne on thunderous wings
On your sharp brightness a shadow to shed.

The winter time has no warmth or light,
If we cannot see your smiling beams.
Long and silent is each and every night
If you must rise so late from your dreams.

Come, dearest sun, and send me new rays
To shorten winter's relentless hold.
Let the warmth of your heart set mine ablaze —
My heart that is almost numb with cold.

[1883]

Júlíana Jónsdóttir

Júlíana Jónsdóttir was born in 1837 at Búrfell in Hálsasveit in Borgarfjörður, the daughter of Jón Sigurðsson and Guðrún Samsonardóttir. She was raised by her grandfather, Samson Jónsson, and his wife, Þorbjörg Þorsteinsdóttir, at Rauðsgil in the same district. Soon after her grandfather's death in 1850, Júlíana Jónsdóttir went to live with her mother, who was married to Brynjólfur Konráðsson and lived at Sólvellir in Helgafellssveit. Because of the couple's poverty, however, Júlíana was forced to leave home early and take employment at various farms in the district and later at Kollsá in Hrútafjörður, where she stayed for four years. In 1860 she moved to Akureyjar to work as a maid in the home of the minister Friðrik Eggerts. Because of an unhappy love affair, Júlíana decided to emigrate, but for financial reasons her plans were disrupted, and instead she moved to Stykkishólmur, where she lived for six years. In 1880 she was finally able to emigrate to North America. She lived first with her half-brother, Jón Hrutfjord, near Garðar in North Dakota; later she moved to Winnipeg and from there to Interbay, near Seattle, Washington, where she made her home in a little log cabin, which she called Skálavík. Due to financial difficulties and ill health, however, she was moved to a poorhouse, then to the home of Anna and Árni Magnússon in Blaine, Washington, where she spent the last years of her life. She died in 1918.

While still in Iceland, Júlíana Jónsdóttir published *Stúlka* (Akureyri, 1876), whereby she became the first Icelandic woman to publish a book of poetry. Her second collection of poems, *Hagalagьar* (Winnipeg, 1916) contains poetry written in North America. In addition, she wrote the drama *Víg Kjartans Ólafssonar*, which was performed in Stykkishólmur in the winter of 1879 and in which Júlíana herself played the role of Guьrún Ósvífrsdóttir. The play, which is preserved in a manuscript (Lbs. 1784 4to) in the hand of Ólafur Thorlacius, was the first play written by a woman to be performed in Iceland.

"I Remain" is translated from "Jeg sit kyr" in *Stúlka* (7-8); "Counsel for the Heart" and "To Iceland" (the latter read in 1896 at a meeting of Icelanders in Victoria, British Columbia) are translated from "Heilræði til hjartans" and "Ávarp til Íslands" in *Hagalagðar* (8-9 and 48-49).

I Remain

I yet persist on my home soil,
I who wanted so much to flee,
For poverty, fate, and hard toil
Still have new lessons for me.

You are my mother, I your child,
Old isle-woman of the North Sea.
Warm me by your heart so mild,
At last in your cloak enfold me.

It is sweet in your arms to sleep
At life's end, so weary and tired.
If friend have I none for me to weep,
My story's lost, with me expired.

[1876]

Counsel for the Heart

My poor heart, so hungry and cold,
What do you think you are struggling for?
You must bear all the sorrows e'er told
And never defend yourself more.

What I have to teach must take its toll,
Is the hardest lesson to learn;
Those who hate you body and soul,
Are those for whom you most dearly yearn.

For love you always paid the price,
Though it has often made you weep
To think that he you thought so nice
Was a wolf disguised as a sheep.

When by all you are misunderstood
You must accept it none the less.
You must never be seen to brood
During these hours of stress.

Loves are lost, and all goes amiss,
Dear heart, you feel sorrow and pain;
But you were created just for this
And thus must never complain.

Once deserted, to heal the blow
No amount of tears will do.
You may swell, fill, and overflow,
But nothing at all will spare you.

You can take comfort, though, very soon,
For the pain eventually goes:
With your final and mortal wound
As the last drop of your blood flows.

[1916]

To Iceland

Ancient isle-woman in the deep eastern sea,
Your green cape, enveiled in white snow,
Beautiful homeland so full of majesty,
Runic history is carved on your noble brow.

You dig your heels into the ocean floor,
Frost and ice attack and surround you.
You do not budge though battered is your shore,
You never fail anyone, are always true.

Your tongue is clear like snow on mountains high.
Your tongue is hard like steel with its clear sound.

Your word is gentle like a mother's lullaby.
Your tongue is gold and will shine though in the ground.
Far away from your bosom, dear mother,
The currents of time have now borne us.
We gather here as friend, son, and brother,
To honour you, and to send you a kiss.

On clipped wings our minds fly home apace,
Greet the land of our fathers with a smile.
In our mother's fond and joyful embrace,
Rest our unchained spirits for a while.

There are many memories on which to dwell
When nothing overshadowed our hope and dream.
Life seemed to smile at us, all went so well,
How fast time's wheel was driven by the stream.

[1916]

Torfhildur Þorsteinsdóttir Holm

Torfhildur Þorsteinsdóttir (later Holm) was born in 1845 at Kálfafellsstaður in Austur-Skaftafellssýsla, the daughter of the minister Þorsteinn Einarsson and Guðríður Torfadóttir. At the age of seventeen she went to Reykjavík to study English and needlework, and from there she went to Copenhagen to continue her studies. Upon her return to Iceland, she was briefly employed as a private teacher at Hnaus and then returned to Kálfafellsstaður. A year after her father's death in 1871, she moved with her mother to Höskuldsstaðir in Húnavatnssýsla to stay with her sister Ragnhildur, who was married to the minister Eggert Briem. In 1874 she married Jakob Holm, a businessman from Hólanes, but was widowed a year after their wedding. She then returned to Höskuldsstaðir, where Reverend Eggert Briem's sister, Rannveig, was staying at the time. When in 1876 Rannveig decided to emigrate to Canada to join her husband, Sigtryggur Jónasson ("the father of Icelandic settlement in Canada"), Torfhildur decided to go with Rannveig. She stayed with Rannveig and Sigtryggur in New Iceland on and off for nine years. In 1885 she moved to Winnipeg, where she worked as a teacher and a writer until 1889, when she returned to Iceland. She died in Reykjavík in 1918.

Torfhildur Þorsteinsdóttir Holm dedicated her life chiefly to her literary activities. In fact, she has the distinction not only to be the first woman novelist in Iceland, but also to be the first to write on historical subjects. While in Canada she wrote and published two novels. *Brynjólfur Sveinsson biskup* (Reykjavík, 1882) won her instant recognition as an author and was soon followed by *Kjartan og Guðrún* (Reykjavík, 1886). In addition, she published two collections of short stories, *Sögur og ævintýri* (Reykjavík, 1884) and *Smásögur handa börnum og unglingum* (Reykjavík, 1886), the latter intended for children. During her first two years in Canada, she also collected and recorded a large number of oral tales by Icelandic immigrants, which were later edited and published by Finnur Sigmundsson under the title *Þjóðsögur og sagnir* (Reykjavík, 1962). She also published a few short stories in *Framfari* and in Danish and English newspapers in Winnipeg. Upon her return to Iceland, she published *Elding* (Reykjavík, 1889), *Högni og Ingibjörg* (Reykjavík, 1889) and *Barnasögur* (Reykjavík, 1890); she also established and edited the annual journal *Draupnir* (1891-1908), the monthly journal *Dvöl* (1901-1917) and the children's magazine *Tíbrá* (1892-1893). In *Draupnir* she published her novels *Jón biskup Vídalín* (*Draupnir* 1-2 [1891-1893]) and *Jón biskup Arason* (*Draupnir* 6-12 [1902-1908]).

"Two Different Marriages," "The Hourglass" and "The ABC and Worldly Wisdom" are translated from "Tvenn ólík hjón," "Tímaglasið" and "Stafrófskverið" in *Sögur og ævintýri* (51-65, 76-80 and 96-103).

Two Different Marriages

"It's difficult to find an excellent wife. How true that is! It can't be exaggerated how difficult it is. The priest Sæmundur the Learned in Oddi is supposed to have said that if it were known what was hidden in the sea, no one would dare dip his little finger into it. What would this learned man have said about marriage if it had been then as it is now? No doubt something worse than about the sea. Everything is going wrong these days where freedom and heresy reign. Women are no longer satisfied with being in charge of domestic affairs, but demand equality with men. They are more disposed to conform to foreign news in the papers than the words of the apostle which say that woman is subservient to man. They care about neither laws nor regulations and don't obey the king's orders. It would be most sensible never to marry. And yet men continuously do so. As late as today two banns were announced. It really would be best for me not to ask for Rósa's hand in marriage. It's too bad that I've already dressed up like this for that purpose."

"What is it you're mumbling to yourself, Jón?" said a man who had just arrived. "You're all dressed up, and yet, you weren't in church today."

"I've become thoroughly fed up with all these weddings. Because I'm the choir-leader, I'm forced to be present and listen to ten or twelve of them a year. At first, I wasn't too bored, but now I've had it. But how's the service going?"

"It's finished. Otherwise I wouldn't be here."

"That's true. The banns for you and Ingunn of Borg were announced today. How do you feel about getting married?"

"Obviously, I'm favourable. Otherwise, the banns wouldn't have been announced today. Nothing compelled me to it except love. And when love is mutual, one has nothing to fear."

"I guess so. But have you considered the fact that your wife-to-be is an only child and used to being spoiled? It won't take much before she becomes both master and mistress of the house. One has to tame these dear women if things are to go well."

"You really do have a bee in your bonnet as far as marriage is concerned. I've never seen you in such a state. Won't you tell me who the bride of your choice is?"

"It's hard to say whom one should choose when the choice is from those already excluded! Still, I've considered the matter and Rósa of Tjörn has been foremost in my mind, not so much because she's wealthy, but because from a young age she's learned to obey and yield to the will of those who are her superiors. Her father is a strict man and her step-mother even stricter. If one cannot make an obedient wife out of her, there will hardly be many to choose from in the whole district."

"You're going to treat your wife as a slave, I hear. I don't approve of that at all. But it's probably best for those who think like that to get the most compliant wife," the man who was called Gísli said. "But actually, I need to get hold of my neighbour Friðrik in Háholt. Goodbye." They then parted.

After the service, there was a lot of hustle and bustle among the church-goers. Some went to the vicarage, others to their horses and left. Among those who left were Gísli and Ingunn, who lived on the same farm. Gísli had just inherited a considerable sum of money from his parents and wanted to start farming, but Ingunn was poor and of humble descent. Nonetheless, Gísli was optimistic about their marriage, because they loved each other dearly, and, quite frankly, it had never occurred to him to tame his wife or make her submissive like Jón, the man he had spoken to, intended to do. In addition to being the choir-leader, Jón was the minister's farm manager. He was suspicious and strict, but was otherwise considered a nice man. As we have discovered, he was also thinking about getting married just like Gísli, although his thoughts in that direction had a different objective. Jón thought to himself: "If I can just make Rósa subservient to me, then the marriage will be as it ought to be." Gísli, on the other hand, thought: "If I can just win Ingunn's love, then the marriage will be as it ought to be." One believed in love, the other in reason. And yet, are

55

these so different that they cannot be combined? Let us now examine these two men's married lives.

Although Jón had his doubts, he carried out his intention of proposing. A little later that day, he rode with his master to Tjörn to ask for the hand of Rósa, the daughter of the farmer there. She was not at home when they arrived, but her father was, and that was sufficient. Jón broached the subject. The farmer took it well, for he knew that Jón was reasonably well off, tight-fisted, and likely to become a good farmer. These were qualities he seemed to know would and should be appreciated by all women. The farmer thus promised him his daughter in marriage, although she was not present.

About this time, the minister had to consecrate his neighbouring minister, and for this reason Gísli and Ingunn's wedding had to be postponed, because one bann still had to be announced. Jón made use of this delay and hurried to buy a special licence in order to be able to celebrate his wedding together with Gísli's and thus save some money on the banquet.

In due time, the minister married both couples. Gísli moved to a place called Núpakot, in which he owned a share, and Jón bought a very good piece of land called Miðskáli. Both hired servants and started farming, and time passed without any noteworthy events.

One day, when the minister had finished the service and the members of the congregation were about to leave the church, the minister said that he had to discuss a problem with the foremost farmers and requested to speak with them.

"The fact of the matter is," he began by saying, "that the children in Kambselur are in deep trouble. Both of their parents are now dead; their mother passed away yesterday. All the district's funds have been allocated to other causes, so the parish executive officer and I now have no other choice but to knock on the door of mercy of those who can help and ask that they take them until the next district meeting. We cannot at this point promise any recompense. But we all know that charitable work is never unpaid and constitutes in itself great merit."

Everyone became silent at this speech, and the minister continued: "I've promised to take one child, and Jón, my assistant, another, or at least share it with Hálfdan, his neighbour. But there are four left.

We trust in your benevolence, that you give sympathetic considera-
tion to this matter."

Now those who were present began to deliberate the matter at
length, and after some discussion some men agreed together to take
two children. But still two were left, the youngest.

"How about you, Gísli," the minister said. "Aren't you going to
give a helping hand? You can afford it."

"Yes, I probably will, but to what extent I cannot say until I've
spoken with my wife."

Those who were present looked at each other with raised eyebrows, but it was Jón of Miðskáli who said out loud what everyone
was thinking:

"Since you're so henpecked, you ought to bring your wife to
meetings, so that you don't have to go to so much trouble to get
permission."

"That's uncalled for," said Gísli. "I don't mind going to the trouble
of letting you know the outcome when I've spoken with her. And I
don't take your calling me henpecked to heart. On the contrary, I'm
happy to have a wife whom I can consult. Her advice has always
brought me luck and honour. Is it better to suppress one's wife rather
than to have her as one's adviser? It's not that she won't allow me to
do as I see fit; the fact is that I won't, because I love her."

Having said this, Gísli took his hat and left. The others remained
at the meeting until the early evening, and yet no solution was found.

"I've agreed to take one of the Selur children part-time until the
spring," Jón of Miðskáli said to his wife when he came home from
church in the evening. "I prefer to take Stína, because she can look
after the child. It's better to make that kind of use of her than none."

"Yes, we have to get someone for that," Rósa said, "but I'd
promised to hire Ingibjörg of Gerður's eldest daughter for a while.
Ingibjörg is so very poor that I consider it a deed of charity to give her
preference. As a matter of fact, we could take both of them."

"Nonsense. I won't take any of that riff-raff."

"You weren't against the idea last winter when I mentioned it to
you," said Rósa.

"So what! I'm against it now and won't hear any more about it. I'm
the one who decides and not you."

Having said this, he sat down to eat, but she went to the kitchen without saying anything and cried.

"Why are you so sad, Mum?" asked the two children who just came in.

"Because Dad wouldn't let her hire Gudda of Gerður," said the third child, a seven-year-old boy.

"Yet he once said that she might," one of the children said.

"Yes, but he always lets her down when he's promised her something," another child interrupted.

Rósa either didn't hear the children's conversation or pretended that she didn't and sat and stared into the fire. She probably knew the proverb which says: Sit by the fire if you are ill or life is no thrill. But all of a sudden, she heard the blustering voice of her husband, who said:

"What's the meaning of this? I need my everyday clothes. I want them immediately."

His wife jumped up from the fire, and the children rushed into a dark corner.

"Now Dad is angry," they said.

It took her a while to find the clothes, because Jón had flung them far and wide in the morning, and his wife hadn't gathered them together, because her neighbour had been visiting during the day. The hours when Jón was away were the only happy ones in this miserable home, because miserable it was even though it had more than enough money. His wife, his children, and his servants — they were all trembling and fearful. His wife was, however, his most obedient servant, because when he beckoned she ran. As one would expect, he never asked for her advice, because he considered it an insult to his honour to say: "Should I do this?" He was accustomed to saying "I did this," whether she liked it or not. Everywhere he dogged her footsteps with bickering and reprimands. The minute he rode into the farmyard or if he made his appearance somewhere, a dark cloud spread over the face of everyone in the household. But despite this life which was so far from what it ought to be, his wealth did not leave him in the lurch. Thus ended this and all other evenings in Jón's home. — But let us now turn to Gísli as he rode from the church.

He was in a bad mood, but was not quite sure why. The word

'henpecked' had hit him harder than he wanted to admit. When he rode into the farmyard his wife stood outside to greet him.

"I was getting bored of waiting for you," she said, "and I was beginning to think that you'd stayed overnight with the minister. But thank God you're home."

"Yes, I was held up at the church longer than I'd anticipated. There was some sort of district meeting after the service about the children at Selur."

"Does the district have to make arrangements for them?" Ingunn asked.

"Yes, I think so. The minister said that the mother has also died."

"That's dreadful! The poor children!"

"Do you think it's dreadful that an old woman kicks the bucket?" asked Gísli.

"Yes, under such circumstances. But come in. I can hear that you're not in the best of moods."

"I was told by Jón of Miðskáli that he thought I was in a hurry to speak with you. He said it would be best for me to bring you to each meeting, so that I'd know what I should do. He accused me of being henpecked."

"Why did he do that?"

"Because I wouldn't take any of the children before I'd discussed the matter with you."

"But why don't you ever want to do anything before you've discussed it with me? Am I such a shrew? Or don't you know that I do everything you want?"

"That's exactly why I don't want to do anything without your knowledge. Besides, what was I to do? I didn't know the exact situation with regard to beds or food supply, and least of all if I could place such a burden on you. I also find that the best solution to a problem is found when we discuss it."

"But do we have to be embarrassed about that?" said Ingunn.

"I admitted that I loved you and that I didn't think a good solution could be found except if you were present. But never mind about that. — What kind of help should we offer in this situation? We have five children ourselves. Can we take on more?"

"Let's think about that tomorrow. But that reminds me. Gunnlaugur of Eyr came here today. He lost the cow that calves early in the spring and asked if we could lend him a cow for a while."

"What did you say?"

"I told him to come back tomorrow when you were at home."

"What business is that of mine? Do I know how much milk you have? People probably think that I'm always watching over you and that you daren't do anything without my permission. And yet you know that I'd never overrule you. You ought to have lent him the cow if you can be without it. The poor man probably needed the milk."

"And the poor children probably needed shelter," said Ingunn and smiled. "But since we're both so dependent on each other in each our own way, we should discuss things as we always do and then not talk more about it for the time being."

Every sign of discontent had left Gísli's face, and peace, happiness, and harmony reigned in Núpakot between the couple and among the children and the servants, and they always all looked forward to his coming home.

The next morning the couple sent for two children, Þorketill and Kristveig, for whom no arrangements had been made. And that was the end of the matter. Both children were very young, because others had taken the older ones. When, at the meeting of the district in the spring, the children were to be placed on the various farms as farmhands and maids, they didn't have the heart to let them be sent from place to place and kept them without any payment.

Jón of Miðskáli kept his child for half of the season, as he had promised, and although his wife wanted to keep her longer, it was out of the question. She didn't get to hire Gudda of Gerður either, even though she had promised to do so, but in order not to be a complete cheat or in order to make good as best she could, Rósa often tried to slip to her clothes or food without her husband's knowing.

Thus time passed until Jón's and Gísli's children had grown up. Then fate decided that after twenty-six years Jón and Gísli once again shared a wedding celebration. Gísli's son Jónas married his foster-sister Kristveig, whom he loved and who loved him, and Brynjólfur, Jón of Miðskáli's son, married a well-to-do farmer's daughter in the area and intended to take over his father's farm, as Jón was becoming tired of all the work. The wedding celebration took place in the vicarage. After the wedding, Jón and Gísli met at the exact same spot where they had spoken about marriage before their own weddings. Both were a little tipsy from the wine. Gísli initiated the conversation and said:

"Hello, fellow! How are you? Many things have happened since we sat here by the brook many years ago. Let the young people enjoy themselves singing inside while you tell me your views on marriage now. When we last spoke, we had different opinions on it, but now we both have the experience."

"Both good and bad can be said about it," answered Jón, "depending on how one approaches the matter, but 'the fewest words bear the least responsibility.'"

"Yes, that's what the proverb says," said Gísli, "but there's also another proverb which says that 'a drunken man speaks from the bottom of his heart' and that may prove true of both of us."

"Alright. I don't mind giving you my opinion. Marriage is, like life itself, nothing but difficulties and worries which no amount of sunshine can brighten."

"Ugh! Don't speak like that, man! Can anybody possibly think like that?"

"Yes, my wife and I are so very different, and I've always had to keep an eye on her, so that she doesn't slacken off on her housework, and her wailing and worrying have often annoyed me. But I have taken care not to give in to her whims, because then things would really have gotten out of hand."

"Yes, but in this respect you have overlooked something. If you'd given in to her, you'd have won her love and trust, and when that has been won, a solid and proper basis for a happy marriage has been laid. But the children have no doubt brought you much joy."

"Oh no! Far from it! They are all very different from me in character. They have their mother's temperament. As a result, they have turned to her and cling to her. What I request them to do, they do with a sour face. When they want something, they demand instead of asking, just like their mother. If they get what they want, they grab it like dogs. If they don't, they go their own way with a defiant smile on their faces. You can imagine how depressing this ingratitude and indifference are."

"My dear Jón. It's all because you've alienated them from you already in childhood by being inconsiderate and harsh. Children are sensitive and cannot take such treatment. But doesn't your wealth bring you joy?"

"No, not my wealth either! Of course, I cannot help doing my best to take care of it. But there are too many parasites — my wife, my children, the paupers, the minister, the church, the sheriff, and many others, so I cannot really enjoy it. I'm all these people's slave. My own personal pleasure is to put my lips to this."

As he said this, he took a flask out of his pocket, took a sip, and handed it to Gísli.

"When I slake my thirst on this, Gísli, I drown my worries for a while, but later they awaken again with renewed vigour. It also happens that when I've had a little, I almost become so gentle that I want to embrace and kiss my wife, but then she avoids me as if I were a ravenous lion or I don't know what."

"That's because you're normally so difficult. But it's also because we from early on had different views on married life, and indeed, it's turned out a very different experience for both of us. In my opinion all your unhappiness is due to the fact that you chose a wife according to your head and not your heart. In other words: you chose a woman whom you didn't love. You wanted a compliant wife, but paid no attention to the fact that love and compliance go hand in hand. If the heart is left out in these matters, then things turn out the way they have — or worse, if worse men are involved. It's obvious when a husband's and a wife's relationship is no better than that between cats and dogs. I was happy when a long time ago the banns were announced for Ingunn and me, but I'm even happier now. Back then I lived in hope, but now in knowledge, as the Bible says. The two of us have always been in agreement and harmony. Neither of us has dominated the other, and we have always consulted each other. That's why you once called me henpecked. Yet my being henpecked has proven to be better than your and other people's dictatorship. The child from Kambselur, which you took for a part of the season, still hardly earns her keep, and yet Stína, poor thing, is not so stupid. But she was sent from place to place, because you wouldn't give in to your wife and keep her longer, not even for the entire winter. At Hálfdan's, she led a life of misery, so that your good deed was all for nothing. Then she continuously got bad positions, poor soul! But the children we took are faring well, I think. At least it seems to me that my Veiga looks pretty good as a bride today. She's been as dutiful to me as my own children, and she has truly brought me much joy. Little Ketill is now apprenticed to a carpenter in the north, and I hope he'll become an industrious and fine lad. If I hadn't consulted my wife, I'd have taken only one child and it's uncertain for how long. But thank God things worked out the way they did. I'm quite well off, but there's no wealth which I cherish more than my wife and my children. We share good and bad times, and for them I save whatever may be left from what I owe the servants, the parish, and whoever, and I hope there will be no parasites, because I'm sure I haven't exploited the homes of widows and fatherless children. Yes, I'm much happier today than I was as a bridegroom. But we've been here much too long reviving old memories. Let's go home. I think my wife must have begun wondering about me."

"My wife doesn't worry about me. The longer I'm away the happier she probably is," said Jón and took a sip from the flask in order to console himself. After that they went home.

The festivities were held with pomp and propriety. The guests drank to the bridal pair's health and then to the parents-in-law. The men smilingly raised their glasses, and Gísli said:

"Long live love and reason. And may they always come hand in hand."

After the festivities, everyone went home. But there is nothing further said about what part love and reason played in the life of the young couples.

[1884]

The Hourglass

"Dad," said little Sigvaldi, "look how the margin on the upper glass gets bigger while the bottom of the hourglass slowly fills up, and yet so very little sand runs down, only a few grains at a time!"

"They are very many, my boy," said the father, "and even if only one grain of sand ran through at a time, it would nonetheless slowly make a difference, because many a little makes a mickle, as the saying goes. All the beaches are in reality nothing but numerous grains of sand, and even though each grain is tiny, every little bit helps, and so it is with everything. The sea consists of many drops of water and the earth of many specks of dust. But enough of this. We must attend to our daily work and see how the hourglass fares when we return home."

Father and son went to the field and ploughed and levelled the soil until noon. The heat from the sun was strong, and they were glad to take a few minutes' rest at home.

"Dad! Look how the margin on the upper part of the hourglass has increased. And now the sand runs much faster than this morning," said little Sigvaldi.

"That's how it looks, my boy," said his father. "The hours do not wait, and we must not dawdle either but work while it is still daytime. But tonight when we've finished the field, I shall explain this to you in more detail. Look! Just while we've spoken these few words, many, many grains of sand have run through. Nonetheless, each has its fixed and apportioned time to complete its work."

After these words father and son got up to continue working, to bear up under the daily toil, and when they finished they had completed the work required for the day.

When they came in, Sigvaldi said: "Look how fast the sand is running! It's impossible to count the grains. Now the upper part is almost empty. And now — now the last grain of sand has gone. What happens next?"

"Now I turn it around — like this. And so I do every evening. And now I shall explain to you the meaning of the hourglass and its resemblance to human life. The glass is used to indicate time. It is very useful and almost indispensable when one cannot see the sun and where there isn't a clock. There are various kinds of hourglasses. This one measures a night and a day, and one merely has to turn it as soon as the upper part is empty in order for it to show the right time. When the glass is empty, the day has gone and it is time to rest. A new day dawns and ends for all people, rich as well as poor, whether it is a grain of sand that tells him to rise, as here, or whether it is shiny and chiming bells that announce the hours. But whether the bells chime the hours or the grains of sand run through silently, they both pronounce the death sentence of the day, whether it has been bright or dark, easy or strenuous. The days pass, the years pass, and the queen of time, eternity, keeps on collecting the hours, both from the fading sound of the decorated clock and from the murmur of the sands. She does not lose a single hour but saves them all in an equally beautiful place. In fact, she collects with the same care tears of joy and tears of grief, vicious laughter and sad smiles — in short, everything that time brings her, whether its hours are marked by the golden works of a clock or by the black grains of sand. And let me tell you, these grains of sand which now ran through took with them gemstones of vigilance and virtue as well as misdeeds. Sometimes time passes slowly and smiles to its fortunate children and gives them all kinds of nice things. But the same time flies fast and carries along everything that is in its way, and within it all events take place. Nonetheless, its journey is always the same and always even. It never hurries in one instance more than in another. The difference consists merely of its influence on the differing character of the individual and stems from the various outer circumstances it brings the individual. It reports everything it hears and sees in its homeland. — But I still haven't told you why the grains of sand run faster as the day passes. In reality the grains of sand run evenly. It only seems that they run faster as the margin of the upper part of the glass becomes wider, and one is less inclined to notice it when the margin is slim. The hourglass is like a young man, who impatiently spreads out his wings of hope and feels as if the years will never pass. Through the magnifying glass of hope he sees ahead of him the rosy path of adult years, which his imagination glorifies to the extreme. He looks at the freedom and enterprises of the adults and adds to that the peace and joy of youth. But these things rarely go hand in hand as he himself is later to learn. If the youth looks at the hourglass of his life from this viewpoint, it is very natural that to him the grains of sand — whether one calls them seconds or days or years — run slowly. He knows about the seriousness of time. And that knowledge is acquired only through experience. But despite his impatience the time runs incessantly, and he reaches adulthood with all its concerns. Then either the roses wither and lose their beautiful colour or he discovers on them thorns that sting painfully. There is no rose without thorns, as the saying goes, and that is true. But each trial has its redeeming aspects just like each joy has its sting.

Each smile from the sun brings warmth, and the warmth brings weariness to the manual labourer. The greater the blessings, the greater the worries. This does not mean that life is bad. But the magic veil in which the young man has clothed his remaining journey disappears. Life is in itself good, but it is nonetheless often difficult and tiring, and he is often keen to seek the shadow although it is only noon. If he looks at the hourglass there is still much left, but nonetheless more sand has run through than he had expected. He is not pleased with everything and wants to search for something else. He pauses and tries to find a better way. But meanwhile the days and years pass incessantly. And in this way time is wasted again and again. He looks at the hourglass and is surprised how many grains of sand have run through, and still he has not reached what earlier seemed to him so near. Energy still wriggles in his veins and his heart is still hopeful. He continues his journey, but the heat from the sun reduces his energy and the thorns hurt his feet, so that his walk makes him weary. But showers often follow sunshine, and dark clouds may be seen gathering over his head. The sky is both gentle and grim, and now the traveller is overcome by thunder and lightning which he had not expected. He is about to drop with fatigue. He looks at the hourglass. 'Oh, one day passes quickly,' he says to himself. 'Now it's late; I shall welcome the evening and rest.' In this way, my child, life goes on and on. But it treats people very differently with respect to circumstances and in terms of how much and how useful a day's work they leave behind. But it treats people the same insofar as the years seem to pass faster the more numerous they are and insofar as everyone is called to rest when the sands of the hourglass have run out — and most welcome the rest. But since we are all labourers in the Lord's vineyard and have been placed there to work for Him, then He himself portions out the rewards which He mercifully bestows upon us, because we are all useless servants. But when the sands of this earthly hourglass have run out, a new hourglass begins in eternity. — But now we must go to bed and sleep. You are tired after the day's work, which you completed well and according to expectations, and I hope you will receive the same testimony from your Lord at the completion of your life's work."

[1884]

The ABC and Worldly Wisdom

Nikulás, my brother, who was Count Súmet's valet, had received permission to visit our parents, who lived out in the country. Nikulás's visits were always joyous. He could tell so many entertaining stories and aroused an uncontrollable desire in me to go with him to the city. Besides, he did his best to convince me and promised me all kinds of fun if I should come with him. My father eventually let himself be persuaded to let me go, and we took off.

The count's castle was situated a few miles outside the city, and we arrived there in the evening. Nikulás immediately took me to the kitchen where servants and maids were busy preparing a big banquet.

"The whole castle is decorated and illuminated. What's happening?" Nikulás asked.

"Don't you remember that it's your master's birthday today? He always invites many guests," the girls answered and continued working.

I looked in amazement at everything around me. Never before had I seen such splendour. From the distance the many illuminated halls looked magical. But how could I get to see their inner splendour? From the kitchen a long staircase led up to a little room, and past that room there was another hall, big and beautiful. It was adorned with three chandeliers, and in each of them, as far as I recall, twelve candles were burning. A round table stood in the middle of the floor, and around it there were twelve plush-covered chairs; along both sides of the room were sofas also upholstered with expensive plush. In one corner there was a tiny table laden with a variety of treasures.

At the table was sitting an old man with silver-white hair; he had a high and stately forehead, bushy eyebrows, and a sad expression on his face. He was resting his head on his hand as if he was thinking of bygone days more beautiful that those which were now passing. Did I say more beautiful? Was not the hall magnificent enough, and were not the lights sufficient in number? Were not his beautiful garments costly enough? Or was his heart veiled in darkness despite the brightness of the hall? So it seemed to me when I saw him get up to receive the guests, who were now entering, and wish them welcome.

The happiness which then spread over his face looked to me like mock civility. But then congratulations and wishes for a long life streamed from all lips. It was clear that this pleased the old man, so I thought to myself that I must have been mistaken and that he was a happy man.

I saw all this from the doorway, and since Nikulás and I looked very much alike both in terms of size and facial appearance, he promised me that this evening I might take his place as count's valet and gave me various instructions on how to conduct myself. He dressed me up in his uniform, and undauntedly I entered the room.

The party went exceedingly well as indeed one would expect in the home of such a nobleman. The dancing and music went on for a long time, and although the count didn't himself take part in the entertainment, he enjoyed looking on. Most of those who came were either his friends or relatives, and they all gave him costly gifts as befitted such a man.

Nonetheless, one of his birthday gifts was neither expensive nor conspicuous. It was a primer wrapped in black cloth. It so happened that the cook was a poor widow who had a child. She made a living chiefly from cooking at banquets, and since she was an honourable woman and had a reputation for being a master of culinary art, Mrs. Skesteð, the count's housekeeper, hired her as her assistant when banquets were held in the castle. Her daughter, Friðrika, who was six years old, always came with her as indeed she did this evening. The count, who was generally considered a man of few words, had sometimes spoken with her when she played outside and even given her a shilling.

Consequently, the little girl, who was ignorant of the rules governing the social hierarchy, spoke as freely to him as to anyone else. Admittedly, he didn't consider it very proper, but he attributed it to poor habits and childish simplicity and didn't pay attention to the fact that sometimes she forgot about his nobility. This day she had upon her mother's advice bought herself an ABC, because soon she had to learn to read.

She was sitting with her book in the kitchen looking at the picture on the front cover when I came down and began to describe the birthday presents. Everyone listened attentively, but little Friðrika shot up and said:

"I want to give him my beautiful book."

We laughed at her simplicity, but the child ran off after the servants, who were serving the meal, and before anyone could prevent it, she was standing in front of the count.

She handed him the book, but not with trembling hands like some who nonetheless had bigger gifts to give; instead, she triumphantly said:

"I want to give you this for your birthday; you are always so nice to me."

All the guests watched in wide-eyed surprise, but the count smiled, took the gift, and said:

"Thank you, Friðrika. In return I give you this gold coin, so that you can buy yourself another ABC."

Because the master of this house took this so well, the guests followed his example and vied with each other in praising the frankness of the little girl.

The party went on until late in the evening. When the guests had departed, Nikulás gave me some clothes, which I had to hang in a closet in the count's bedroom. But just as I had entered the closet, he came in, and when he saw that the closet door was open and that no one was in the room, he locked the door to the room, placed the candle on the table, and sat down.

Because I was acutely aware of not being the right valet, I dared not draw attention to my presence and decided to wait for an opportune moment to escape my prison.

First the count sat down and sat for about a quarter of an hour resting his head on his hand. Then he got up and went over to the birthday presents, because he had requested that they be brought to his room. One of them was a chair, beautifully carved and widely inlaid with gold, with a brocaded cushion in the seat. He took the chair and sat down in it. Then he took a bottle of perfume which was made with such skill that never before had such a treasure been seen; indeed, the person who gave it to him claimed to have acquired it from China. He refreshed himself with the perfume and looked at the other presents. Finally he muttered to himself:

"These things resemble their owner. The chair is made only for the eye. It is beautiful to look at, but uncomfortable; it is indeed soft, but it makes the owner indolent. Life is a struggle, not rest. Like me, it is made to show outer glamour, while its inner structure is feeble and sick. I have a weak heart and you weak feet, my friend!"

As he held the bottle of perfume to his nostrils, he said: "You were created to make me swoon with vanity. Tomorrow, I will be a wealthy and happy count; tonight I am who I really am: an unlucky man. Does a sadder heart than mine beat in the breast of a human being?"

As he was saying this he hid his face in his hands, and it looked to me as if he was crying. After a short while he stood up, took a photograph out of his breast pocket, looked at it with tears in his eyes, and said:

"Hard decree of fate! I still love her as dearly as I did then. I reproach myself every day. I have cried. I have carried a gnawing pain in my heart day after day for many years. But what does that help? I am convinced that she is innocent. I saw it before I made my decision. But what does that help? What is done is done. If I had overcome my pride, it could have worked out. Now it is too late."

He put down the photograph and took without thinking Friðrika's ABC, which had been brought in together with the other presents, and opened it. The book was intended for children and not adults and therefore he had to spell out the words that first appeared to him: "Try to redress your misdeeds, so that you can again become content; be innocent, kind, and honest; and you will do well in this world and the next."

"That I should have to spell in this manner in my old age! But who knows, maybe it will do me good. To redress one's misdeeds, to be kind, to be innocent! If I had made that effort, I would have been content. I have read in the book of worldly wisdom, and yet I am not happy. I must look into this further."

He put the book away and undressed, and now his gold-embroidered clothes lay on the floor.

The count fell asleep, and I got out of the closet and down to my brother. He was cheerful and asked me how I liked this kind of life and what had delayed me. I told him, but while he was laughing at my mishap, I was serious. I was young and had seen little of the world; I had, for example, never seen so much glamour and never such great sadness. I could not sleep that night. Everything I had heard and seen was so vivid in my mind's eye. The following day the count was the same nobleman whom everyone respected and feared. I gave Nikulás his clothes and left, pleased to have had the opportunity to look into the soul of this important man, whom no one knew, and yet saddened by the misery which it contained.

Seven years later I visited Count Súmet, not as a servant but as a respected man, the son-in-law of merchant George and his co-owner. My circumstances had changed miraculously, and the count had changed no less. He still held his position and sat in the beautiful hall, but neither before nor since have I seen a kinder or more humble man. He spoke to the servants in the presence of the visitors like a father to his children, not with feigned humility or hypocrisy, but with a goodwill as natural and sincere as that of a father. "Maybe you did learn to spell when you read those words many years ago? They certainly did you a lot of good," I thought to myself.

At this time a beautiful and dignified woman entered the room, whom he introduced as Countess Súmet. Now I understood the reason for this change for the better, because although I had only seen the photograph unclearly, I was sure I recognized her face.

In the evening, I asked the restaurateur with whom I was lodging about the count, because Nikulás my brother had long since left. He told me that for six years the count had been living with his wife; they had been married for twenty years, but for unknown reasons, probably because of some misunderstanding, he had never lived with her before. He told me that since then the count had been a different man. He, whom everyone had feared, was now as placid as a child. But how this change had come about no one knew, because it had taken place before he took back his wife. The talkative host was busy all evening describing the count's life then and now, and he gave many examples of the benevolence and piety of this great man. But he mentioned in particular a poor and destitute young girl called Friðrika, whose keep and education the count financed, and to whom he had bequeathed a considerable sum of money after his death.

"And one can say about this man that his left hand does not know what his right hand is doing," the restaurateur continued, "because if somebody expresses admiration for these good deeds, he plays them down, and he won't ever hear of gratitude. It's as if he feels he owes much more."

I enjoyed listening to him, because I knew who this girl was, and I also felt convinced that the words of innocence in the ABC had settled the misunderstanding and broken the chain of misery which many years of worldly wisdom and learning had linked, or at least not managed to undo.

[1884]

Margrjet J. Benedictsson

Margrjet Jónsdóttir (later Benedictsson) was born in 1866 in Hrappsstaðir in Víðidalur, the daughter of Jón Jónsson and Kristjana Ebenesarsdóttir. At the age of thirteen she had to fend for herself. She emigrated to North America in 1887, residing for the first four years in North Dakota, and later in Manitoba. In North Dakota she earned her keep while studying at Bathgate College, and at the Central Business College in Winnipeg she took evening classes in shorthand, typing and bookkeeping. In 1893, she married Sigfús B. Benedictsson, later a well-known writer and printer in the Icelandic community, with whom she had two children, Ingi and Helen. For the first ten years of their married life they made their home variously in Mikley, in Winnipeg, on Hecla Island and in Selkirk, but in 1902 they returned to Winnipeg for a prolonged period.

In 1893 Margrjet delivered her first lecture on women's rights to members of Winnipeg's Icelandic community. Many other lectures followed, and, in addition to serving as the first president of the Winnipeg Unitarian Church's Ladies Aid and on the board of *Heimskringla*, she later founded an Icelandic women's suffrage society in Winnipeg. The Canadian Suffrage Association recognized her work by inviting her to attend the quinquennial convention of the International Women's Suffrage Alliance in Toronto in 1909 and their own annual convention immediately following, but lack of funds prevented her from going. Moreover, in 1898 when her husband set up a printing press, the couple commenced the publication of *Freyja*, the only women's suffrage paper published in Canada at the time. Margrjet served as the editor of the journal and also as a frequent contributor of articles, poetry and short stories (most of which she published under a variety of pen names) until 1910, when she divorced Sigfús. In 1912 she left Manitoba to make her home on the west coast, first in Seattle and later in Blaine, Washington. Public appreciation for her work was shown in 1930 when, chiefly at the instigation of the women on the west coast, funds were collected to enable her to attend the Icelandic millennial celebration. Margrjet died in the home of her daughter in Anacortes, Washington, in 1956.

"The Widow" is translated from "Ekkjan" in *Freyja* 2:4 (1899):2-3; "They: A Biography in Few Words" from "Þau: Ǽfisaga í fám orðum" in *Freyja* 4:8-9 (1901):154-156; and "The Messenger of Peace" from "Friðboðinn" in *Freyja* 10:5 (1907):132-134. "Ekkjan" and "Þau: Ǽfisaga í fám orðum" were written under the pen name Herold; "Friðboðinn" was written under the pen name Brynhildur.

The Widow

It was cold and dark. A chilly northern wind blew over the plains and the streets. The snow piled high and howled pitifully at the windows and along the roof. But few people noticed, because they were all so comfortable inside the church with its beautiful seats and the golden chandelier with the many lights that twinkled like glowing stars in the sky, because today was a celebration of victory — it was Easter Sunday.

The singing was finished, and the minister had chanted the epistle and the text for the day. "This celebration is the celebration of victory for Christian people, and therefore they are exceptionally happy today. Oh Death, where is thy sting? Hell, where is thy victory? Charity has conquered — charity for all mankind," the minister said, and he continued to speak about charity until the sermon ended. Then the collection plate was passed round, and the contributions were substantial, because people thought that the minister had spoken beautifully — beautifully about charity — and they were deeply moved. The man who passed around the plate went to each person, and everyone gave something, even little children. In the corner sat a woman, poorly but respectably clad. She gave nothing. The man who passed around the plate looked at her for a moment, and his look said much. The woman turned pale. "I gave while I was able to," she thought, "and if I'm lucky, I'll give again, but not now. Now I have nothing except hungry and poorly clad children. But charity has conquered death itself — charity for all mankind," she thought.

Then the last hymn was sung, and after that people started going home. When they came out, they put on their outer garments and pulled down their warm fur caps. The pretty girls with the beautiful hats pulled down their fur collars, despite the fact that the cold wind and snow blew uncomfortably around their cheeks and ears, so they hurried home. The widow also went home, but her coat was worn and had no fur collar, so she began to shiver and shivered all the way. "Charity has conquered — charity for all mankind," resounded in her ears. "I must also conquer," she thought and hurried home.

The house was cold and the light dim. The children, a boy and a girl, were lying in bed, clinging to one another; they were so cold. "Mum, dear Mum, are you bringing something to eat?" the boy asked when he heard his mother arrive.

"No, sweetheart, not now. Tomorrow I'm going to try and sell Dad's book, and then I'll get you something to eat, my little darlings," their mother said, bent down, and kissed her children, who, like her, were shivering. She didn't know which was worse, hunger or cold, but worst of all was being unable to give her children bread, because they were so hungry.

"Oh, I'm so hungry," the little girl cried and hid her face in the pillow. "I'm so hungry."

The mother also cried. She could say nothing, only cry. The children sobbed and fell asleep from the grief, the cold, and the hunger, and their little chests gasped for air from the sobbing.

The mother sat by them in the cold for a long time thinking about past and present times and forgot that she was cold. "He'd have sold the book and not paid to have it published himself if he'd known that he was going to die," she thought. "Tomorrow I'm going to sell some copies myself. I know it'll sell well. I need to get some help while the distributors are still selling copies of the book. I cannot ask more people for loans, and I cannot manage any longer. But where shall I go first? To some old friends of my late husband?" Thus she pondered. But then she felt that she could not possibly sell the book herself, go from door to door and offer a product which no one needed. No, that was quite unthinkable. And yet it was a book by a man who had a reputation among a few intellectuals, a few ... yes, they were few. Wasn't there a danger that people would not understand him now considering that they hadn't understood him when he was alive? What did people know about human rights? But then the words echoed in her heart: "Charity has conquered — charity for all mankind." He, her husband, had also written about charity, the kind of charity that acknowledges and supports human rights. Yes, they must understand him now that he was dead and buy the book out of charity for the widow and the fatherless children. But could she sell it herself? No, no; it was like begging. But then how should she manage while waiting for any profits from its sales? Eventually, she got a new idea. Her husband had planned to send the book as a present to his friends; those who received books in this way paid for them at their own discretion and usually a generous amount. Yes, this was the way to go about it. Accordingly, she made up her mind to go to the publisher and get from him a few copies of the book for herself. But to whom should she first go with the book? To the merchant L.; he and his wife had been their friends while her husband was alive. They would certainly pay handsomely for the book. And then there were the honourable Mrs. V., Mr. B., the minister, and others. Sleepy, cold, and hungry, but somewhat more hopeful and happier, she lay down and slept after she had bent over her children and kissed away the tears which still hadn't dried.

It was Easter Monday. The weather had improved. A mild southerly breeze gently caressed the widow's cheeks as she left merchant L. and his wife's house. The tears which she had tried to suppress while inside were now allowed to run freely. They were not tears of gratitude, but tears of disappointment. The merchant and his wife had not accepted the book. Their friendship went no farther than to her husband's grave. The widow, who was now poor and lonely, had no share in it, and her husband's work on "Human Rights" had in their eyes no value. Charity for all mankind was forgotten, at least it didn't include the widow in this instance.

The tears streamed down her pale and unrecognizable cheeks. The need had been so great, and therefore the disappointment was so painful. She didn't have the courage to approach others and wanted to go home, but then she saw in her mind her children crying for bread. She wandered about as if in a trance. The sun was burning hot, and the brightness was intolerable. Tired and grieved, she sat down in the shade on the stone steps by the church door, hid her face in her hands, and cried.

There she sat thinking about past and present times, and her thoughts were dark and sorrowful. Why had the world turned its back on her? What had she done to deserve this? And yet her dear children were innocent. She almost became desperate. But then the minister's words sounded even louder in her ears: "Charity has conquered — charity for all mankind." Surely, he, the minister, would not have forgotten these words, she thought, and decided to find him. But just as she got up, the minister arrived and opened the church door, walked in, and closed it again, without noticing the woman who stood in the shade.

The widow stood still, uncertain what to do. The minister was not, nor ever had been, a friend of her late husband, although obviously he was not an enemy either. But between their opinions there had been an abyss, and that meant a lot these days. All this flew quickly and unpleasantly through her mind. "Charity has conquered — charity for all mankind," sounded again in her mind, so she resolved to go into the church after the minister.

The minister sat writing in front of the altar.

"What brings you here?" he asked when he saw her.

"I have a book, Sir, which I'd like to show you," she said quietly and handed him the book.

"It is written: my house shall be called the house of prayer, but you have made it a den of thieves," the minister mumbled while opening the book and looking at its title.

"No, I don't want this book. You're wasting your time, my good woman, by distributing it," the minister said and handed the book back to her.

"I ... I wanted to give you the book, Sir," the woman now moaned.

"You put nothing on the collection plate last night," the minister said and looked firmly at her. "It's inappropriate for a Christian woman to distribute this book. Indeed, its author seems not to have been a member of any congregation ..."

What more he said she didn't know, because she hurried out. "Charity for all mankind" echoed in her heart. But where was charity now? Had they all closed their hearts to her, or had charity been completely ousted from this world?

She found that she heard her children crying for bread, so she decided to hurry home. She walked faster and faster. "You put nothing on the collection plate" buzzed in her ears. "I couldn't, I couldn't," she said out loud again and again, and she hurried even more in order to silence this accusing voice. Then she seemed to hear her children calling "bread, bread" and crying pitifully. Something buzzed in her ears so much. She was so tired. Her head felt hot and heavy. She stopped for a moment to see where she was but could not possibly get her bearings. Countless events from the past whirled through her mind. Where was she going? Home, home, and so she set off again. Suddenly, she tripped. She tried to grab hold of something to support herself, but everything went black, and she felt she was falling down, and then everything was darkness, emptiness, and oblivion. The night spread its dark wings over the earth and hid sorrow in its lap.

The merchant added up the day's profit, and the minister went over the sermon he had written in the church (it was another sermon about charity). Both were pleased with the day's work and fell asleep with a good conscience.

There was a mild southerly breeze. The flowers had come to life; they lifted their heads from the breast of mother nature and looked around. The sun sent them loving kisses, and they joyfully nodded their heads to her as if they wanted to say: "Oh, nature is so very beautiful; how wonderful it is to live and breathe in the gentle spring air." Then they sent out their fragrance in return for everything that nature gave them.

"Look at that flower," little Ívan said to his sister. "We should pick it for Mum. Smell its beautiful scent."

"Won't it die if we pick it?" asked little María and looked longingly at the flower in her brother's hand.

"Yes, it'll die, but we all will at some point. Dad said that if we could please and care for others, we should. Mum likes flowers, and since she can't come to them, we'll have to bring them to her," said little Ívan.

"That's true," said the girl, but her voice was mixed with doubts. "But isn't it sad that the flower has to die?"

"Yes, it's sad. But let's go in and find Mum. The doctor says that she may come outside tomorrow. Isn't that great?" said Ívan and ran inside.

Little María ran after her brother. They gave the flowers to their mother, the widow, whom the good Samaritan, Ingersoll of these times, had picked up from the street, taken home, and nursed. The ordeal which she went through on the unforgettable Easter Monday combined with the loss of her loved one and the worries and want of the last few days had been too much for her physical and mental strength. She was unconscious for a long time. Deliriously she spoke about her children, and her benefactor brought them to his home. But now the widow was no longer poor. The book about human rights had obtaincd recognition from a number of the best known intellectuals. The minister was proud of this book, which his friend W. C. W. on his deathbed had decided should be sent to him as an honorary gift, and now he showed it to everybody. "Yes, he deserves it. Such people know how to appreciate one another," people said. But the widow knew the true story behind this gift.

[1899]

They: A Biography in Few Words

Once upon a time many years ago when the mid-winter sun had set and the first freezing cold winds blew over the frozen earth, they, he and she, married. They did so voluntarily and of their own accord, and in their hearts lived the sisters Hope and Love, and that was to them more than sufficient.

They foresaw a path filled with troubles and tribulations. Poverty surrounded them on all sides just like the frozen snow covered the carth. But they were not afraid of anything, because love and hope were to them suns that melted away doubts and difficulties, just like the spring sun melts away the winter ice and brings life and fragrant flowers.

The years passed, but love and hope, which had blessed the bridal pair with passionate love, stood firm. Side by side they fought the battle of life and overcame one difficulty after another. They carried the heat and burden of life and found happiness only in each other's presence.

But then finally it happened that they had a serious argument. The first hurtful words were like razor-sharp sword cuts in the hearts of the lovers. The argument ended, but its consequences spread and created a distance between them.

She felt that he neglected the home, because all her thoughts concerned his and their children's well-being.

He felt that she obstructed his freedom. He was responsible for providing everything for the home and therefore had to be away, and besides, it was so enjoyable to visit the neighbours and chat with them. Sometimes he got delayed, but what business was that of hers?

How many men haven't thought the same?

She waited for him at home, tired and worried, and worked and worked for him and the children.

How many women haven't done the same?

But all of this brought about an increasing coldness and more discord, so that their relationship became unsatisfactory. They were not bad people and considered this both improper and harmful, so when they recovered from each and every disagreement, they thought up various ways to reawaken the pleasure and the intimacy which had formerly blessed their relationship. But there were always more and more things that charmed him away from the home as more and more things tied her down there. However, when they thought that the love in their hearts had died and that hope had disappeared, something happened that became decisive in the course of their lives.

Once when the wife was sitting by herself lamenting false hopes and a comatose love, a man came to her and said:

"You're dissatisfied with life. I'll take you with me over the black river which some call the Sea of Death — because I'm Death. Do you want to come?"

She thought about it. She had children, and it was so hard to die and leave them behind. After a while she said:

"If you'd come when I was destitute and alone, then I'd gladly have accepted your offer. But now I love my children and my husband, and for their sake I want to live."

Death shrugged and said: "Weren't you just complaining about false hopes and a comatose love?"

"Yes, but what about my children? I love them, and for their sake I want to live and …"

Here she fell silent and hid her face in her hands.

"And your husband too, you were going to say," Death interrupted.

"Yes," she answered quietly.

"So you want to live a little longer?"

"Yes, please," she answered.

"Then stay here longer, but when I next visit you, you must be ready to depart. Farewell," said Death and went.

"While this went on, the husband was pacing the floor very agitated.

"Oh, I'm so tired. Oh, if just I could love as I used to and rest my head on the bosom of the woman I love."

Then he looked around and saw a woman sitting on a chair, looking at him longingly.

"Who are you?" he asked.

"I'm Compassion," she answered.

"Will you comfort me?" he asked and laid his head on her bosom.

She said nothing and gently caressed his cheeks, and then he found rest.

From then on, Compassion often visited him, and his heart turned towards her, because with her he always found rest.

He found Compassion more tolerant than his wife at home. He forgot that all Compassion ever did was to enjoy and love, but his wife to tolerate and suffer.

Then once when the couple were together, Death came in and after him Compassion. Death turned to the wife and said:

"Now you must come with me, because the wounds you received in the battle of life cannot heal."

Her husband looked up and said:

"No, you must not take her. She's my wife, and I love her."

Then he stretched out his hand to draw her towards him, because now he felt that he loved her in spite of everything. But now it was too late.

"Oh, Death. Give me a little more time, for I love . . . ," the wife said and reached out both of her hands to her husband.

Then Compassion went over to the husband, laid her head on his chest and said:

"Come to me, your wife's wounding words won't hurt you any more."

The wife's hands sank down. She looked at Compassion and her husband, sighed, and said:

"I understand."

"Are you ready now?" said Death.

"But my children?" the wife moaned.

"They'll come after you," Death answered, and all of a sudden the expression on his face, which had previously been cold and contemptuous, became gentle and kind.

Then the wife sank into Death's arms, and he carried her out onto his ferry and sailed her across the black river to the unknown land.

The husband watched the ferry until it had disappeared. From then on he had only ungratified desires. He found that the pleasures which had been so sweet turned bitter, because they were the cause of the hurtful words and the sorrow and the wounds which the battle of life had given his wife. Now he was at least free. But of what use was that? Compassion took his hand and led him away, but because he could not forget, Compassion became tired of leading him. So when Death finally came to sail him across the river, he too had had enough of life.

[1901]

The Messenger of Peace

He glided on the wings of the quivering northern lights through the dark blue night among the multitude of twinkling stars and didn't stop his journey until he descended to the earth in the dusk of the holy Christmas night. The earth was covered with snow, and in the silvery gleam of the moon, the ice pearls glittered as if they were the most precious diamonds. Everywhere it was bright as if it were broad daylight, not only from the moon, which shone in its fullness in the clear sky, but also from the thousands of electric lights. Huge buildings stretched their towers up into the air, as if they were asking God to bless them and their inhabitants. The streets of the capital city were crowded with people, and everyone was in a hurry. In the crowd was a paper boy, clad in rags, cold and voiceless from offering his newspapers to every passer-by, but few noticed him, because he was so little and poor.

"Peace on earth and goodwill to men" now resounded from countless churches and chapels. The messenger of peace went into the nearest church. Far within on the middle of the floor stood the Christmas tree decorated with countless colourful electric lights and silver tinsel and flowers. On its branches hung small brocaded socks and baskets full of all kinds of things that gladden the hearts of children. On the platform twelve young girls were singing Christmas carols. They were all dressed in white, symbolizing the celebration of innocence and youth. Before the altar the minister was preaching "peace on earth and goodwill to men." The messenger of peace looked around; in the expressions of the children of humankind he read their souls, and he smiled gently, because at this time most were happy. For the time being, they had left their sorrows and worries behind them. The happiness many felt at this moment was the most sincere and the holiest in the human soul, the happiness that grows out of the conscious knowledge of making others happy. There were, however, some who in the midst of the holiness of the Christmas night harboured vindictive thoughts and used the opportunity to irritate imaginary enemies with ludicrous presents. The messenger of peace saw this and grieved. But many, many had also completely forgotten themselves when they shared their modest possessions with their friends and kinsmen, and when the gifts were distributed these were the happiest of all, although no one remembered them, and then the heart of the messenger of peace became filled with love for humankind.

After the service and the distribution of the gifts, the messenger of peace went outside. He looked over the crowds of people coming out of the churches, watching them recede until everyone had disappeared, had come home. Then he went to a big building, where trumpets were blown, drums beaten, and hymns sung. A large crowd of people had gathered there as well, men and women, children and elderly, and most of them were dressed poorly. These were the poor and the destitute whom the Salvation Army had gathered at its tables. When the people had eaten, they prayed and thanked God and good men for this one meal, although many of them didn't know where or how they would get the next one. And yet these people live in the land of plenty, where no one has to starve!

At the end of the meal, people got up, went out, and scattered in small groups as each went home. But what a homecoming! Many places had no heat and no light — a little of everything but none of the many real necessities. Crowds of people were crammed in small and inadequate lodgings, sometimes in a single room to save light, firewood, and rent. And yet there were empty houses here and there all over the city. The people who a short while ago had given thanks to God now shivered, because the night was cold, much too cold to be without firewood. Pale, skinny, and shivering women suckled their babies at their breasts and fed them the only kind of food they had so far known, although they were almost a year old or more, because the scraps which society gives to its outcasts are not suitable for infants. And yet the world shouts: More children! More children! Give us more people! Nonetheless, mothers and children starve, and desperate fathers fight over employment and snatch the bread from one another's mouths — the crumbs that fall from the tables of the rich.

From this sight the messenger of peace turned in sorrow and went out on the streets. Still the words echoed: "Peace on earth and goodwill to men." Otherwise everything was silent and still, and God's peace enveloped the poor earth in its tragedies. The stars twinkled in the sky's blue arch, the ice pearls glittered in the snow, and the electric lights illuminated the empty streets. The messenger of peace glided over the city and looked at the homes of humankind. He saw, in turn, wealth and poverty, sorrow and happiness. The rich praised their good fortune to live in the land of plenty where no one had to starve. Their tables were loaded with expensive dishes. To their right sat Happiness. They praised their own good sense and thanked God for being "different from others" — such as these poor wretches who didn't know how to make a living or whom God refused to bless because of their sins. But behind these people two supernatural beings whom people call Conceit and Greed sat and grinned sarcastically.

From here he went in sadness and came to the houses of the poor, the widows and the orphans: the people who just managed to survive and the people who despite their utmost efforts couldn't meet their most vital needs but lived with what little they had. Had the rich remembered them? Why should they do that in the land of plenty, where no one has to starve? The messenger of peace saw the poor paper boy warm his half-frozen feet by the fading embers while his mother with loving hands divided the result of his toil among four hungry mouths. In countless homes, he saw poverty of which no one knew except those who struggled against it. In countless homes, he saw sorrow which no one felt except those who suffered it. The poor and the sorrowful retire, but over the groans of sorrow and misery the joy of the Christmas celebration rose, and in its midst the words resounded: "Peace on earth and goodwill to men!"

On the wings of the quivering northern lights among the multitude of twinkling stars the messenger of peace glided up to the high seat of the Almighty God and His Son to describe what he had experienced in the capital city of the land of plenty. Then the Son grieved, bowed His head, and said: "So it still isn't consummated."

[1907]

Guðrún H. Finnsdóttir

Guðrún Helga Finnsdóttir was born in 1884 at Geirólfsstaðir in Skriðdalur, Suður-Múlasýsla, the daughter of Finnur Björnsson and Bergþóra Helgadóttir. In 1900 she entered the Women's Academy (Kvennaskólinn) in Akureyri. There, in the home of her aunt, Helga Helgadóttir, and uncle, Björn Jónsson (who was the editor of *Stefnir*), she met the poet Gísli Jónsson, a printer by trade, and married him in 1902. In 1903, the couple emigrated to Canada and settled in Winnipeg, where they raised five children: Helgi, Bergþóra, Gyða, Ragnar and Unnur.

Guðrún H. Finnsdóttir was a member of the Winnipeg Unitarian Church's Ladies Aid and served as its president in 1927-1928. She was also the first editor of the women's section of *Brautin*, the publication of the United Conference of Icelandic Unitarian and Liberal Christian Churches of North America, in which she also published the articles "Clara Barton" (*Brautin* 1 [1944]:95-103) and "Erasmus frá Rotterdam" (*Brautin* 3 [1946]:96-103). She was one of the founders of the Jón Sigurðsson Chapter IODE and provided many contributions to the Chapter's *Minningarrit Íslenzkra hermanna* (Winnipeg, 1923), a memorial book of the men and women of Icelandic descent who served in the Canadian and the United States forces in World War I. Finally, she was an active member of The Icelandic National League, in whose journal, *Tímarit Þjóðræknisfélags Íslendinga* (of which her husband was editor, 1940-1958, and co-editor, 1959-1968), she published most of her short stories.

Guðrún H. Finnsdóttir's first published short story was "Landskuld," which appeared in *Tímarit Þjóðræknisfélags Íslendinga* 2 (1920):114-119. It is generally believed, however, that the first story she wrote was "Utangarðs," which appeared in print in 1938. Many other stories followed in succeeding issues of *Tímarit Þjóðræknisfélags Íslendinga* as well as in *Heimskringla*, *Lögberg* and *Saga*. Most of these were later reprinted in *Hillingalönd* (Reykjavík, 1938) and *Dagshríðar spor* (Akureyri, 1946). A number of her lectures were printed in a book entitled *Ferðalok: Fyrirlestrar, ræður, æviminningar, erfiljóð* (Winnipeg, 1950), which was published by her husband after her death in 1946.

The first section of "Lost Tracks" is translated from "Fýkur í sporin" in *Tímarit Þjóðræknisfélags Íslendinga* 3 (1921):89-93, and the second from *Dagshríðar spor* (207-230); "Beyond the Pale" is translated from "Utangarðs" in *Hillingalönd* (9-36) and "Not Everything Is As It Seems" from "Ekki er alt sem sýnist" in *Heimskringla,* 19 December 1945 (4).

Lost Tracks

I

Spring had arrived with warmth, growth, and song, and with a youthfulness that penetrated everything. The trees spread out their branches with the young, light-green foliage that quivered in the soft southerly breeze. The sun sparkled on the lake, which was like a glittering mirror in the stillness of the morning. The scent of forest and the song of birds filled the air. It was as if spring and youth would reign forever.

Ingólfur in Vík felt and saw the beauty and the spring, but still he was in low spirits today, and he had not slept well. All night he had been pondering his past. All the weary and distressful footsteps were clear in his mind. One such step, and not the easiest, he had to take today. It was his daughter Ragnhildur's wedding day; she was to marry an Englishman, a doctor who lived in Winnipeg.

Her father had expected her to continue being the mistress in Vík, to marry some exemplary man in the neighbourhood — an Icelander. But these daydreams had now all been shattered.

For many years Ingólfur had prepared to hand over to his daughter his life's work as completed as best he could. He had spent all his time improving and enlarging his land, meadows and fields, and also decorating and improving the house. But for what purpose?

Ingólfur looked at his farm as it was today: the house, large and impressive, of light-grey concrete with a red roof, a well-kept garden all around it, and a wide avenue of trees extending to the main road. Behind the house was a good-sized thicket, and in the clearing to the west stood a granary, a stable, and a storehouse. Everything reflected orderliness and prosperity. Level fields and meadows spread north and west of the farmhouse. And the lake, full of fish, was only a good hundred feet from the house. It had kept them alive a long time ago in their pioneering years while he was raising livestock and breaking the land.

In his mind he saw the first log cabin he had built in Vík, small and low, with an earthen floor and with clay packed into the cracks where the logs did not fit. Now it would not even be suitable for a cowshed.

What little was bought for the household, he had carried on his back over long distances. For two years they had tasted no other meat than wild fowl and game he occasionally shot. They could not slaughter any of their few cattle. Then he managed to raise oxen for driving and ploughing. He built the first cart himself, and that was quite an improvement. But the oxen were not as fast as automobiles nowadays. At that time there was no alternative but to work and save to keep body and soul together.

The only thing of which there was plenty was firewood. The forest was dense and tall all the way to the edge of the lake. It had to be cut down and cleared before it was possible to plant potatoes, never mind growing grain. Where there was no dense forest, there were impassable bogs and morasses that had to be drained.

Old Ingólfur was now amazed at the foolhardiness and courage his wife Þórdís and he had had when they settled there. He doubted that they would have tried to set up a household there, had they had any idea of half of all the difficulties that awaited them. But then there was no alternative in those days; they had no choice. The north-western part of the country was a virgin forest and uninhabited prairie when the immigrants had been assigned there in small scattered groups.

Ingólfur remembered his neighbours with gratitude; how they helped one another both with regard to work and necessities. There was as much helpfulness as there was poverty. Often he had looked over the district and been amazed at how much these people had accomplished with their bare hands. Most of them had passed away or moved. Those who had settled and cultivated the land were forgotten; they had been replaced by others, who reaped the fruits of their labour.

Yes, it was beautiful and prosperous in Vík nowadays. Ingólfur looked at his hands, gnarled and bony from drudgery and toil. Indeed, he had won a victory over poverty, single-handed farming, and all the difficulties that only the pioneer experiences. But that was all. Everything else he had lost.

Þórdís, his wife, died young, just over thirty years of age; she developed consumption from all the hardship. No house, no conveniences, only drudgery and toil, poverty and difficulties. And what really ruined her health was when they lost the children, one after another, for lack of nursing and medical care.

Vík had cost him dearly. And why had he struggled? Now he had also lost Ragnhildur, the apple of his eye, on whom he had based all his hopes. He felt he had chiefly himself to blame. If he had kept her at home and not been concerned about educating her, then his dreams would have come true; she would have stayed on her ancestral farm.

It was in the city that she had become acquainted with this future husband of hers. Then when she had graduated and come home, there were constant visits from Winnipeg all summer. Every weekend Vík was full of young people, Icelandic and English, who came to visit Ragnhildur and to relax in the country over the weekends. And it was rare that the doctor was not in the group. Ingólfur had suspected nothing. To be sure, he had found the relaxation these young people sought somewhat peculiar. Driving in automobiles back and forth all over the district, boating and sailing all over the lake, playing ball games and then dancing and singing until the early morning. He saw that Ragnhildur was enjoying herself, and he did not grudge her that, because there had not been much joy in Vík while she was growing up.

Ingólfur had often looked with amazement at his daughter in this group of strangers; sometimes he felt that she was a stranger as well. His little girl, the farmer's daughter, raised by him in isolation and on almost uninhabited land, not only held her own, but also surpassed all others in beauty, intelligence, and graciousness. And he was sincerely pleased and thankful to have such a daughter.

One Sunday evening last summer, Ingólfur had walked west to the meadow to check on his livestock. Having found everything in order, he walked leisurely home. The moon was shining and it was calm; over everything there lay a pale-white brightness like a magic veil. In the forest everything was on the move — a world of its own that came alive in the evening. The trees stood like guardians, silent and quiet, and cast long shadows. It was one of those beautiful evenings that often follow hot days. It was as if the earth took all life that is tired after the heat and toils of the day into its soft, cool arms like a gentle mother. Ingólfur had reached the pavement in front of the farmhouse. Unconsciously and out of habit he stopped and looked out over the lake that quivered and glittered in the moonlight. He looked south along the beach, a short distance south of the farmhouse. There they came walking, Ragnhildur and the doctor — holding hands.

Ingólfur stood petrified, overwhelmed by pain, disappointment, and anger. One feeling succeeded the other. So this was the doctor's errand to Vík, not relaxation. Some relaxation this was! What a fool he had been. And Ragnhildur, she had forsaken him, she had let him down for the first time in her life, and for an Englishman — she, his only child.

There they came holding hands.

He was not prepared to meet them now. He needed time to think, to try to get control of himself. It was best for him to walk, to walk himself out of the storm and the vehemence like he had so often done before. He hurried away from the farmhouse, away from Ragnhildur and the doctor, away from everything, into the stillness of the night. He was alone, all alone. He walked a long distance along the beach, back and forth, back and forth.

Often he had wished that Þórdís had been allowed to live, but never as poignantly painfully as now. It was as if his loneliness mocked him. He wanted to be able to retrieve her from eternity, see her, feel her, receive the sympathy and strength he could always count on from her, even after she had fallen ill.

Suddenly, Ingólfur stopped short. What had been Þórdís's last and only request? Didn't she entrust little Ragnhildur, who was then in her second year, to his care? He had tried not to let her down. He felt that he owed Þórdís in her grave the youth and happiness of which she had been deprived so early. This debt he had tried to pay Ragnhildur. And until now it had been a pleasure to him. But now it had come to the point that one of them had to yield to the will of the other.

Ragnhildur was not fickle; no one knew her deep and firm mind better than he. Now he understood why lately she had sometimes looked at him with worried, serious eyes.

All of a sudden Ingólfur felt tired — in soul and body. He sat down on the sand and rested his chin in his hand. His thoughts were gradually becoming clearer and more calm. The memory of Þórdís, her presence, the murmur from the lake, the peace and quiet of the night — all this touched his tired soul like the soft hands of a loved one.

The lake had often before been to him a companion and a friend when the storm or commotion in his own mind had almost gotten the better of him. Here he had knelt in solitude and desolation. Here he had prayed fervently and sincerely. And here he had also doubted the existence of a god. Life seemed a merciless aggregate that crushed those who got in the way of the unfeeling wheels of chance. Here he had cried tears, the bitter tears of a grown man, out of whom life had almost squeezed all willpower. Here he had also found peace, peace after having been overcome by his emotions. As the waves on the lake abated after the storm, so he had also gradually found peace of mind as the years went by — learned to be grateful for God's smile in the sunshine, His tears in the rain, learned to be grateful for life itself. And it was little Ragnhildur who played the main part in lighting and warming his soul again — ever since she was a little girl and came running to him with open arms, happy face, blue sparkling eyes, blonde hair, and clear voice of a child. It was she and no one else who had spread around him light, hope, love, and faith in life. On her he had based all his dreams for the future. She was to enjoy all the things that Þórdís and he had been deprived of. Now she had failed him for the first time. But was it fair to look at it in such a way? She had the right to marry the man of her choice, and it was only natural that she would marry. But he had hoped, actually expected, that it would be an Icelander.

What could he do? Put his foot down and simply forbid her to marry the doctor? No, those days were long gone. He could do nothing, could not say a word. He knew that although he protested now, he would have to give in eventually. But he was her father, he had raised her. Didn't he have a right to demand that she respect his will in this matter? She surely knew that he was against her marrying an Englishman. Was he to repay Ragnhildur all her love by depriving her of happiness? Did he dare do that? What had her mother gained by marrying him, becoming his wife? Poverty, poor health, grief, and death. He had not managed his own life well enough to dare manage other people's lives. He had to accept this like other Icelandic parents who had been in the same situation. And he had blamed them for not having prevented such marriages. What hurt the most was the feeling that Ragnhildur was lost, not only to him but to the Icelandic community in which she had been born and raised, and to the Icelandic social life. It was the same story with most of the Icelanders who married North Americans. They were lost to the Icelanders, were absorbed by the English.

Old Ingólfur sighed and wished in his mind that the Icelanders had been as wise as the Jews and made it a breach of religion to marry into other ethnic groups. Therefore they had remained a nation through the centuries, despite the fact that they had been scattered throughout the world and suffered persecution and humiliation.

Ingólfur stood up. A cold gust of air came from the water. He looked east and saw that dawn was breaking. A new day — a new generation that must have its own history, its own calling, and its own experience. Ingólfur had won a victory over himself — over his selfishness and wilfulness. Ragnhildur had to decide for herself.

All these memories had filled his mind last night, and now he had come out into the beautiful spring morning to shake them off. It was Ragnhildur's wedding day, and it was supposed to make her happy and pleased; no expense would be spared. No disagreements and nothing but sincere prayers and congratulations would accompany her from the ancestral farm.

Ingólfur looked over his farmhouse and the land. Yes, it was beautiful in Vík, and he had worked hard to make the farm look like this; yet he felt he had done it all in vain. The property of Vík was of little use to him except to rest his bones — if it would be granted to him to be buried next to Þórdís and the children.

The wages of the immigrant are often meagre and always the same. To be sure, he is given land, but in return he gives his life, his health, and all his abilities. Yes, the land absorbs him, body and soul, and his children for a thousand generations.

[1921]

II

The car backed slowly out of the carport behind the house, turned around, and then drove north, until it turned at the next street corner and disappeared. Ragnhildur waved in the direction of her husband;

he was on his way to the general hospital, where many patients were waiting for him, for he was a successful and well-known doctor.

Her heart was tender and her mood in harmony with this wonderful, bright morning. The breeze, cool and refreshing, played in the foliage of the trees, which gently rocked its green branches far above the gables of the houses. It was as if they were raising themselves on tiptoe and stretching their arms toward light and sun. The rows of houses on both sides of the street seemed to nestle in the green gardens under the branches of the trees. But Ragnhildur found nonetheless that at this time they must also stare longingly up into the blue universe, because sun and summer, life and vegetation, also make their way into the homes of humankind.

And yet she knew that there were homes in which the spirit of spring could not penetrate the icy cold and the frosty atmosphere. People's houses cannot be measured only in terms of square feet; rather, the size of the homes depends on the warmth and the height of the ceiling in the minds of those who live in the houses. It is the attitude that creates size. It makes no difference whether it is a castle or a hovel. Some people's homes are halls of sunshine, others' graves of dead men and women.

Ragnhildur loved spring and everything it represented — spring mood, spring growth, new life, new hopes, new dreams. Each spring the earth itself rose from the dead and gave humankind new vitality. Nature in its entirety was then a harmonious poem of praise to life and light.

Although Ragnhildur had long become used to city life, she was still such a country child that especially in the spring she found the streets narrow and the horizon small. On a bright spring morning like this, she often longed to be back home in Vík and to be able to run her eyes over the blue and glittering lake, to lie in the sand and listen to the dialogue between the waves and the rustle of the forest. There she could return to her youth and feel her father's love and care. Now she understood his good sense and intuition better when he was counselling her, and now she often listened to what she had then only listened to with one ear, because in those years life was a song and the voices of youth were loud.

Her thoughts often travelled to Vík in bad weather as well, when the sky was covered with heavy, dark banks of clouds and the wind howled in each crack like a hungry wolf in search of prey. She knew that in this weather the lake was grim, rough, and grey, the forest sinister and dark, groaning from the struggle with the storm, and that there was an ominous feeling of depression over the entire area. She was only a little child when she knew that such weather was dangerous for the fishermen's small boats looking for sustenance out on the water — boats that had not always all come back.

But when the weather was good and the lake calm, her little world was bright and safe. She had often played by herself in the sand in front of the house. Her playmates were the birds on the beach and the small fish in the little lagoon that cut into the sand. There she had built for herself a sandcastle and a throne — and on that beach she had later made a castle from different material.

Ingólfur, her father, had died many years ago, and Vík had been sold; she herself had moved away for good. But the parts of Vík that could neither be bought nor sold were still in her possession, and her mind often drifted to the lands of memory. It warmed her heart to recall the kindness of the poor pioneers, who were their friends and neighbours. The hovels of many of these people had been small, but spiritually their homes had not been cramped, because the spirit of spring, the spirit of plans for the future and brotherly love filled the minds of most of these people. Yes, she remembered these people well, who, despite their worn and weather-beaten appearances, were open-minded and cheerful. Their souls had not shrunk nor had their hearts frozen from the difficulties of the first pioneering years. But she remembered most clearly the kind women who took care of her after her mother had died. On holidays and feast days, they cared for her like their own children. She could not recall a single Christmas when they hadn't taken turns giving her a new dress, although some of these women were so poor that their own everyday dresses were pieced together from dyed wheatsacks.

It was not until she was an adult that Ragnhildur had realized how much of an entrepreneur and a fine manager her father was, because by the time she had grown up and was studying at the University of Manitoba, Vík had become one of the main estates in the district. And she lacked nothing during her college years. To Ragnhildur those years were like a beautiful dream in a fairy tale. Her studies went well; she enjoyed popularity and much respect. For that reason the changes and the disappointments were hard on her when through marriage she moved into a new environment that was both narrow and cold.

Her parents-in-law were called Mr. and Mrs. Gray, and the name suited them well, because they were grey and cold. Materialism and contemptuous ambition had made them difficult. Their home was open only to those whom they considered it honourable to associate with and who in turn reflected well on their social position.

She did not belong to their class. Her husband had bitterly disappointed his parents when he chose a farmer's daughter as his wife — a foreigner. In their eyes all foreigners were lower-class people — beasts of burden in the shape of humans. She was, of course, not unaware of the stigma that was attached to foreigners, especially by ignorant and arrogant people, but personally she had met with little of this sort of thing. She had never considered herself or her people inferior, and therefore the disappointment was the more painful.

Ragnhildur brushed her grey hair from her forehead and breathed in the scent of the flowers in the garden. When she thought about the first years of her marriage, it was always as if a cloud covered the sun. Her story was the same old story. She was not welcome in the family, and no opportunity had been missed to put her down and humiliate her. She had often been amazed at the low-mindedness of petty people, who puff themselves up by trying to step on those who seem inferior. Some of the attempts had been painful stabs while others had been ridiculous like, for example, when her mother-in-law insisted on changing her name to Ruby, because her foreign name was similar to the name of the maidservants in the neighbourhood. By then Ragnhildur had got used to a number of things and answered calmly that she had no intention of changing her name and that indeed there was no similarity, because the maids were all called Kate or Mary regardless of what their names were. Her mother-in-law's name was Catherine Mary. She didn't often respond in this way and usually tried to ignore things in silence. But she absolutely refused to conceal her ethnic background. She neither would nor could deny the best in herself — her family, her background, and her spiritual heritage. She did not want to change herself for the sake of accommodating ignorance and arrogance.

Her parents-in-law had shares in coal mines and coal businesses. With their wealth in such volumes of heat they intended to break her will and conviction — to melt her soul in the foundry ladle. But in return she kindled her own fire, perhaps more out of eagerness than foresight, because her domestic peace had begun to get burnt in this battle. She knew that she was standing on live coals or between two fires.

If her husband saw or understood some of what was happening within the family, he completely passed it over in silence. Ragnhildur was hurt and interpreted his lack of involvement as a sign of support for his parents' absurdities. Instead of joy, peace, and sympathy, which had reigned in their house and in their relationship in the beginning, the atmosphere in the home gradually became heavier, harsher, and less sincere. The reason was that neither of them was now open or honest. Between them there were unspoken thoughts — thoughts that neither of them would be the first to put into words. Although Ragnhildur didn't believe that her husband agreed with his parents, her suspicion gradually became an accusation mixed with gall, which brought poison and dejection into her life and marriage.

People's inner lives and thoughts are not woven from one thread; rather, they are a complex web that makes up the whole. She knew and understood that her husband was raised in a home that was spiritually poor and weak, marked by the prejudice and fear of those who lack inner strength and who think that they can live on material things alone — this superficial life, which cultivates all outward form and sells its soul, conscience, and self-esteem in the hope that on false values it can get one step higher on the ladder of society.

Right from the outset Ragnhildur had been scared of her parents-in-law. Her mother-in-law was a big, grim-looking, and unattractive woman. She shuffled around the house in rustling silk dresses; the skirt, wide and long, flapped round her like a kind of ferule; and her heavy steps gave Ragnhildur the unpleasant feeling that the woman would be happy to tread on everything in more ways than one.

Her father-in-law was no gentler. His protruding jaw, long nose, and cold and deeply set eyes gave evidence of that. And the glimpses of greed which came over his face and eyes when he spoke about money told their story.

During those years, Ragnhildur had looked upon her parents-in-law with the merciless eyes of youth, and the contempt they showed her did not make her mitigate her judgement. Nonetheless, after she had married, she had tried hard to be friendly. She had shown them due respect as the parents of her husband, and at times the obligations of kinship had asserted themselves so much that she was annoyed on their behalf when she saw and felt that some of the people they coveted passed them over but nonetheless accepted and sought after their money.

At other times she longed to strike at her mother-in-law's obsessive ambition, by telling her the shattering truth, or to put an end to her father-in-law's political and social speculations. But just as often she was ashamed of her thoughts — felt she was deceiving her husband, when the disgust against his parents flared up in her mind. She often wondered whether one's thoughts were in fact spontaneous, at least sometimes. They appear uninvited and flutter about — not least the ones that one would rather be without.

Everything was still calm on the surface, but the politeness within the family had become cold and ugly. Ragnhildur had usually remained silent, but in many areas she had opposed her parents-in-law's opinions. And then this quarrelling had affected her to such an extent that her joy and security had become like birds with clipped wings. Her honesty and boldness could no longer fly so high, because her soul was filled with resentment and suspicion. She longed to tell her husband all her troubled thoughts, but his silence had hurt her so much that she could not bring herself to open her heart to him on this topic. She also knew that spoken words cannot be taken back, and that maybe alone she would be able to get through the difficulties of her feelings and the commotion of her mind. Perhaps her husband was wiser than she by pretending that nothing was wrong and by smothering his parents' unmotivated judgements and her dissatisfaction. And love is strange and unpredictable, because when she accused her husband she at the same time excused him and called to mind all his virtues, his devotion, and his care. She realized his noble-mindedness in not backbiting or judging his parents and she defended his silence; but then she always arrived at the most tender spot: Was he of the same mind and opinion as his parents? Was there also hidden in him a spark of contempt for foreigners? And her thoughts would then travel the same, endless circle. Day after day, week after week she pondered, blind and bewildered. She still loved her husband, but nevertheless she did not trust him completely. Could it be that this hostile atmosphere was affecting her love?

She often longed to ask her father's advice, but she did not want to discuss these matters with him, because he had disapproved of her marrying a "foreigner," to use his words. In his eyes people who were not Icelanders were foreigners, so in this respect both sides were equal. The difference was that her father had never come between her and her husband, although he disliked her marrying a man of a different ethnic background. And he had pointed out to her some of the things that had come up later, but which had seemed absurd to her then. Ragnhildur had never regarded herself as a foreigner; she was a child of this country like her husband. Both were born and raised here, and both by parents who had moved to the country. And she had found the bitterness in her father's words unnecessary when he spoke of the difficulties and hardships the immigrants had met with here in this society, which was literally falling apart.

Experience is a harsh school, and now she had more understanding with regard to these matters. But she wanted to remain faithful to her ethnic background; that she had promised her father. Of course, life demands so many promises, and so few of them are in fact kept. Circumstance twists people round its little finger. She now knew that her father had been right when he told her that in their co-existence with people of other nationalities the Icelanders had woken up to a harsh reality: they had lost their heritage, lost their people, language and mentality.

But love had never requested that she put on alien clothes. Her husband had never attempted to erase her national feelings — not with a single word. She must show herself to be enough of a person to save her domestic peace and her love; everything else was a defeat and a breach of her most sincere promise. She must be a persevering and pure settler.

This was what was on her mind on that bright June morning when everything went up in flames. She wanted to visit her father and stay with him for a fortnight with little Þórdís Mary, who was named after her grandmothers. Ragnhildur had never gone to Vík except for short visits. She had decided to teach little Dísa a bit of Icelandic, because she knew that it would please her father. The little one would then not be one of the English children who made the old Icelandic grand-mothers so weary because they did not understand what they were saying. She had spoken both English and Icelandic with her daughter. Moreover, she had taught her Icelandic jingles and nursery rhymes so the little one could recite in Icelandic "Bí, bí, and flutter by," "Moon, moon, take me," "The bird on the beach," "She stepped out of bed," and "Fine fish," and more. Ragnhildur was looking forward to seeing the expression on her father's face when little Þórdís started reciting the same verses he had taught her when she was little.

In this unusually good mood she went to her parents-in-law around lunchtime to let little Dísa say goodbye. Ragnhildur walked in, greeted them cheerfully, and told the elderly woman her errand. Her mother-in-law immediately looked like Fury and said she would not allow her to take the child along — she had heard that in these foreign homes people and pigs lived together in the same filth. Ragnhildur was so surprised that she was at a loss for words. Why bother to speak with this woman, who believed all filthy stories and mixed all ethnic groups? Nonetheless, after a moment she answered dryly: "Ask your son about the house in Vík." At the same moment she looked into the sitting room, where her father-in-law was sitting. In front of him stood little Þórdís resting her hands on his knees. She was busy talking to her grandfather and looked at him with bright and happy eyes. But there was something about his expression that Ragnhildur didn't like. And now she heard that her daughter was reciting Icelandic rhymes with all her might. Little Dísa had confused her grandfathers. "What are you saying?" he asked the child irritably. And it occurred to Ragnhildur that this was the same question many Icelandic grandfathers and grandmothers asked their grandchildren.

She hurried in and said: "Speak English to this grandfather, Dísa." Then she smiled and said kindly: "These are Icelandic jingles and nursery rhymes I've taught her for fun." Her father-in-law looked at her for a moment, and his eyes were like ice-cubes. Then he pushed the child aside so that she shrank back, got up, walked across the floor and stopped opposite Ragnhildur. They stared right into each other's eyes, and neither of them looked away. "I won't allow you to teach this child any of this foreign nonsense; English is sufficient. I intend to give her a portion of my property, but I also intend to keep an eye on her upbringing so that she will be worthy of it. I want her to be brought up in an English manner as a God-fearing child." And then he added with emphasis and with defiance in his voice: "I want you to know that I'm serious."

Ragnhildur stood dumbfounded and looked with eyes of amazement at her father-in-law as if she had never seen him before. Pushing her about in various ways was nothing new, but she had never doubted that he was fond of the child. Now, because of her mother, he had pushed little Þórdís about, this little, innocent child, with gruffness. But his wheeler-dealer spirit wanted to buy her with hopes of an inheritance and with threats and to influence her child's upbringing, thoughts, and inner life. She swore that the dark hand of fear and hardness would never squeeze the happiness and vitality out of the mind and heart of little Þórdís. She was so angry that her legs were shaking, but she controlled her temper so that she appeared calm when she answered slowly and with a firm voice:

"The only man who has any say in Þórdís's upbringing is her father, and as far as her education is concerned our priority is for her to become an upright and good girl; and she will almost certainly learn more languages than English. I also intend to teach her to work, to teach her to value the working hands of humankind, so that she will understand that it is dishonest to live on other people's blood and sweat — and her soul will not be sold for the hope of an inheritance."

As soon as Ragnhildur had finished, she looked down, patted Dísa's head, and said: "Say goodbye to grandfather and grandmother, Dísa. We're going home." She snatched her hat and gloves from the table in the entrance and hurried out of the house. Little Þórdís was running after her. Fortunately, the child understood nothing of what had been said.

Well, what a visit that had been! She had arrived with all good intentions, and this was how the visit ended. This was not her only trip to that house that had been in vain. Usually, she had left either hurt or angry. She knew that she had said too much, but that was that. They had declared war and she had fought back; she was tired of endless retreats and decided to break the silence between her husband and herself no matter what the outcome.

Lunch was prepared and Ragnhildur was waiting for her husband. When he finally arrived, she immediately saw that something was wrong. He was serious and silent as if he was busy with his thoughts, and there were sadness and tiredness in his expression and his eyes. They ate in silence, because Ragnhildur also had much on her mind. She saw that he was not feeling well — did she have the heart to burden him with her complaints? And yet she had to speak with him; her soul smarted from the morning's whipping. All of a sudden the food did not taste right and she stopped eating. She herself was so depressed that she could not hide it. Therefore, there was neither mildness in her eyes nor sympathy in her voice when she looked at him and asked: "Has something special happened?"

He looked at her for a moment, and there was reprimand in his eyes, when he answered: "Why did you have to quarrel with my parents this morning? They say that you confronted them with contempt and threats. In spite of everything, they are my parents, and it's going too far, Ragnhildur, to forbid them to enjoy the company of their grandchild. You will have to see to it that this be smoothed out again — apologize for this in some way."

Ragnhildur was pale, and her face was as carved in stone. Only her eyes were alive, because they became dark and deep from inner torment. Each word he spoke was like a stab in her heart. There was the answer to all her questions. They had twisted the story in their favour and their son agreed with them, and therefore it would be of no use to try and tell him the truth. Fear and doubt, these evil spirits, who had whispered poisonous words in her mind, were then the voices of truth. She looked at him as if she wanted to read his innermost thoughts, looked at him with different eyes than she had ever done before. So he expected her to apologize for what she had said this morning! It was she who had to crawl on her knees before their inconsideration. She had been so ignorant, so ridiculously naive, to think that she could flee to him with all her problems. From him she had expected sympathy and security. She had hoped that he would acknowledge her rights as a human being, as a wife, as a mother. But she was the foreigner in this family, and what was said about foreigners never had to be excused. They had to accept everything with gratitude and humility. Although they were sometimes told that they were free people in a free country, the feeling of powerlessness was continuously being rubbed into them, until the weakest of them denied the very nationality, language, and culture they had been born with. Amongst these people her parents-in-law intended to place her — and her husband agreed with them!

The anger and hurt burnt in her heart. She looked daggers at her husband and said with much emphasis on each word: "You're welcome to believe of me whatever you think is likely, but I'll never apologize for what I said this morning. It's sufficient for your parents to have your sympathy and your magnanimous participation in their injustice and hostility towards me and my people."

The doctor flushed, and there was resentment in his voice when he answered: "You take my parents' nonsense about foreigners much too seriously. I see no reason why you should always be defending all foreigners here. For one thing, they are not all worth it, and secondly, everyone is, as far as I know, equal before the law. Instead of turning a deaf ear to this nonsense, you make a big thing out of it. There would be more peace within this family, and it would be more appropriate if you were less proud and more tolerant."

Ragnhildur got up quickly, and the words fell from her lips with cold despite: "It has long been more appropriate for the coward to buy peace by submitting to violence, agreeing with falseness, and by falling on one's knees before arrogance. Now I finally have proof that in your view I should put up with almost anything. After this day I can testify to equal rights of foreigners in this society. With unwritten laws it is possible to denude people of their culture and to kill them psychologically — to make them lose their belief in their own worth and spiritual value. Nobody will succeed in forcing me to do such things — nobody, and least of all had I expected you to use such tactics. But then even you deceived me . . . "

All of a sudden they realized that the phone had been ringing several times, and the doctor hurried out of the dining room to answer. Ragnhildur heard him say "Yes, yes, in a moment," and when he had hung up, he rushed out of the house and ran down the steps. She stood silent as the grave and listened to his footsteps until they disappeared, stood silent as the grave and shook with emotion. She hid her head in her hands, and the tears, hot and heavy, streamed down her cheeks, because she cried like those who are lonely, helpless, and who see no light ahead.

Ragnhildur never forgot the first days at home in Vík. It was as though everything helped give her peace of mind. The weather was wonderful and her father so sincerely happy about their visit. Little Þórdís immediately took to this quiet, cultivated grandfather of hers and followed him wherever he went. He showed her the foals, the lambs, the calves, the chickens, and the birds on the beach and in the forest, and taught her the Icelandic names for them. Otherwise he found little Dísa's Icelandic poor, but made fun of it all nonetheless. Old friends and neighbours came to see Ragnhildur and invited her home. The kindness and warmth worked liked an antidote in her heart. She was once again in a bright world in which she could bring out the best in herself when need be. She made an effort to seem cheerful and happy, although underneath she was sad, and the angry hopelessness sat around her soul night and day. She would under no circumstances spoil her father's happiness about their visit by letting him get an idea of her unhappiness or her and her husband's disagreement. She didn't want to disturb her father's inner peace. This weary, experienced man had somehow learned the art of living. And in her heart of hearts she was so faithful to her husband that she did not want to complain to anybody. Sometimes she noticed that her father looked at her with mild but serious and inquisitive eyes; but if he had an idea of her state of mind, he showed no sign of it.

One day after another passed. The warmth of summer and the peacefulness of the countryside and the harmonious atmosphere around them brought peace to Ragnhildur's mind. Man's soul is like an instrument that circumstance plays variously with soft or hard hands, so that the nuances of the tones vary. She found that her thoughts were becoming milder and were more in balance — her soul was being freed from the bonds of constraint and antipathy. She found peace of mind in the quiet conversations with her father, because in spite of the difference in age, their opinions were similar in so many ways that their attitudes towards life in general were the same. She recognized the spiritual panorama — she was home again where her thoughts were given scope to fly unhindered and to search and to ask. Here she was not a foreigner.

And yet she felt that in a certain way she was now a guest in Vík. Her home was no longer there but in her own house which, despite the sunshine and the summer glory, was now a home of darkness and cold because of misunderstandings and conflicts. She had left her home hurt and angry and not without reason. She had blamed her parents-in-law for everything and then, in her quick anger, her husband, who had probably got the wrong idea of what had happened. But was she then completely innocent herself? Didn't she perhaps have some part in the discord and misunderstanding? The voice of truth spoke to Ragnhildur there in the tranquility and threw the first rays of light into her soul. She admitted that her husband had been right — she had not been tolerant lately. She had shaken her fist at her parents-in-law and made them feel the strength she had over them. On countless occasions she had made them feel that she thought nothing of them. She had made her mother-in-law feel that she hardly considered her worth speaking to. She had also made it plain to her father-in-law that she considered him to be a coarse and barefaced speculator. She had done it all in such a way that it was impossible to pounce upon her. When they spoke disdainfully about the foreigners' lack of culture, she had often out of spite spoken to them in difficult and polished English, spiced with words and sentences in other languages with the result that they didn't understand half of what she was saying. And there were other things she had done out of revenge. Social life was a case in point. Her mother-in-law had not considered Ragnhildur good enough for those with whom she was trying to ingratiate herself. But Ragnhildur had soon driven her into a corner, because not only did she have a higher education and more charm, she also had from her school years farther-ranging connections than the old woman suspected. Some of Ragnhildur's acquaintances held the types of positions that her mother-in-law looked up to and spoke of in the same voice as when she spoke of the Almighty. Thus had Ragnhildur got even in the petty way that many centuries of psychological suppression have taught women to use as a weapon. Spiritual decline is reminiscent of poor business life; those who are spiritually weak often succumb by trying to beautify themselves in the reflection of others and thereby cause deliberate jealousy of those who seek prosperity. In a sweet voice and with an innocent expression, she had told her mother-in-law about visits and parties of which she knew the old woman's vanity was jealous. She had not told her of many of those whom she had met and in whom she had found intellectual qualities, talented and interesting people, who had never had their names on the banquet lists in the newspapers or on the invitation lists of social life. And as Ragnhildur's revelations increased, the more clearly she saw how despicable all this in reality was. She had a black mark on her conscience for having let petty-mindedness lead her astray to such an extent that she herself had used the same weapons she despised in the hands of others. She had repaid arrogance with arrogance — an eye for an eye and a tooth for a tooth — and had become a lesser person.

Increasingly, she doubted if in the thoughtlessness and vehemence of her youth she hadn't used the wrong tactics against her parents-in-law. Obviously, they must have some virtues — otherwise they could hardly have Charles, her husband, as their son. Now she found that without becoming demoralized she could well have appealed to their vanity, patted the old man's cheeks by letting him understand that she respected his financial expertise and economic know-how. With her education and her cultivated manners, she could have helped her mother-in-law reach the goal she desired. She could have given in and pretended she did not hear this nonsense about foreigners, like her husband had told her. She could have . . . but why rack her brains about this now that she had burned all her bridges behind her?

Moreover, what her father had told her at the outset was beginning to disturb her more and more. By marrying a man of another nationality, she had got herself into this difficult situation, and no one but herself could get her out of it. Her marriage had also expedited the dissolution of her nationality and was the first cause for her losing this as far as her people were concerned. Of course, she would always be Icelandic no less in spirit than of descent, but what about little Þórdís Mary? No one called her Þórdís and only she and her husband called her Dísa. In about two decades no one but she, her mother, if she was still alive, would know or remember that Mary Gray was of anything but pure Anglo-Saxon descent. Wasn't it somewhat impetuous of her not to wait and see what time and circumstances brought to light? If the unlikely happened, that Þórdís would in time fall in love with a nice and well-educated Icelander and marry him, the kinship line would only be brought back one generation, but this was improbable, because they did not take part in Icelandic social life.

She began to doubt if she would have been so firm about the matter of her nationality if her parents-in-law hadn't always been putting down all foreigners. Human nature is such that suppression normally breeds resistance — only the weak, the cowards, retreat. But the tranquility and sultriness in one's mind no less than in nature are followed by peace of mind, rest, and often sleep in the end. She had never liked to retreat, nor had she liked to compromise on what she considered and knew to be true and right; but now she was in a situation where she had only two alternatives — to break all ties, and that she could not bear, or to slacken the reins, give in, and overcome her pride. When she weighed the two options, the same face appeared in her mind, first glad and smiling, then serious, and later reserved and disappointed — the face of her husband, the man she found she loved more than anything else and for whom she was prepared to risk anything. It was in this frame of mind the doctor found her when he came to Vík to visit her almost three weeks later.

When the doctor came home from his rounds, his wife and daughter had left, and the house was unpleasantly empty. Although everything was tidy and the evening sun brightened up the rooms, he nonetheless found everything gloomy, drab, and desolate. He was in such a bad mood that he hardly knew what to do with himself. He was angry at his parents, angry at Ragnhildur, and most of all angry at himself. On his way home at noon he had quickly stopped by his parents' and found them both highly incensed. Although he believed portions of what they said, he picked up the gauntlet for his wife, and for the first time in his life he had an argument with them. All this had led to the fact that when he came home everything he had said had sounded like accusations against her. He realized this immediately and also that he ought to have been a fine enough doctor to see what she had to put up with under the circumstances.

In this way the first days passed, and his mind was not with his patients. In his solitude he began to think about various things that he had never before contemplated. Ragnhildur had said so many things that he had let go in at one ear and out at the other, but which now became a topic for speculation. And he found in her words the bitter truth and the sincerity of her opinions. The thought that she had fought her battle alone and that he had never defended her or showed his parents that he was wholly on her side made him ashamed. She had revealed a number of things he had never noticed before nor opposed. In his heart of hearts he had always looked down upon the weather-beaten and ragged foreign miners who worked for his father. But somehow he had never realized that by doing so he was casting a shadow over all foreigners, including his wife. He now saw her as a queen in the group of women his parents happily would have chosen as his wife. And he saw in his mind his father standing next to Ingólfur in Vík, and he found that the comparison was not to his advantage. He realized that it was true what Ragnhildur had so often said, that everyone was a foreigner in this country except for the Indians and the Eskimos. The loneliness, stinging and biting, gradually opened his mind and calmed his temperament. He saw that he had been a coward — saw that he had never properly valued his wife. As happens to so many others, he had been infatuated with her beauty and charm but had forgotten that behind these qualities lived an independent soul with firm opinions. And before the time she had planned to be away had passed, he had felt uneasy and had become afraid that she would never come back. And then countless wonderful times they had had together — during their college years, during his visits to Vík, and during their few years of marriage — came to mind, and it became increasingly clear to him that without her and little Dísa his life would be worthless. But he knew that he had to settle the matter with his parents before he could ask her to come home. And now he found that the solitude had opened his eyes and given him the strength to convince them without losing his temper.

Before three weeks had passed, he had driven down to Vík in his car. And there in the sand, with little Dísa between them, they strengthened anew the foundations of their future, which had begun to fall apart.

Since then twenty years had passed. Ragnhildur never knew exactly what had taken place between her husband and his parents. But from that time on they had turned over a new leaf, and as the years passed they had become friendlier and easier to deal with. Now they had both passed away.

Ragnhildur still loved her Icelandic heritage and the Icelandic language, but she had acquired the broadness of mind and tolerance only years and experience can provide. And she admitted to herself that the course of events had completely changed her outlook. The young, upcoming Canada was on its way to absorb her nationality, herself, and her child, but she and her husband had managed in time to save from shipwrecking what was most precious to them — their love and their marriage. Like so many others, they had been stranded on the skerries of different temperaments and different backgrounds, but their good fortune had carried them on the highest wave up onto the beach.

Ragnhildur was suddenly awoken from her daydreams by the sound of running feet on the front steps, and a typhoon in the form of a young girl with streaming blonde hair, blue eyes, and a smiling face filled the house. In a youthful and happy voice, she called: "Mamma, mamma, I passed the exam — I passed. It says so in the morning paper." Then she ran out again, because her father's car was stopping outside the house. Ragnhildur took the paper and looked. Yes, there on the first page was the list of medical students, and in alphabetical order she read: D. Mary Gray, distinction.

She felt a short pang in her heart. It had come to what she had earlier feared the most. Ingólfur in Vík's family line had disappeared — was forgotten. She herself was the last link. Mary Gray was a child of her time — she belonged to the new, upcoming generation.

But generations continue to come and go — like the wind that whistles around one's ears — like the leaves that flow on the currents of a river. They continue, century after century, and rarely take the time to look back. And time is like a bird that comes from the direction of sunrise and flies towards the sea until it disappears from sight — or like a cloud of dust that follows a cavalry regiment. The hoof-beats are heard for a while — the tracks, deep or shallow, are imprinted in the sand. The wind blows — the dust of the ages covers the tracks — and before one knows it no traces of them are seen. But the dreams of humankind continue to appear and disappear — and appear anew — and with each new dream a new hope is raised — and with the hope new life.

[1950]

Beyond the Pale

Why do people always desire the most what is farthest away and impossible to grasp? Why do the lands of a mirage seem so much more beautiful and attractive to those who have solid ground under their feet?

The longing to explore endless horizons wins a victory over all common sense. The desire to search for these bright lands overcomes most people at some point, and then they take off into the tempting uncertainty.

I have arrived here, all the long way from Iceland, and am one of the many who today, on the 2nd of August, are taking part in the Íslendingadagur, the Western Icelanders' annual festival, to celebrate and honour our fatherland far north in the ocean.

In the tall maple forest south of the Red River, a great number of people have gathered from all classes of society and all ages, from decrepit old men to infants. The weather is wonderful. Indeed, an elderly woman told me this morning that the Lord always gives the Icelanders good weather on the 2nd of August. I can well believe that, because it would be unfeeling of the Creator to let the weather ruin people's joy on this particular day.

The day is ceremoniously celebrated with speeches, music, sports activities, and festivities. Select people exhibit their athletic talents, and men of letters compose and speak. And today I feel no weakling is placed in the high seat. The speakers' eloquence and the poets' masterpieces warm my heart. Only people who speak with sincerity can speak in such a way.

Memories and pictures of Iceland are everywhere present, and it is clear to me that although these people are resident citizens of this country, they have still not established roots but move about like foreigners in a distant country.

I think about the scattered population at home, and I am overcome by feelings of regret as I watch these promising people strolling about under the arches of the linden trees' foliage along the even, grassy bank. These are all Icelanders who today, and perhaps every day, look longingly to Iceland, the country where they were raised and had their families and lands.

During the formalities people sat quietly and seriously and listened to each word. But when they were over, people began to move, walked about, looked around, greeted and chatted with one another, met friends and acquaintances. Everyone was in a festive mood and looked so happy that I almost came to believe literally what Ásgrímur had said to me on our way to the festival this morning that such a magical force followed the Íslendingadagur that even the frictions between opposing parties, a strong shackle on the minds of our countrymen here, did not manifest themselves. He said that on this day advocates of opposing denominations met with a Christian smile, as if they admitted that each nonetheless had the right to walk on God's green earth in the bright sunshine and breathe the clean, fresh air; fanatical teetotallers and alcoholics greeted each other with hand-shakes and kisses and had coffee together; politicians had friendly discussions about the welfare of the country; leaders of opposing women's organizations looked each other straight in the face with kindness and unanimity while they asked about each other's health and well-being. "A true model of brotherhood to all the rest of us, who just follow in complete naivety, loyalty, and sincerity," Ásgrímur added and laughed.

"The eyes of the guest are sharp, and beware of fooling me, because I'm beginning to see and understand more than you'd expect of an emigrant," I answered in the same tone.

There are so many things I have tried to understand and analyze since I came here. And today, in these crowds of people, I have tried to use both eyes and ears. Despite the fact that people are pleasant to me, I feel I am not considered one of them. The elderly people are very Icelandic both in appearance and demeanour, but still they are a little different from people at home. I find the young people good-looking, and I envy them their openness and informality. Unconstrained and cheerful, they form a group and chat sometimes in Icelandic, some-times in English. They have distinct, Icelandic features, and yet, especially when they speak English, I find that there is something foreign about them.

Today I have seen all kinds of distinguished Western Icelanders: intellectuals, poets and authors, politicians, lawyers, doctors, femi-nists, and leaders and chairpersons of this and that society. A distin-guished temperance agitator, for example, was pointed out to me; in my ignorance I thought he was not quite right in the head, but then I realized that he was just so sincerely happy. Such misunderstandings naturally stem from the naivety of the emigrant, who is unfamiliar with everything.

The older people are busy finding seats at overloaded coffee-tables here and there under the trees, and friends and relatives are offered coffee. All the women of any standing have with them cups and all kinds of cakes which they serve to everyone unsparingly. People chat with friends and acquaintances, walk from one table to another, eat cakes and drink coffee to their hearts' delight.

One woman immediately caught my attention. She was extraordinarily eloquent, but strange and coarse in appearance. She was big and fat and dressed in a tight, red, and shiny silk dress. All kinds of golden fineries, which were literally dangling on her, clearly satisfied an untamed love of finery. The belt around her waist was especially conspicuous. It was made from silver dollars that were linked together, showing alternatively the head of Queen Victoria and the Statue of Liberty of the United States with the engraved words "In God we trust." The belt was naturally valuable, because a lot of silver dollars were required to reach around the waist of this woman. Its aesthetic value was not the same — but what does that matter compared with the power of wealth — the god in which most people trust.

Somehow I have become separated from my travel companions, and in the crowds I am almost losing heart and becoming homesick. I drift down to the river. Here it is good to sit alone, to rest, think, and daydream. The sun throws rays of light onto the river and turns the grey, muddy water into a stream of gold. The river is calm on the surface, but its strong, deep, and powerful current turns and twists along the prairie forming promontories and tongues of land. One of these promontories is Elm Park, the place on which we are standing. It lies like a gigantic hoof-mark, around which the river bends. It washes the hills, erodes and carries away both the dark, fragrant soil and the yellow clay. Thence the river flows onward to the sea — a symbol of the people here. The living stream of people continues generation after generation while the sands of time run in the hourglass. People continue, strong and powerful, while those who settled the land disappear into the sea of oblivion like obscure folktales.

Una from Holt comes walking in my direction, but she does not see me and walks past. Since I left Iceland, her house has almost been my home. Una has been here in the West for many years. She is now an elderly lady and has grown children with whom she is living, because her husband died some time ago. Una is always asking me for news from Iceland; it is as if she cannot get enough. She asks about

everything — people and politics, farming and cattle, and all the
changes that have taken place in the district since she left. She often
mentions Holt, where she was born and raised. There she lived with
her husband Sveinn in great poverty and difficulty until Eiríkur, the
reeve, Jón of Hvammur's father, managed to get the parish to pay their
fare to America, so that they would no longer be a burden to the
district. I never let Una — never mind her son Ásgrímur — feel that
I remember that they were sent West by the district. But I have often
thought about Eiríkur and Jón since I came here, for it is also their
doing that I went to America. And I shall not deny that I smile to
myself when I think about the fact that the people I like the best and
visit most often are the family the reeve rid the district of. But my
smile always disappears when the picture of Jón appears in my mind,
and strange though it may seem, it happens most often when I am with
Ásgrímur, although they are different — and the comparison is not in
Jón's favour. He was born and raised to be the ornament and leader
of the district, to rule and govern, to live on the largest estate, and to
choose the woman he liked best — buy her if he cannot get her in any
other way. Ásgrímur, on the other hand, was sent away by the district
to avoid more trouble — out into the distance and uncertainty to
another continent to manage as best he could or to disappear into the
deep like his little sister, who died on the voyage and was buried at sea.
I wonder what my parents would say if they knew my thoughts, my
parents who had long intended for me to be the mistress of the house
at Hvammur. But that may have to wait, and so may perhaps my return
to Iceland. And yet, in a peculiar way Iceland towers clearly and
uppermost in my mind just now. It is flowing in the clear, blue sky in
the north — the land of mirage in the distance that no one here can set
foot on.

I am overcome by a strong desire to be back home, by a strange
magic longing for bygone days of beauty and joy. And yet one
particular bright and beautiful spring morning is peculiarly clear in
my mind. I still hear the glad voices of spring resound in the air and
smell the scent of the vegetation. The grass, green and young, is soft
under one's feet, the dew is sparkling and shining like big diamonds
in the heather and on the birch trees, and the moss campion clothes the
grey gravel plains in a pink garb. The morning sun enwraps all growth
in its warmth and brightness. The mountains stretch their sunny peaks

up into the sky, and rivers and streams are running fast on their way to the sea, which is silhouetted against the blue air like a dark line in the distance. A delightful Icelandic spring morning — joie de vivre everywhere. Nature works day and night to compensate for a long and cold winter. The midnight sun shines so bright that the dark wings of the night become light and transparent. When day and night both keep guard over the soil out there in the north magic things happen, because people likewise desire to work day and night, to keep vigil all spring, to enjoy life and light like all other vegetation, and to let dreams take root and hopes grow.

It was out there in the morning sunshine that I decided to give in to this longing of mine to take off on my own out into the world. Within myself I found the strength to make my own decisions instead of tying myself down in Hvammur for the rest of my life. I have still not recovered from Jón of Hvammur's proposal, from the self-exaltation, selfishness, and vanity that shone through in each word. I wanted to tell Jón a few things that would put a dent in his self-esteem, but all I could do was to thank him for the offer — and decline.

Sometimes when one is happy, fearless, and unsuspecting, all sorts of troubles suddenly pour down. I think I will always remember my last carefree and, in fact, happy day in my parents' home. My brother Þorgeir and I were on our way to the sheep pen. We were laughing and chatting and having a good time and felt no tiredness or lack of sleep although we had been up all night helping the boys to pack the wool that had to be taken to town. Our parents left in the evening and rode ahead of the caravanners from the three neighbouring farms. After everyone had gone it did not occur to us to go to sleep; instead we made coffee and stayed up during the bright night until it was time to go to the sheep pen, because the lambs had still not been weaned from the ewes. When we arrived at the pen, we saw the ewes scattered south over the entire promontory, which was flat and covered with grass along the river. We soon managed to gather the sheep together, and when we had let the lambs out of the pen it did not take them long to find their mothers. Then we had to decide who was to stay behind with the ewes while they were calming down. It became my job, and when I was alone I sat down on the bank of the brook south of the pen and listened to the murmur of the water. The birds sang patriotic songs to their hearts' content in tones more beautiful and sincere than Barroclough's orchestra's rendition of the national anthem today.

I hummed to myself the tune "Now I see and embrace you, singing spring," and to me it seemed as if all living things joined in. Could there possibly be a more beautiful place on earth than here at home in the Icelandic countryside? And yet one hears the call of distant places. I picked the petals off a few lady's mantles and threw them into the brook. The current caught them and carried them toward the river. Would they all get there? I got up and ran along the brook to see what became of them. A short distance farther down one of the flowers had got caught in an eddy and flowed ceaselessly round and round a little stone. Farther down another was flowing in a little lagoon that had formed at the side of the brook and had no chance of ever getting out. But the third flowed with the stream all the way down to the river, and after a short while I lost sight of it on its way to the sea. How far would it get? In my mind I compared myself with the petals that got nowhere. Here I was in the monotony of everyday existence and wanted so very badly to see a bit of the world and not to sit on the same tussock all my life. But older people don't understand — they are happy to be where they are and to have things the way they have always been. Here my parents have lived and my grandparents before them, and it is as if they are a part of the soil — as if their spirit reigns over us. In this way they have thought and ruled, and in this way everything must continue. But then the voices of nature, the voices of spring, with the youthful power of growth come and sing restlessness into the minds and hearts of those of us who are young. Nowhere is the call clearer than in the solitude of the bright summer night. And I returned home, drunk on spring, beauty, and the longing to be independent; I was happy and determined. But it did not last long, because I truly fell into disfavour with my parents for having rejected Jón of Hvammur. Nonetheless, I insisted on going abroad before I tied myself down for life. I told them that I wanted to go to America — where clearly everyone could go who in one way or another was beyond the pale of society. At first I said this as if it were an absurdity to make them understand that anything would be better than Hvammur — even America. To my surprise they agreed to let me go West rather than to Copenhagen, which was where I would have preferred to go. They probably thought that the boredom there would open my eyes and soon send me back home. It was finally decided that I should go West for a year and stay with some relatives. But I had to promise to keep Jón in mind and to return home. And now I have been here for a few months or since last autumn and am probably in even more trouble regarding my parents and the promise of returning.

There is Una again. I notice that she is looking for me, so I get up and wave to her. She comes over and asks if I am bored because I am here all by myself and not with the young people who are about to start dancing. Then after a moment she adds:

"My Grímsi was asking for you. He said he wanted to dance the last waltz with you."

I watch Una while she is talking. Her son looks so much like her. The only difference is that he is happy and uninhibited in behaviour and speech while she is restrained and quiet. But she always brightens up when she speaks of Ásgrímur; her expression changes, and it is as if the joy comes from within, just like when the sun appears from behind an overcast sky. And indeed why should she not smile and be glad when she thinks of her promising and intelligent son? I had to be careful not to let the happiness show when I heard that he was looking for me to ask for a dance. I did not answer but told Una that I had enjoyed myself today; but I had difficulty understanding much of what I had heard such as, for example, this great patriotism that was expressed in the songs and the speeches, and people's almost childish pride in their nationality, and I added hesitantly: "We at home cannot compare with you, and yet all these people willingly left Iceland."

"Yes, it's exactly the longing for Iceland and the difficulties in remaining Icelandic, the longing that tries to make words, thoughts, and feelings come true. We try to hold Iceland in our minds and hearts here at a distance. And as to leaving Iceland willingly, I doubt if that applies to everybody." Una looked at me as if she thought to herself that I was clearly talking about things about which I knew nothing. I have often had the experience since I left home that I am not credited with more intelligence than I already have, so I answered with a smile: "Perhaps not everybody, but most I imagine."

Una answered oppressively: "I certainly came reluctantly. It's probably best that you know that we were sent here by the district. None of my children knows except Grímsi. He was old enough to understand everything."

116

"One can hardly blame people for being poor," I quickly answered, but I was well aware of the stigma attached to being a pauper, "and now you're better off than most of the farmers in our district at home," I continued. "Have you disliked it here in the West, Una?" I asked in order to change the subject.

"Disliked it," Una repeated. "I wouldn't say that, but so much of me stayed behind which I always wish I could have assembled into one piece instead of dividing. Our entire past is in Iceland, and the roots run deep in the country where our race has developed for more than a thousand years. Here we cannot teach our children their ancestors' history in place names or show them any physical traces except in words, and therefore we try to raise our voices on occasions like today. Then there's the other side, which pertains to life here. The American dream was an incentive to make us work our fingers to the bone. Sveinn's back was bent and his hands were rough when he died, but he paved the way for our children's future and gained confidence in his own abilities. I'm not ashamed and I'm not being ostentatious when I say that I've often felt proud of being able to manage on my own, of owning my own home, and of knowing that my children and I will never be treated as paupers. In my mind I often saw my children as if they had been raised in the district and, say, Grímsi been sent as a shepherd boy to Eiríkur of Hvammur. What would have become of him? And my girls — by the time they had worked at humiliating and poorly paid jobs here and there in the district, they would probably have considered themselves lucky if some farmer had hired them as maids. I've seen it all. Those who are in a bad way and all alone are often grateful for very little. When these pictures come before my eyes, I find that a great 'thank you' may come from the lips of those who have done well here but who have experienced the same conditions as I have. That feeling will, I think, become the first seed to take root here."

"Why don't you return, Una? I'm sure you'd do just fine now." I felt I had finally found the right solution.

Una smiled and answered: "It's not quite as simple as it may seem. We've become familiar with this place and are settled here; we have our possessions and jobs here, and my children might feel like foreigners back home. I wouldn't want to see them in that situation, and, as I told you, I'm divided; a part of me feels at home here and wants to be nowhere else. You probably find this a lot of nonsense after all the wisdom you've been listening to today," said Una on the way to where the band was striking up dance tunes.

I did not like what Una had said. No Icelander had the right to love any other country but Iceland, and no one could truly love two countries at the same time. I was overcome by disappointment and pain. Everyone here was like that.

"So these are then the fleshpots," I said a little impatiently. — "I'd better get home before I develop a taste for them."

Una stopped and looked at me in surprise. She did not know how much was going on in my mind at this moment.

"Let's not misunderstand one another," Una said quietly. "If you return shortly, your memories of this place will only be a superficial travel recollection. But if you stay here, you'll realize that what I've been telling you is true. The western world does not easily let go of those who settle here. And if you settle here, you'll feel like I and probably most people who've come here as adults do. In one's mind there's always the longing for what is impossible to bring along and then a comparison — a comparison that for a long time doesn't work in favour of this place, but which changes nonetheless. In the evenings, when I was standing outside looking at the prairie, the mountains at home appeared in their glory. Now the prairie often seems beautiful to me. In times of heat and drought that caused everything to wither and burn, I remembered and longed for the cooling drizzle at home and saw the scattered showers in the sunshine on the mountainsides. And when the hot winds were blowing mercilessly, I recalled the mild southerly breeze and the cool wind from the sea. Now I remember as well the raw cold and the pouring rain. In the dark nights here I saw before my eyes the light summer nights and the long bright days. But now I also remember the long winter nights and the solstice. I could go on, but it's unnecessary, because you know what I mean. But what weighs heaviest on the scales is to know oneself and one's family are free and independent, and for that I am grateful. I'm also grateful for the fleshpots, because the child I lost at sea died from starvation. You've no idea of how such an experience affects a mother. It can make her a savage beast, a madwoman, or it can turn her into a helpless, miserable wretch. My child died from starvation — from too little and unwholesome food, the doctor said. For many years I started up from my sleep because in my dreams I felt the grief and pain I suffered then."

"Perhaps it was only a vague notion," I said in an apologetic tone, because I felt I had touched a sensitive chord.

Perhaps only a vague notion, I repeated to myself. Nonetheless, I knew that two things were quickly becoming clear to me: in the first place, that if I became Jón of Hvammur's wife, I would be a bondswoman all my life, and, in the second place, that even if I left for Iceland tomorrow, my love and happiness would remain here — the part of existence that elevates the human soul to the highest pinnacles and that also lets it explore the deepest depths.

There is Ásgrímur walking toward us, and the happiness shines from his eyes. He gives me his hand and asks me to dance, and hand in hand we enter the hall where young people float around light-footed and dressed in pale-coloured clothes. The older people stand at the side in groups talking and watching their children, the young people, enjoy themselves. They look a little tired, because day has turned into night.

Ásgrímur and I begin to dance and follow the rhythm. I feel that we dance well and are in complete harmony. I feel Ásgrímur's eyes resting on me, but I do not meet them, because I am not completely certain how I will answer what they are asking for.

But now it is clear to me that if I return to Iceland, if I leave this big, sunny country, then I will for a long time see it as a mirage farthest out toward the west, this country and Ásgrímur, silhouetted against the sky.

[1938]

Not Everything Is As It Seems

Some years ago I was at one of those coffee parties which Icelandic women arrange shortly before Christmas in support of this or that charitable cause. The hall was crowded, but still I found a seat on a sofa by the wall facing the entrance. The nicest thing about these parties is that often old acquaintances, who perhaps haven't seen each other for a long time, get a chance to meet and chat and renew their friendship.

I had seen many people there whom I enjoyed talking with, but the woman whom I had arranged to meet had not yet arrived, and therefore I had chosen a seat from where I could keep an eye on the door. At that moment I saw Þórunn Hall enter the room. She was a woman who didn't usually frequent Icelandic gatherings, and it was a long time since I had seen her. I had known her well as a child and a young girl, but when she married our ways had parted and I only saw her occasionally in public. But I never spoke with her, because I sensed that she avoided Icelanders, and I found that rather contemptible.

Nonetheless, I had often defended Þórunn, when people spoke badly of her. Her marriage in particular was a topic of much discussion. Some said that she had sold herself to a hardhearted businessman; others maintained that she had been taken by his glamour. I didn't know, because after her mother died and her father remarried, I lost contact with the family. She was now very different from the pretty little girl I had been fond of, and as she floated through the room, there was an uncomfortably strong similarity between her and the mannequins in shop windows, who move according to specific rules to display as best they can the fineries the shops are advertising. I did not find her charming. Perhaps there was some truth in what people said about her complacency and vanity.

My eyes followed her as she walked in, tall, beautiful, and stately. Apart from the deathly emptiness in her expression, she was so amazingly like her grandmother that I found it hard to believe that a drop of old Þórunn Böðvarsson's warm blood wasn't still pulsating in the veins of this doll.

The hostesses approached Þórunn and greeted her with the kind of sweet sales smile which welcomes everybody at such gatherings. Apart from them, no one took any notice of her and neither greeted her nor spoke with her.

The young woman stood deathly still and looked around. Her eyes were cold, and her face was like a closed book. I couldn't help thinking that this woman clearly felt herself worthy of the many looks and covert glances from the corner of this eye and that. But I also sensed rather than saw something else. There was something hesitant and lonely about this masked woman. She probably felt my eyes on her, because suddenly she noticed me and came over and sat down beside me. She greeted me with a firm handshake, and her eyes became gentle when she said:

"It's a long time since we've talked. Do you remember me? When I came to visit grandma and grandpa, you were often there. I've long wanted to ask you about them and their life here when they were younger. But there's never the time on the rare occasions that we see each other — at a distance," she added and fell silent for a moment. "I remember grandpa well, because he stayed with us after grandma died, but I've fewer memories of her."

Her many questions about the old Böðvarsson couple convinced me that the memory of them was dear to her. When the coffee was brought our conversation collapsed for a while, but when the women who served the coffee had gone, she broke the silence and asked vivaciously:

"Am I right that grandma was a beautiful woman with a friendly smile and easy bearing? It showed that life treated her well, didn't it?"

"Your grandmother was a beautiful woman. You look like her. But it would, perhaps, be more accurate to say that she lived her life well. She handled flaws with gentle hands, because she was a strong, sensible, and loving woman. It was these qualities that moulded her features. Would you like to hear a Christmas story your grandmother told me the last Christmas she lived?"

"Christmas is almost here and Christmas stories are in season. I'd very much like to hear especially this one."

"Your grandmother and my mother were close friends, and as far back as I can remember, I spent much time in the Böðvarsson home. After both my parents had died it became for me a second home. I was always invited to spend Christmas with them, and when I married I made a habit of looking in on them every Christmas Eve. With this gentle, old couple, I truly had a spiritual home, because their devotion and friendship were always constant.

"On your grandmother's last Christmas, I went there early, because I had my children and my own Christmas festivities to attend to. When I arrived at the Böðvarssons', old Leifi, the driver, was there with his horse, Jarpur, and his big sleigh in front of the house; the sleigh was loaded with parcels and boxes. Jón, your grandfather, was helping Leifi arrange the boxes on the sleigh. Your grandfather was in an excellent mood, ready to go, and had clearly given old Leifi a drink, because couplets were pouring out of him, and he spoke loudly in good Icelandic with his horse, which was a fine horse with such a talent for language that it had no problems understanding Leifi's Icelandic. Indeed, Leifi expected it to have such intelligence, and that is more than people nowadays expect from Icelandic youngsters.

"Your grandfather told me to go in and see Þórunn, because he was about to go on an official trip with Leifi and would soon be joining Santa Claus. They said goodbye and Merry Christmas and with that they vanished into the dusk. But I heard Leifi saying to his horse that it had better get a move on so that they would be home before midnight.

"I went into the house, and your grandmother received me with open arms. I told her that I'd spoken with Jón. She looked at me with a smile and said:

"'So you know what this is all about?'

"'Hardly,' I answered.

"'You mustn't tell anyone. Leifi is as silent as the grave. He has transported such goods for us before and never said anything. We send them anonymously to those who are in need, because some have too little and others too much, and unfortunately this will never change. In this way we're paying back an old debt.' She was silent for a minute and then added:

"'One Christmas Eve a long time ago, I learned to understand those who are lonely, afraid of life and the future, and who dare not trust other people's sympathy and helpfulness. But it was nonetheless my good fortune that that Christmas became one of the happiest Christmases I've had in my life.'

"I'd become very curious and asked your grandmother to tell me her Christmas story, because I suspected this was no ordinary story.

"'Well, my dear,' your grandmother began, 'I don't mind trying to tell you about this event in my life. But it's not a story and also I don't know if I can describe in words my state of mind then, because the emotions and attitudes of youth are forgotten at my age.

"'In the autumn of the second year of our marriage Jón and I moved into the first house we owned here in this country. Jón had built it in his spare time that summer in the part that was called West on the prairie. He had bought the lot cash at a low price, and for the timber he got a loan on good terms. Moving into the house was something very special. To me the house was a castle, and I felt like a queen in a fairy tale. It was a tiny three-room house with a family room, bedroom, and a small kitchen. But it was pretty and comfortable, and there was more than enough space for the two of us and little Sigga, who was then only a few weeks old. Getting settled cost us more than we had anticipated, careful though we tried to be, and we had very little money left. Jón had steady work during the summer until the end of September. He searched all over town for employment, but there was nothing available until the spring. The only job he could get was cutting timber in the wilderness, which he gladly accepted, and he was hired until the middle of December. Before he left he attended to the house and the cowshed, because we had one cow and a few hens. We had plenty of firewood, and he bought feed for our animals before he left. We calculated that I would be able to manage with what little we had left of his summer earnings.

"'In the beginning, the housekeeping went well, and I got used to the work in the cowshed. But at the end of November, the child became so ill that a doctor and medicine were needed. Little Sigga soon got better, but I had to take every precaution while she was recovering.

"'On top of that the weather was very bad with blizzards for days on end, and then, when that stopped, came merciless frosts. I managed to keep the house warm, but the cowshed was so cold that the hens completely stopped laying eggs, and the cow gave only very little milk. I tried to keep everything going, but in my mind I was counting the days until Jón would come back. There I was alone, day after day, with nothing before my eyes except for the mass of snow, covering the prairies as far as the eye could see. To me it seemed as if the snow stretched from dawn in the east to sunset in the west. But sometimes the evening clouds were so beautiful that I saw in them mountains and valleys which reminded me of my childhood in Iceland. I neither could nor would leave the child except to go to the cowshed to attend to the cow and the hens. The acquaintances we had lived far away in the north-east end of town, and I did not know our neighbours, because they, too, lived a good distance away. I contacted one of these men, who sold drinking water from door to door. He came twice a week and I paid him my last cent, because after the child had fallen ill and the snow had become impassable, it was impossible for me to fetch water at a long distance. I lived as thriftily as a person possibly can, but nonetheless the food supply was giving out. Jón had said he would be back a week before Christmas.

"'The journey home took three to four days, and in the morning of the 19th of December I was cheerful, because I felt confident he would come home in the evening. I cleaned the house from top to bottom, and the cowshed looked like a parlour. The day flew by. Not even the lack of food bothered me. I had a bit of flour and oatmeal, a sprinkle of sugar in a bowl, and a few potatoes. Nothing else except what I could get from the cow. Jón was coming home and everything was all right.

"'As the day had gone fast, the evening was endless, because Jón didn't come. Day after day passed, and I heard nothing from him. I was either consoling myself by the thought that he'd decided to work longer than he'd originally planned or seeing in my mind all the things that could have happened to him, and they were many and ranged from having had an accident to having frozen to death. Those were dull days and the nights no better. My little child now laughed and prattled in her cradle; she and the work helped me keep my composure.

"'On Christmas Eve I kept myself busy. I cleaned the entire house and baked Icelandic pancakes from the last handful of flour. The oatmeal was finished, but I still had six potatoes and a litre of milk for Christmas dinner. "He's coming tonight," I said out loud to myself, "or he's" — I dared not think farther. I took out his best suit and brushed and pressed it, laid out his shirt and starched collar on our bed. Everything had to be ready when he arrived. It was getting dark and my fear was beginning to get the better of me. Fervent, wordless prayers were travelling around in my mind, and to avoid crying I had to absorb myself in work. I dressed the child in the prettiest dress she had, and she was as beautiful as a flower in bloom. The family room was warm and bright, but I was cold with fear and perhaps also because I was hungry.

"'The evening went slowly, one hour after another, and seemed like an eternity. I put on my Sunday dress, for it was Christmas Eve. It did occur to me that I was stupid not to take the child and look for help. But I was afraid that people would talk about it and give me gifts of charity if my situation became known. Enough people might blame Jón for not having provided properly for me before he left. The merchants sold on credit, but I didn't want to ask anything of anybody. I didn't know then how helpful the Icelanders here were.

"'It was past nine o'clock. The child had fallen asleep, and I turned down the lamp to save oil. I was filling up the stove in the kitchen, and the kettle was boiling so that everything would be in order when Jón arrived, because I was still a bit hopeful. Suddenly I seemed to hear a noise by the front door, so I ran to the door and listened but heard nothing except for sleigh bells in the distance. I opened the door nonetheless and almost tripped over a big box that stood in the small entrance hall. Our name was written on a card that was attached to the box.

"'I opened the door and looked out. There were deep footprints and the tracks of a sleigh in the snow, but I saw nobody.

"'I dragged the box into the kitchen and opened it. It contained all the Christmas goodies that one can imagine. A bird, smoked lamb, fruit, sweets, coffee, sugar, and all sorts of groceries. There was also a bottle of Jón's favourite wine and a packet of the tobacco he smoked. Around the bottle was a note on which was written in a disguised hand: "From a friend with thanks to both of you." I stood there staring at all these nice things. And I had not dared to trust people's kindness! The tears I had fought all day finally got the upper hand. How long I sat by the table I do not know, but suddenly I heard the slam of the door in the entrance hall. I quickly dried my eyes and heard Jón's unmistakable knock on the door. I dashed to the door and opened thinking that if this was not Jón himself then it must be his ghost. Jón had arrived, tired, hungry, and cold, but alive and well. Now everything was all right, and Christmas was in our home. He'd tell me nothing about his hazardous journey until after the holidays, but when he did, I knew I had virtually claimed him from hell.

"'That Christmas taught me to understand those who are helpless, destitute, hungry, and fearful, and I also learned to trust people's kindness. To the friend who sent us the Christmas food we made the promise that we would always remember him by making a similar gesture to others in a situation similar to the one in which we were then. We've tried to keep that promise according to our means, but nonetheless that Christmas will never be fully repaid.'"

While I had been speaking the young woman had not moved and had been staring into space. And it may sound strange, but when she turned to look at me some yearning in her eyes reminded me of a river coursing under transparent ice. She tried to hide her emotions which broke through her cold shell.

"This, then, is your grandmother's story. It is short, but it gives a good idea of her character and qualities," I said slowly as I got up, because now I saw that the woman I had been waiting for had arrived.

Þórunn Hall shook my hand warmly and said: "Thank you for your story. One day I'll tell it to my children and to a young woman who is so unlucky as to have lost faith in most of the good things life has to offer. She could have learned from a grandmother who'd rather go hungry than risk the reputation of her husband."

She quickly walked to the door as if she were in a hurry. In her movements there was spirit and life. I looked at her with sad eyes until she disappeared out of the door. And it occurred to me that there was more of her grandmother in her than I had expected.

Hunger has many faces . . .

[1945]

Arnrún from Fell

Arnrún from Fell (the pen name of Guðrún Tómasdóttir) was born in 1886, in Uppkot, Norðurárdalur, the daughter of Tómas Guðmundsson and Ástrós Sumarliðadóttir. She graduated as a midwife in Reykjavík in 1905, then went to Copenhagen and completed her degree in nursing in 1908. She worked as a midwife in Ísafjarðarkaupstaður until 1917, when she emigrated to the United States where, in 1918, she married Karl Friðrik Bjarnason, a professor at Harvard University. From around the time of her husband's death in 1949 until 1966, Guðrún Tómasdóttir worked as a nurse in a hospital in Boston. She died in Boston in 1972.

Guðrún Tómasdóttir had already written short stories for *Eimreiðin* and *Iðunn* before she left for the United States. Her later stories have appeared mainly in *Tímarit Þjóðræknisfélags Íslendinga*. A collection of some of her stories was published under the title *Margs verða hjúin vís* (Reykjavík, 1956).

"In Old Haunts," "Much Do Servants Know" and "Goody" are translated from "Á fornum stöðvum," "Margs verða hjúin vís" and "Goody" in *Margs verða hjúin vís* (7-15, 16-25 and 110-125).

In Old Haunts

Goðafoss moored at the quay with the morning tide. So, now they had gotten a quay at Stafnfjörður, but otherwise the village seemed to have changed mighty little from the time when Jói rowed with him out to old Vesta in the early spring of 1908. Actually, as he looked more closely he noticed that the eastern end of Möller's store's drying place for fish now belonged to an apartment building, and over the door of the old man's store could be seen a sign saying "The Ísafold Society's Store" which was said to be Danish property. He smiled. Greek people in the States usually called their restaurants "American

Restaurant." Would some of the small Naust cottages still be there? Ólafur's cottage, Gunnar's cottage, Sveinn's cottage. He came all the way from America to see Ólafur's cottage. Could it possibly still be there considering how decrepit it was twenty years ago? He turned his binoculars in the direction of Naust. Well, well! If it wasn't standing there all by itself! Or was it Sveinn's cottage? No, it was their "nest," as Lína called it. Lína — poor little Lína.

Would any of his friends in Berwick believe that he had lived in this turf hut? Yet it was true. In fact, for almost five years. And although the rent was only sixty kroners per year, it was extremely difficult to pay on time.

He had been terribly poor back then. A twenty-year-old boy, who was resolved to become a captain and, as time passed, a ship owner. He had had little else than the clothes he wore — and Lína. Well, he became a captain and later a ship owner — but in the States. The castles in the air which he built in Stafnfjörður had materialized in another country. He had often been impatient and dissatisfied in those days. All his contemporaries seemed to do better than he did. Jón from Lón, who had arrived in Stafnfjörður a year earlier than he, had a share in a boat and lived upstairs at his father-in-law's. Mundi from Meiðastaðir went to each entertainment in the Templar's Lodge. But he and Lína were so poor and had so few clothes that they were ashamed to go to church.

He had grown up in the country, and until his confirmation, he had roamed from place to place. He was fifteen years old when he came to Reverend Halldór at Hof, where he met Lína Hermannsdóttir, who looked after the minister's children. Lína was wonderfully gentle and good, the first person who had been kind to him. She was a good-looking girl, small and thin, with dark hair. But she was not intelligent and hardly looked at a book. He hadn't thought about that until a while after he had married her. Then he called to mind that he had heard that her mother had been dismissed — and more than once.

Sometimes he made only very little money, but Lína never complained about their poverty. She was always in the same mood, equally gentle and compliant, and took good care of the home. Nonetheless, he became tired of her relatively soon; he even wished that once she would become really angry, so that he would have the opportunity to ingratiate himself with her and mollify her. (He now knew that it was also possible to become tired of that.)

He had read all the papers and books he could get his hands on, especially those that concerned fishing and finances. But sometimes he could not concentrate on what he read. The thought became ever more pressing how crazy it had been to marry so young.

Their little boys brought much joy, at least in the beginning. But they soon became like toys with which one gets bored; he had been too young to appreciate that precious gift — had arrived at that conclusion much, much later.

His mind was wandering so much at that time; he didn't know what he wanted. Yes, he knew that he wanted to be wealthy, and that Lína and the boys seemed to be dragging him deeper and deeper down into the swamp of poverty.

It was as if everything turned against them almost two years after they had married. The lack of fish, bad weather, and then Lína's poor health after she had the twins caused them to spend what little they had — and more. He became more and more worried and anxious each week. The time passed like sand between his fingers. All his hopes for prosperity became more and more distant. Here in this peaceful fjord the difficulties had almost overpowered him. Here he had almost given up.

A great peace and calm was resting over the fjord. The sea was as still as a stagnant puddle; the waves were so innocent, as if they didn't have the ability to foam. How this beautiful late summer day reminded him of a similar day more than twenty-five years ago! Would he ever be able to forget the day when they arrived here, he and Lína, newly wed? There wasn't a single little cloud in the sky, neither literally nor figuratively.

But the sea ice was not far from land, as they say. Shortly after the boys turned two, little Halldór fell ill with enteritis, which was going around the fjord, and shortly before he died Hermann was infected. There were only four days between them. They were placed in the same coffin and buried at Hof in a fierce March snowstorm. He couldn't afford a funeral, though they each received one later. It was as if his heart had broken and life had lost all purpose. It was not just a wave that broke on him — the sea goddess Rán had waded ashore.

He had come here to visit old haunts. Look, there were the beginnings of a flower garden behind Möller's house. Here was a bakery where Halta-Leifi's cobbler's workshop had been. This must be the doctor's house. He had heard that his doctor had resigned. Perhaps his successor lived there. "Man's life runs fast and doesn't linger." Wishes and interests change. About twenty years ago he would have been speechless with joy if he had all of a sudden received one hundred kroners. He would have to pay that amount many times over in tips before the end of his journey.

He still clearly remembered when he and Lína came here the first time. Giddy with joy they walked hand in hand out along the fjord — out to Naust. To think of all the adversity they faced since then while they were living in this little turf hut!

He walked faster. Here was the consul's house, newly painted and expanded. But where Hannes's house had been now stood an ugly new concrete house. Hannes's Þorgerður often helped Lína while the boys were on their deathbeds. She must be in her eighties, if she was still alive.

Yes, there Ólafur's cottage stood like an old faded monument. The memories crowded in on him. It had often been good to come home, to see the light in the window, to meet Lína inside the door, her face flushed from the stove — to be swaddled with gentleness and love. No, he hadn't always been unhappy here.

Ólafur's cottage seemed to have changed remarkably little. It was as ramshackle as one would expect with broken windows and a sunken roof, but still recognizable.

He himself had changed more, both mentally and physically. He had aged and his hair was greying at the edges. And Lína — Lína had died from measles, which had gone the rounds here in 1916, eight years after he had left. For seven years she continued to write to him. When he had gotten three or four letters in a row, he wrote her a couple of lines and sent a few dollars. She was so childishly grateful for what little she received and always ended the next letter with the sentence "It came in very handy."

Came in very handy! Why hadn't he worked his fingers to the bone for her?

Lína often listened with rapt attention to his building of castles in the air, like a child listening to a fairy tale: He owned more ships than old Geir. They had a house much bigger than Vikness's house. He called the consul Henrik and addressed the doctor informally. They had both an organ and a piano, and all their walls were covered with pictures. Lína was dressed in Danish clothes and wore boots on week-days. It took so little to please her.

If she only knew how little his wealth and reputation weighed on the scales in comparison with what it took to please her. But what's the point in thinking about that now?

It was strange how the same person could look on things with such different eyes. Perhaps it had something to do with the duality in most people's character. Why had he been unable to be content here with Lína and the boys, at least as content as most people are? Why hadn't he sent her money for a ticket to the States? It might have saved her and the boys' lives. He didn't have so much as a photograph of this son of his, who was named after him and who was born seven months after he left. He wished he could believe that fate is unavoidable.

He stopped for a moment, looked at the village, saw Vikness's house, and was amazed at how unimpressive it was. Someone on the ship said that Vikness was on his deathbed. How clearly he remembered when he and Lína quietly walked back and forth on the street in front of the house and listened to Mrs. Vikness playing the piano, the first instrument of that kind in Stafnfjörður. Then Lína had asked: "Do you think there is as fine a house anywhere else?"

Now he had arrived at his destination. Only Ólafur's cottage was left. All the other shacks had been demolished. It looked as if a big house was going to be built here. An enormous mound of gravel and sand and a high pile of timber. Would anyone still be living here? A fellow stood there taking a pinch of snuff. — "Hello!"

"Hello," the man repeated and put the snuffbox in his pocket. "What's your name, Sir, if I may ask?"

"Eymundur Eymundsson."

"You must be a passenger on the *Goðafoss*."

"Yes."

"Where do you come from, Sir?"

"From America."

"From America! I guess I should stop addressing you so formally.

One knows one's countrymen's preferences. Where are you going?"

"To — to Reykjavík."

"To Reykjavík! It seems to me that you're making quite a detour and going the longest way round. Did you take the wrong ship from Leith?"

"Does anyone live in the cottage?"

"No, it has to be torn down next weekend. The Stafnfirðingur Society bought this strip of land. They intend to build a herring boiling plant. There's progress being made in many other countries beside America."

"May I look in?"

"I expect so. But there isn't much to see. Fortunately, these old hovels are on their way out. But, since you're from the capital, dear countryman, you'll never have seen even a fisherman's cottage."

Eymundur walked up to the cottage without saying a word. The man looked after him in surprise. It was a damned lie that all countrymen across the Atlantic were talkative and friendly. This man had a very formal look about him.

The door was bent and didn't close properly; it had worn a half-circle off the floor inside the threshold. Yes, it was often difficult to close the door in damp weather. And this was their living room; a wooden floor and the normal width of a living room on an Icelandic farm. He had painted the walls light green; now they were dirty brown. The kitchen to the left, but now there was no table under the window. The strips in the plate rack were broken, and the stove was gone. But look, there was the peg which he had carved and hung behind the door! And there was the window sill on which Lína placed the lamp to show him his way home.

He went back into the living room and looked out of the window over the fjord. His eyes stopped at Langafjall. Often the mountain had seemed to him like a prison wall; he had shaken his clenched fist at it and wished that he would never see it again. Yes, here he had said to himself that he wished he had never set eyes on Lína.

They were always poor. But during his last winter in Stafnfjörður, their poverty had become extreme. He had bought a share in a boat, but they had caught no fish, so the guarantors had repossessed it. It was almost impossible to find employment during the winter. He clearly remembered how Lína was always mending clothes whenever she sat down. Her own blouse was colourful from all the patches.

He was not quite sure whether he had dreamed or daydreamed during that winter that a woman came to him and said: "Since you don't appreciate my gifts, I shall take them back. You shall be free and independent and go wherever you want."

The night after little Hermann died, they had been lying silently next to each other. Lína probably thought that he was sleeping and allowed herself to cry. He was filled with compassionate love for her and took back his desire for freedom. A kind of late summer calm came over him for the next weeks. Lína was dearer to him then than she had been for a long time.

But soon his old longing to go away came back again. It didn't take long before he had convinced himself that the boys had been the anchor that held him back in the harbour. Now he spoke uninhibitedly about going south to look for work and suggested that maybe Lína should go home for a while — her father lived in a small holding belonging to the church further up the fjord. He would soon be able to send for her. There were so many opportunities for employment in Reykjavík. Here everything was in ruins. — And so on and so forth.

It was not easy, however, to make Lína approve of this arrangement. Somehow, she seemed scared, she who was always so compliant; it was almost as if she doubted that he would be able to send for her within two months.

He could see the day he left Stafnfjörður as if it were yesterday. Lína was sad and very depressed. Perhaps she had an inkling that they were parting for ever. Nonetheless, she was gentle as always. "You'll send me money for the ticket as soon as you can," she said and smiled through her tears. He solemnly promised to do so. But two months later he was on a trawler sailing from Hull.

Not to say that he hadn't sometimes told himself that the only proper and decent thing to do was to return to Stafnfjörður or at least send for Lína. But it was always possible to find a legitimate reason for delaying things. First he had to pay his debts in Stafnfjörður, then he had to take his helmsman's examination, and then came his journey to America. He had had a good excuse for a long time.

Her letters followed him from place to place. Loving but strangely childish letters. The last one came just before Christmas 1915 and told of the death of little Eymundur. She begged him for money for a ticket, because now she could in no way endure being at home. But by then he felt that it would be impossible to resume the relationship. He didn't answer the letter.

What was the reason for such hard-heartedness? Ambition and wealth? Probably, but not exclusively. Admittedly, he had decided not to stop before he became one of the owners of the Trellis trawler company, and had obviously thought that Lína would be a stumbling block on his path; but the solution to the riddle lay, of course, deeper. However, one thing made him feel good: that no woman had a part in this. He hadn't known then that Theresa Trellis existed, didn't meet her until six months later.

In the early summer of 1917, he wrote to a lawyer in Reykjavík requesting a divorce from Lína and was informed that she had died from measles in 1916 — died in this little turf hut.

During the last few years he had rarely thought about Lína — had made efforts to forget her and the hard times at home. But this summer when he and his wife stayed in England for a while, he had been overcome with an irresistible desire to go to Stafnfjörður. — "I don't understand you, Edmund," Theresa had said. "You have no family there and have been away for so long." Fortunately, she had not suggested that she go with him.

And here he was again in old haunts, unknown to everybody.

"Are you deaf, countryman? *Goðafoss* has sounded its whistle twice. One would think you'd fallen in love with that ramshackle cottage."

Eymundur walked as if in a trance in the direction of the ship. If he could only just turn around and go directly back to England. He had completed his errand, and it was anything but a pleasant thought to have to sail from fjord to fjord for the next ten days with a group of people he didn't know. Fortunately, he could catch a ship to Leith the day after he arrived in Reykjavík. He went to the front of the ship, leaned on the rail, and looked at Hof. All of a sudden, he remembered a long-forgotten sermon by Reverend Halldór: "What would it profit a man to gain the whole world and lose his own soul?"

[1956]

Much Do Servants Know

Nína Jónsdóttir had been in the house of S.P. Larsen in Philadelphia for almost two years. Mrs. Larsen called her "ung pige i huset," which Daisy Hall translated as "maid of all work" — and said it in such a tone as if it were impossible to sink any lower. Still, Daisy was pleasant enough, although she never let her forget that they were as unequal now as when they were schoolmates in Sandfjörður and Daisy was Dísa, the daughter of Hallgrímur the factor.

Nína had the day off and was on the train to New York. She wanted to visit Dagmar Nielsen, who was a nurse and the sister of Mrs. Lange in Chicago, and then, of course, she would drop in on Daisy. Nína had gone to Winnipeg when she left Iceland almost five years ago but had soon moved east. She had heard so much about New York and wanted to live there. Dagmar thought that she would soon be able to find employment at a sanatorium in Brooklyn which unlike the schools of nursing did not require a middle-school qualification. Dagmar was a nice girl just like her sister. Nína had always been staying with Danish people ever since she came west, which was one of the things Daisy criticized her for. "You're foolish," she said, "not to be staying with English-speaking people." Oh! She must not forget that it was Daisy who suggested that she attend evening school and urged her to do something with her life instead of being a "maid-rag," as she called it. Daisy had steady nerves and naturally meant well.

Nína had met her in Chicago. Daisy had gone straight to Chicago instead of making a detour to Winnipeg, because John Hall, her uncle, lived there. He had emigrated at a young age and done well for himself. In Chicago, Daisy took courses in massage, cosmetics, and hairdressing — "beauty culture" she called it. Now she was staying with some wealthy people in New York while she was saving up money to set up her own hairdressing salon.

They had known each other since primary school in Sandfjörður. Hallgrímur Hallsson, Dísa's father, had then recently been appointed manager of the Diehls Company. In her mind Nína saw the classroom and saw Loftur Geirsson, the teacher, mince behind the desk and curl his moustache while he had them recite their lessons. Loftur could be very entertaining if he wanted to, and quite witty, as when, for example, Lóa, the bank manager's daughter, had said that Hamburg was the capital of Germany and he asked if she had been acting "The Lady in Hamburg" last night.

Sveinn, the old teacher, who had then been about to retire, had been most pleased when they repeated word for word what he had taught them. Loftur introduced a few new things — tried to shake the hay before he pressed it into the creel, as he expressed it. He encouraged them to learn and recite poems, preferably from other sources than the schoolbooks. His classes were often a lot of fun, and she would never forget the time when she tried to recite "One is up in the mountains" and started to cry. How stupid of her to choose such a poem, she who was so sensitive as a child and in many ways still was.

Dísa was the last to recite that day, clearly because Loftur knew that she would be able to keep the attention of her schoolmates, who sometimes became restless at the end of the classes. It would be unfair to say that Loftur had favourites, but when it was Dísa's turn it was nonetheless as if his eyes said: "You're one of us." They were both from the north. Dísa recited the verse in a low voice but with such stirring emphasis that the class shuddered:

Brrr! A penetrating wind and a snowstorm from the north
Beats the shrouded ground.
At the mountain pass the sun appears late
To see when spring comes round.
It sees it nowhere, and hides its eyes,
Sinks sadly toward the bay.
In the crusted snow a weak blade of grass
Cries for the warmth and light of day.

The poem was, of course, a satire on Sandfjörður. Dísa was "the outlaw," who mourned "midsummer's heavenly sun." Nína still remembered how hurt she had felt.

But Dísa had steady nerves. Some of the boys, especially Gummi, the son of Siggi the busybody, enjoyed teasing Nína, and the worst thing was that she started blubbering when they sang: "Jónína Sveinsína Engilberta Sigurmunda in Yztakot." Dísa, of course, knew what was behind these names; Nína's father, uncle, and two half-brothers had drowned while putting in at Brimtangi two months before she was born. What Dísa said to Gummi she never knew, but she got him where she wanted him, and he stopped teasing her. It was more fun at school after Dísa came. Nína looked up to her although Dísa usually pretended not to see her.

"Would you like more?" Daisy asked and lifted the coffee pot.

"No thanks, I don't think so," Nína answered. "I've had more than enough."

"Not even to go with a sugar cube?"

"Well, perhaps a few drops."

Daisy sat silently with her hand under her chin. Nína took a sugar cube and asked: "How do you like it here?"

"So, so. Mr. Marlin is wonderful, and I can put away most of my pay, because although I had a good salary and got handsome tips in Madame Juliette's Beauty Salon, I spent most of it on room and board. I hope I'll be able to buy a hairdressing salon soon. I've got tired of waiting on the old biddy."

"Is it an elderly couple?"

"She's forty and he thirty-four, but he looks younger."

"Do they tell you their age?" Nína asked as she put the dishes into the sink.

"Neither of them makes a secret of it — no I'll wash them — and then I've heard them quarrelling about it, or, rather, her reminding him."

"Reminding him of her age?"

"Yes, she says she knows for certain that he often wishes she were younger, and he says he'd have forgotten a long time ago if she wasn't constantly reminding him. — Would you like some fruit? I forgot to offer you."

Nína shook her head.

Daisy washed the china, put it away, and looked over the kitchen to check that everything was in order. "I don't want Esther Rydman to turn up her nose at me when she comes home tonight. She's the cook here, Swedish, and is in the missus's good graces."

"Are you finished?"

"Pretty much. I just have to take the blankets off their beds. Do you want to see the apartment? No one's at home."

"That would be fun."

"This is the dining room," Daisy said in an offhand manner.

Nína could not help comparing it with the Larsen family's dining room, where the furniture was of artificial oak and one had to be careful not to stumble over the children's toys. This dining room looked most of all like a furniture exhibition in Marshall Field in Chicago. "It's really beautiful and luxurious," she said and looked around in humble admiration.

"Do you think so? I can't stand this heavy, carved oak furniture; it's so difficult to polish. Marie and I wouldn't miss it if the antique dealer took it tomorrow. And then this blue carpet which is impossible to keep clean. — This monstrosity is from Italy."

"Is the madam Italian?"

"No, but she lived in Italy for a while with her former husband, an old oil sheik from Oklahoma. That's where the wealth comes from. He was ill for two years — died there. — This is the living room."

Something jumped up from one of the chairs, put its back up, and hissed.

"What kind of creature is that?" Nína asked and stepped back.

"An Angora cat. And only the missus is allowed to touch it. Guess what this puss is called. — Annabelle Marlin, after its owner."

"Really!" Nína giggled. "God knows what people back home would say if they heard that people name their cats after themselves."

"Indeed. It would almost seem more appropriate to name dogs after people."

Nína stood still in amazement and ran her eyes over the silk-covered chairs and sofas, the shiny small tables here and there, and an enormous piano. — "This must have cost a fortune."

"She bought it in France during the depression. She said that it cost only ten thousand dollars."

"*Only* ten thousand dollars," Nína said and gasped for breath. "What a lot of paintings they have," she added.

"Yes," Daisy answered and brightened up. "They make up for all the junk here. They are by Mr. Marlin. He's an artist. — Here's the library which they use as a living room when they're alone, which is rare, because she's always bustling in and out or filling the house with guests. See how many books he's got. Everything from Shakespeare, Goethe, and Dante to even the *Edda* — in English, of course. But it's not often he gets any peace to sit and read, never mind to paint. Fortunately he has a studio in town."

Daisy turned off the light in the library, and they went back into the living room. "Between you and me, I think she's scared to death that he doesn't find her comparable with younger women unless she pretends to be fanatic about dancing and entertaining."

"You think so?"

"Yes, I'm sure. Her daily toil consists of getting herself ready for the evening. She's in bed until noon, sometimes with a face-mask, and I spend half the day massaging and primping her. If she puts on a pound it's as if it's my fault. There's no end to this pampering. I'm sick of it."

"I don't blame you. But you're being well paid for it," Nína said slowly.

"Even so," Daisy answered, somewhat surprised. "Here's her bedroom — wait while I switch on the light."

Nína waited outside the door while Daisy turned on a lamp which looked like a doll in a crinoline.

"What's this — a bedside lamp?" she asked.

"No, but the wrinkles are less noticeable in subdued light. Don't stand there like a lamp-post! Esther isn't at home, Marie lives in town, and the couple usually don't get back until after midnight."

Nína had never seen such a bedroom before except in movies. Sofas full of silk cushions, silk veils, lace curtains, and a four-poster bed with curtains. Daisy took two blankets off the bed, one made of lace and the other of thick silk. She placed a pair of high-heeled silk shoes beside the bed and a kimono and a nightgown on the bed. The kimono looked most of all like an evening wrap, and the nightgown was deep-cut and so thin that one could probably hide it in the hollow of one's hand. This was just like in a movie! Nína stood in the middle of the floor, clutching her purse with both her hands as if clinging onto reality in this dream world.

"Would you like to see the dressing room and her closet?" asked Daisy. She opened the door to an enormous closet extending from the bedroom.

"How does one person manage to use so many clothes?"

"Some of them she uses only once or twice. But do you think she gives us girls any? Oh no. Not that I'd want to wear out her rags. But Marie Petersen, who's seeing her two sisters through school, could use some of them. Do you know what the old biddy does? She sells them! And she and Mrs. Goldstein haggle over the price of each piece."

Nína clicked her tongue. "And they, who are so wealthy!"

"*She* is so wealthy. That's the point. If she hadn't been so wealthy and he so poor, she'd never have got her hands on him. — Sit down for a minute."

They sat down. Daisy folded her hands in her lap and continued: "She'd just arrived from Italy and was walking around in one of the big shops that was exhibiting paintings by beginners and other unknown artists, when one of Mr. Marlin's pictures caught her attention; she liked it so much that she requested to meet the artist and fell in love with him right away."

Daisy paused for a minute, and Nína put in: "Fancy that."

"Yes, just like that," Daisy continued and stressed each word with a snap of her fingers. "She tells this story at each party and even when the two of them sit over a cup of coffee in the library — as if this were hot news."

"Love at first sight, as people here say."

"Clearly on her part. As far as I know Mr. Marlin was in severe financial difficulties at the time. How do I know? Listen. Once last winter — the missus was not at home as usual — his friend and former schoolmate, Mr. Elliott from Boston, was here for the evening. I was clearing the table, because Marie had the day off, and they were having coffee and smoking in the library. I heard only bits and pieces of what was said, of course, but still enough to understand that his friends had been surprised when they heard about his marriage — they felt that Mrs. Geber wasn't 'in his class'. They spoke so quietly for a while that I didn't hear what they were saying until Mr. Elliott said something about divorce, that he ought to leave her. But Mr. Marlin didn't take kindly to that; he said nice things about her, and that he had no real reason to . . ."

"Yes, why should he divorce her?" Nína interrupted. "She picked him up from the street and didn't hide the fact that she was older than he was."

Daisy pretended not to hear and continued: "Mr. Elliott said that she was ruining his future as an artist. — It's true. She's never content unless they're on the go, and then she's always criticizing the women who pose for him — he's primarily a portrait painter."

"She's jealous?"

"I should say so! Even of middle-aged women, never mind professional models like Miss Sullivan, who posed for three paintings of the Virgin Mary. If the paintings look like her, she must have been a beautiful and lovely girl. He said that she was the best model for the Madonna he'd ever had. But the older one didn't stop before he let her go. I've heard that Miss Sullivan became a nun."

"Are you sure that Mrs. Marlin had no reason to be concerned?"

"Absolutely. Mr. Marlin is a proper and honest man."

Nína felt like making a comment but contented herself by asking: "How long have they been married?"

"Six or seven years, I think," Daisy answered and seemed to find the question alien to the topic. "Now everything looks different for him. He could have a good income and probably be rich if he had peace to work. He pays for half of the management of the household, but she wants so much luxury that he probably cannot save much. Do you know what I think?" Anger and hatred were in her eyes. "She does it on purpose — she wants him to be financially dependent on her, so that she can keep him tethered."

For a moment they were both silent.

"Did you see the photo of him?" asked Daisy. "The one on her bedside table?"

"No," said Nína, "I didn't see it."

"Come, I'll show you. That's him. Isn't he cute?"

"Yes, he's very good-looking."

"More than that. He's exceptionally handsome. As usual with good-looking people, the photo doesn't do him justice. He's got the most beautiful smile I've ever seen, for example. It spreads slowly over his face and reminds me of — of sunrise in Akureyri."

Nína said nothing and tried to suppress a smile. Daisy seemed to wake from a reverie and quickly said: "There's a photo of her in his room. Do you want to see it? I have to take the blanket off his bed anyway."

"Oh, they each have their own room?" Nína said as they went out.

"Yes, 'grand it must be' — as Marie says. This is the photo of the missus there on the tall chest of drawers."

"She's also good-looking," said Nína. Daisy folded the blanket and shook the pillows. She was flushing and seemed quite disconcerted. Nína noticed, and it was as if a weight had been lifted from her shoulders. The awe she had felt for Daisy had gone. "One hardly notices the difference in age between the two of them, if any at all," she added. Daisy continued straightening the bed. Nína gained even more courage. "And what do a few years matter? No one would raise an eyebrow if a young girl married an old dodderer who could be her father." Nína looked up and said defiantly: "I feel sorry for Mrs. Marlin."

Daisy showed signs of leaving. She was still red in the face but no longer perplexed. She was back to her usual self, proud and dignified. She smiled a chilly smile. "Well, well, my friend, that's for you to decide."

Nína felt like saying that this wonderful Mr. Marlin had married for money and that she knew that Daisy was not impartial in her judgement. But her inferiority complex made itself felt again, and she contented herself by saying: "If I were you, Dísa, I'd leave as soon as possible."

[1956]

Goody

"Goody is the only one of us who hasn't married," her girlfriends and former schoolmates said when they mentioned her to others. They had all studied at Putnam Academy, and most of them had degrees from there and were (if anyone cared to check the city records) between thirty-four and thirty-eight. They had started becoming surprised how the time had flown. "There's the son of Thelma Mardal, for example, now on his way to Princeton," "Pearl Johnson's eldest son is in his final year at Putnam Academy," "Vigdís Ahlfeld's daughter's a head taller than she," "Lolla Hemmert has divorced her husband," and "Stieva Thurston is no longer talking about adopting a child," they said.

Goody had been baptized Guðríður Þóra after her grandmother, been called Gudda, and been registered in primary school under the name 'Goodman, Thora G.,' because no teacher wanted to attempt to spell Guðríður, never mind pronounce it. After that Gudda became Goody — "and that's that," Miss Taylor said.

People had started calling Goody "one of the older ones," because they liked her too much to lump her with, for instance, Molly Davis, who swept the streets with her skirts when the fashion demanded knee-length or shorter skirts, or Beryl Schmidt, who talked to herself and called her cat General Ike. Molly and Beryl fitted people's general image of spinsters; they were thin, gawky, and sour-looking. Goody was the exact opposite: fat, healthy, and cheerful. Those who did not know her thought she was a married woman and probably the mother of many children.

She was always laughing, made fun of everything, and put people in a good mood.

She had always had a rather round face, but now it was beginning to resemble a full moon. She had a large but not unattractive mouth with white, healthy teeth. "To grin from ear to ear" was almost literally correct with regard to Goody.

Most people agreed that she was not bad-looking, but too big and fat. She was called "the tall and the monstrous" when she was younger. Now she had long become overweight, and the weight was most conspicuous above her waist. "I'm so exceptionally well-endowed," she said and laughed. She always joked about herself.

Few people liked bright colours more than she. Red, sky-blue, and copper or Spanish-green hats, and checked and flowered dresses were for her a strong force of attraction. In the summer, she often wore sleeveless dresses that looked as if she had grown out of them. "She emphasizes what ought to be hidden," Lolla Hemmert said.

When voluntary work was to be done or money had to be raised, she was often the first to be approached, because not only was she very obliging, but she was also considered to be quite well off financially. She was the only heir of her father, Jóhannes Goodman, who had come from Iceland as an infant and been a hardworking and enterprising man. He took over and expanded the smithy his father, Kristján Guðmundsson, had established, and was for some time believed to be exceedingly wealthy. He had suffered great losses during the depression, and some thought that this had been the cause of his premature death. Arendt Ahlfeld, who had then not yet become a judge, had assisted Goody in assessing his estate. When the debts had been paid, it turned out that there was more left than they had both expected.

Jóhannes had built a large and beautiful house on the corner of Pioneer Street and Jefferson Avenue when Goody was in her second year of primary school. His wife, Ísafold, who was born in New Iceland, had always been in poor health and died the year before her daughter finished primary school. As far back as Goody could remember, they had had housekeepers. Mrs. Blatz had just been hired when Jóhannes died. This was eight years ago, and she was still living with Goody.

When people in Centerville showed their guests the town, the Goodman house was one of the sights that was pointed out to them, because although it was no longer fashionable to have lions, deer, or dogs of marble, copper or other metals in the flower beds in the garden, the Goodman house was an exception. Two copper lions guarded the main entrance from Pioneer Street and two iron watch-dogs the door of the storehouse behind the house, which was, among other things, used as a garage. People had started calling this and some of the other houses built at the same time "old manor houses." "Grandfather would have liked to hear that," Goody thought, because the house was on his land, and the storehouse had been built by him.

She had once tried to sell the house but was glad that she had not succeeded. When her father died, her friends had urged her to get rid of it, because what use did she have for a house with fifteen rooms? They did have a point. But the most likely buyers, young people who were establishing a home, chose rather to live in modern apartment buildings where everything was new and where they didn't have to worry about the heating bills. People came in great numbers to see the house, but mostly out of curiosity, she feared. When she later saw some of the newest apartments, which consisted of "tiny living rooms, kitchen dens, and bathroom holes," to use her words, she said she thanked the Lord that she still had the house, even though it was large.

Goody took good care of the house, both inside and outside. She was often seen working in the garden in broad-striped plus-fours, a checked cardigan, and a broad-brimmed hat. If it had been anyone other than Goody, people would have said that she looked like a troll. But they found it strange that she, who had a gardener, should be doing hard work, and said that she was making old Jim lazy and ought to find another. She answered that no one had a better knack of handling the furnace than he, and then he had a special way of keeping the rose bushes alive during the winter — he did more than most people thought. And if she was talking with Pearl or Stieva, she reminded them that Jim Sands had been there as far back as she could remember and that if she let him go, he might become a burden to the tax payers or might have to sell his shack, "and he's so proud of owning a house."

This was typical of Goody. And the same was the case with Mrs. Blatz, née Ingibjörg Jónsdóttir, who still bore the title of housekeeper, at least when she was listening. She was more trouble and inconvenience than anything else, because she usually fell ill when Goody was entertaining and needed her help. If Goody offered to call a doctor, Mrs. Blatz started to cry, went upstairs, and took to her bed. When Goody received the guests in a smock over her evening dress, they knew what was up. They had also become used to seeing her go upstairs with food on a tray to "serve Mrs. Blatz in bed and butter her up, so that the house doesn't fall apart," as Goody said with a laugh.

She was known for her hospitality, and everyone felt at home there. She sometimes said: "If you expect that Emily Post's rules are being observed here, you've come to the wrong place." "Help yourself. Enjoy yourself as if you were playing blind man's buff. Make yourself comfortable," was her refrain. The men sat in shirt sleeves, and some of the women slipped off their shoes without apologizing. No one was surprised, and least of all the hostess.

Although she never said so, she enjoyed most of all having what she called "spouse parties." It was stimulating to hear deep men's voices and smell a good cigar. She then always served what Hermann Johnson called "men's food," such as ham or steak with baked potatoes and peas, warm buns, and apple pie with cheese. She also preferred to play cards with men rather than women — bridge was the main entertainment in her circle. And when her partner said: "You play like an angel, Goody," she was half-ashamed of feeling flattered.

But the spouse parties were rather rare; indeed, she never showed any signs that she preferred them, and her women friends did not hide the fact that they enjoyed themselves better without the men. It was much freer and more fun, they thought, to be able to talk unchallenged and to let the games rest for a while (even though the cards had been dealt) and listen to jokes or juicy gossip. They didn't have to fear being interrupted by "Play ball!" or "Are we playing or aren't we?" Moreover, different kinds of foods were served, which was more to their taste, such as chicken with mushrooms in a cream sauce, salad, light puddings with whipped cream, and all kinds of cookies. And if they met in the evening and their husbands were in the club or at meetings, some of them talked about them or relationships between men and women in general. As the evening passed, they often offered advice and were quite outspoken — at least their mothers would have thought so.

Goody never joined in, but they did not have to restrict themselves because of her — that was one of the reasons for her popularity. She was not a prude like other spinsters. Nothing seemed to affect her or arouse her indignation. Still, sometimes when one of them had been outspoken, they looked sideways at her and wondered what she was thinking. But she sat and shuffled the cards, went over the score, or looked down as if no one was present. Nonetheless, she seemed to hear what they were saying, although she did not show it.

But they didn't know what to think, because Goody often went to fetch soda or snacks when one of them was making her confessions and all the others waited with bated breath for the rest of the story. They had started doubting that she was completely free of prudishness. Once Sue Dirksen had asked her: "I hope we haven't shocked you?" and Goody had blushed crimson. "Look at her!" said Lolla Hemmert. "She's blushing to the roots of her hair."

"Nonsense! I haven't blushed since I was in third grade and Miss Kull's underskirt fell down," said Goody, roaring with laughter.

She hoped that they took her answer at face value and that nothing was behind their question. She was angry at herself for not being more in control of her feelings. Stieva might suspect something — she turned pale with fear, because it was to avoid having to listen to Stieva talk about her married life that she made herself errands to the kitchen. All the other trips were a pretence in order to deceive them.

Stieva (Stefanía) Bergson, now Mrs. Guy J. Thurston, and Goody had been close friends since they started school; and they and Pearl Paulsen, now Mrs. Hermann L. Johnson, had been inseparable and the innermost kernel of a large group of friends. Stieva and Goody graduated from Putnam Academy on the same day, but Pearl had dropped out a year earlier, because she and Herm had run away and got married the day after he graduated. Pearl was now expecting her sixth child and was getting enormously fat. But she didn't care. "I'm not like Stieva," she said, "to be content with eating grass, and I'd become grumpy if I starved myself like she does." Stieva was always trying out the most recent diets recommended by the stars in Hollywood and usually lived primarily on raw vegetables and fruit. She talked much about the duty of each woman to preserve her looks. "It is a self-inflicted misfortune to be fat and old," she said and knew what she was talking about. She was half a year older than Pearl but looked ten years younger. She was a living example of the fact that it paid to eat carefully and do what the magazines said. It was also important to aim at "a long married life likened to a courtship," as it said in black and white.

Whether that was the reason or not, no one in their circle was like Guy Thurston, although many of them considered themselves happily married. He worshipped Stieva and didn't hide it. The two behaved as if they were still in their third year at Putnam Academy, and he didn't care if people smiled.

Stieva had as a result become spoilt and could hardly sit down or stand up unless Guy helped her, and although she was, as Ethel Benson said, "extravagant as a soldier on leave," Guy just laughed as one laughs at childish tricks. He was truly special, Goody thought. He had been married to Stieva for sixteen years, and he still behaved as if he were engaged.

Guy was not born in Centerville but in a little village called Haycoat. He was the grandson of Guðmundur Þorsteinsson, a friend and neighbour of Kristján, Goody's grandfather. Dóra, his aunt, was married and lived in Centerville, and when she and her husband lost their only son, they "borrowed" Guy for a while. He was then eighteen years old and graduated from Putnam Academy a year before Stieva and the other girls. He was precocious, almost six feet tall, blond, very sporty, and everyone's favourite. Goody remembered that she had involuntarily compared him with Jerry Peterson, who was called "her boy," because she went with him to the Christmas dance and the school play. "We had no other choice," she had said laughing. Jerry stuttered and was a little squint-eyed, but he was a nice boy. May McIntire and Lulu Benson immediately competed for Guy. He invited May to the Christmas dance and Lulu to the school play. But after Stieva and Dick Dirksen had parted in anger just before the Easter vacation and she and Guy began dating when the school started again, all other girls disappeared from the horizon as far as he was concerned.

One thing followed another after Stieva, Pearl, and Goody graduated. Jerry got a job with his uncle in Chicago, Pearl had Junior, Guy married Stieva, Goody folded napkins and knitted baby clothes, invited Pearl and Herm, Guy and Stieva over, and was invited to parties others held for them.

Around this time Jóhannes Goodman got a new bookkeeper. His name was Thaddeus Kowalsky, and he was from Cleveland, Ohio. He didn't know anyone in Centerville, so it was only natural that he gratefully accepted his boss's invitations and often came to the house. Some people said that he sucked up to his boss, but Goody's friends would not hear of such a thing and said that it was clear that it was his unmarried daughter who was the attraction. Soon people started saying that the next wedding would no doubt be held in the Goodman house.

But that was not the case. Thad returned to Cleveland after a few months. His father soon fell ill, died shortly after, and Thad took over Kowalsky's Bakery, which he had often mentioned to Goody. The two corresponded for a while. But soon it was heard that he had married a girl by the name of Olga. "I hope you don't think that Thad was interested in *me!*" Goody said roaring with laughter, as if nothing was more absurd. What were people to make of this? Goody seemed to take nothing seriously. It was still the same today.

After their wedding, Stieva and Guy moved to his childhood home. Even though Centerville had only thirty-five thousand inhabitants, it was a big town in comparison with Haycoat — "Hayseed would be a better name," said Stieva, who missed her friends in Centerville. Once when she was belittling the village, Goody saw the hurt in Guy's eyes. She knew that he was proud of the fact that his father had been the first settler there — had built a farm from turf

148

and stones and called it Hákot. Later he built a nice house a short distance from the old farm and started a small business, which gradually grew. A good part of the village was built on his lands, and when it got a postal service the English pronunciation of Hákot became the name of the village. John G. Thurston, Guy's father, was the first postmaster in Haycoat.

Stieva popped over to Centerville as often as she could, sometimes three times a year, and had quite lengthy visits. She said that she was praying to get away from Haycoat as soon as possible, but her prayers were not heard until nine years later. Matti Thurston, or, rather, his wife Louise, had become tired of farming and would be happy to take over Guy's job in the business, and around the same time their aunt, Dóra, and her husband, Niels Bartelsen, died as a result of a car accident. They had bequeathed all their possessions to Guy. "When things happen, they really happen," said Stieva.

Guy did not visit Centerville as often as Stieva, and when he came he only stayed for a short while. Goody saw him only once or twice when she invited them over or at Pearl's or Stieva's parents' place. She was always looking forward to seeing him, because he was cheerful and entertaining. He was always the same: "Well, if it isn't my old Goody," he said, shook her hand firmly and long, laughed, and slapped her on the back as if he had met an old buddy of his.

She was the only one with whom he would whisper at parties. "Isn't she sweet?" he asked and was, of course, referring to Stieva. "Doesn't she look good in this dress?" And Goody said that everything looked good on her. "No one compares with her." Goody nodded. "Thanks, matey!" said Guy.

A few years after Guy and Stieva had moved to Haycoat, Goody took over the entire management of the house, although in name they still had a housekeeper. She had long established a reputation as an excellent housewife. She was also heavily involved in the Red Cross and served on many committees associated with the Lutheran Church there.

It was during those years that she was actively involved in the group of those who fought for the building of a swimming pool in the city, because as the summer wore on the water in the De Soto River became so polluted that bathing in the river would be banned altogether. There was a general celebration when the pool was opened. A swimming teacher by the name of Michael Miller had been brought in from Minneapolis. When Goody saw him, she thought: "If Guy had a twin, Mike must be his brother." She was a daily guest at the swimming pool and took lessons, although like most people her age she had learned to swim in the river without the help of a teacher. People had started teasing her and asking her what she was doing there all the time. "So, you have a crush on Mike?" her acquaintances said jokingly. "That's right!" she answered. "For once, be serious!" "I am being serious. I'm madly in love with him," said Goody. It didn't occur to them to believe her. As the summer passed and she was asked how her love affair was going, she answered that it wasn't going at all — "no one would even want to look at my house and my bank book if I was included in the deal!" It was impossible to figure her out: she ought to have been a revue artist; everyone agreed that she was a court jester reincarnate.

She was a drudge without peer, her interests were endless, and she was always ready to try something new. When she was about thirty, she suddenly decided to learn to play the mandolin. She had a player-piano, which was rarely used, because most of her acquaintances preferred bridge to song and music, although on rare occasions Guy got it to play a tune before they became absorbed in the cards. The last time he had come, he brought his mandolin, and the cards were given a rest, which was unusual. She thought it might be fun to be able to play the guitar or mandolin, and this resulted in her getting together with Paul Potter — the Reverend Paul Potter, he said, if people forgot his title; although he was not an ordained minister he sometimes acted as *locum tenens* for the ministers in the Methodist church and held services at revivalist meetings. In addition, he gave lessons in stringed instruments, which was his primary occupation these days. He had recently become a widower for the third time and had seven grown-up children. Three of his daughters were still living at home; two of them gave piano lessons for beginners, but the third was his housekeeper and was about to get married. He was fifty-two years old.

He taught his students in their homes, because "it gets on my nerves to hear the kids practising," he said. At the end of the seventh lesson, he asked for Goody's hand in marriage. She thanked him for the honour but declined. With that the mandolin lessons came to an end. She went to the window in the living room after having seen him to the door and stood behind the curtain, so that he would not see her if he looked toward the window, which he didn't. He was wearing a high-crowned hat with a narrow brim, which reminded her of a chamber pot without a handle. She started laughing, and laughed until she cried with laughter, cried as if her heart were going to break.

Guy and Stieva had again joined the circle of friends for good. They had made themselves comfortable in the Bartelsen house, which Stieva had named "The Oaks," although there were no oak trees on their property. Guy had brought new life into the old Bartelsen business, and this year the two had taken a three-month vacation and gone to California.

It was about a week after they had left that Pearl called Goody and invited her for dinner. "If you aren't busy, do me the favour and come over," she said. "Guess what Herm did?" she continued. "He invited some young man in the bank for dinner. This is just typical of Herm. And Bibby's teething!"

This was the beginning of Goody's and Mr. Robert S. Bluecher's acquaintance. She was then almost thirty-two and he three years older. Mr. Bluecher was from Cincinnati and had been hired for three months as a replacement for old Petersen, who remembered when the First National Bank was housed in a rented shack. Mr. Bluecher was staying at the Pioneer Club.

Goody arrived in a flower-patterned dress, which suited her exceptionally well. She brought a big bowl of strawberries, a bouquet of flowers, both from her garden, and a fresh layer cake. They played bridge for a good part of the evening, and she offered to drive Mr. Bluecher home, because the club was on her way anyway. The offer was accepted.

This was in the middle of June. Shortly after, she invited Pearl, Herm, and Mr. Bluecher over for lunch, and he came a few days later to thank her. She said that she hoped he would drop by again, which he did. A month later it was rumoured that the new accountant from Cincinnati was sweet on Goody. In August everyone seemed to know for sure that they were serious, because he had come to her birthday party. And the first thing Guy and Stieva heard when they returned at the end of September was that Goody was probably engaged.

"No, really!" they both said with one voice. "What's he like?" Stieva added.

"Quiet and not unattractive," was the answer. "Better late than never."

"Yes, that's true," Stieva said laughing. Guy nodded and said that they might look in on her that evening.

They did. "This is Robert Bluecher — Stieva and Guy Thurston," said Goody and blushed. Stieva thought: "He's big and strong. They're a fine match." Mr. Bluecher had brownish hair, dark brown eyes, and a dimple in his left cheek. He greeted them cheerfully, said he was delighted to meet Goody's friends, and asked them to please call him Robert. He listened with much attention to the account of their journey and didn't take his eyes off them except when he quickly turned to Goody with a smile. He nodded now and then to show that he was listening. When Stieva asked if he could sing — "it's said that everyone in Cincinnati can sing," she added — he immediately said yes, sat down by the piano, and played and sang German songs, which they had all heard with Icelandic texts when they were young. He had a beautiful voice and was a good performer. When he had sung three songs, he turned around and asked: "Do you want more or have you had enough?" Goody said that this would suffice for the time being. "Let's play some cards."

He laughed happily: "See! She's started training me."

When they had played for a while and it was about eleven o'clock, Goody said that it was time to think of a few snacks. Stieva seized the opportunity and went with her.

"Finally!" she said and closed the door. "I could hardly wait. He's a very attractive man. I really like him."

"I'm happy to hear that," said Goody and put on the kettle.

"I'm serious. He's unassuming and straightforward, and, of course, charming — and that's quite something. I'm glad to see that he's tall and big since you are —" (she almost said "so big and fat") "— since you are so tall. And then he's mad about you. A blind man could see that."

Goody put cups on a tray but said nothing.

"I can't tell you how happy I am for you. You deserve a good husband. You're engaged aren't you? You don't mind my asking, do you? He's mentioned it to you hasn't he?"

"Yes."

"But it's as if you're hesitant!" Stieva burst out. "I mean — I wanted to say . . ."

"Yes, I'd expect you to say that this — this is my last chance."

"Dear Goody! It didn't even occur to me to . . ."

"Whether it occurred to you or not, it's a fact. I ought to accept him with open arms and be grateful. No one knows that better than I do."

Since Goody is being so frank, then I can be, too, Stieva thought. "Yes, so why on earth don't you?"

"Who knows? Maybe I will."

"I can't understand that you should even hesitate. Are you never lonely? Don't you get bored pottering about all alone in this big house?"

"Yes, sometimes."

"Of course. And it'll get worse as you grow older. I know that you've good friends, but that's not the same as having a husband, even if he were worse than Robert Bluecher. And then it's really too bad that such a fine housekeeper as you shouldn't marry now that you have the chance." Stieva lowered her voice and looked worried. "And who knows, you might have a child. Have you thought about that?"

Goody was putting cakes on a plate, and Stieva couldn't see her face. "Yes," she said quietly, "I've thought about that."

"My dear Goody. Here's an attractive man," Stieva said quickly, "who's fond of you, who would be good to you, who doesn't seem pigheaded or selfish . . ."

"He's neither."

"But what's the matter then? I hope it's not because you think you're not in love with him? If that's all," Stieva said emphatically, "then I can tell you something: it's not as important as you think. Even if you were in love with him now, it wouldn't last long — one grows out of it. Do you think that Pearl is still in love with Herm? Don't make me laugh! Or do you think I'm as mad about Guy as I was in the old days? Well, don't let this come as a shock: I'm not. Of course, I'm still fond of him; I couldn't be otherwise, for he's a wonderful person. But I'm certainly not in love with him."

But I am, Goody thought. I've probably always loved him, although it hasn't become clear to me until now.

Robert Bluecher was the only one who solved the riddle all

Goody's friends were puzzling over that autumn. He guessed it right away. His sadness and disappointment gave him second sight. "I know who's between us," he said. "It's this Guy Thurston. You became quite a different person after he was here the other night."

"Nonsense!" said Goody. "He's married, and besides . . ."

"It doesn't matter."

". . . and moreover he loves Stieva more than anything. I wouldn't have much of a chance competing with her, even if I wanted to get between the two of them, which doesn't enter my mind, or do you think so?"

"No," he said sadly. "But one can't help one's feelings."

No one else had guessed her secret, and Robert was enough of a gentleman to keep it to himself.

She was turning thirty-six — on the 20th of August. It reminded her of Robert Bluecher. Herm had met him at a meeting in Cincinnati and said that he was still unmarried. That made no difference as far as she was concerned. She had known what she wanted then as she did now, knew that her love was hopeless and had never expected anything else.

It seemed almost paradoxical considering the state of affairs, but she now had more peace of mind and was in many respects happier than she had been for many years. For her it was sufficient to know that she and Guy would always be neighbours. She was pleased to see him in church, at parties, and at meetings, and she had managed to break Stieva of the habit of inviting her for dinner unless there were other guests — she had reminded her how bored she was of playing three-handed bridge, and Stieva had finally accepted the excuse. But maybe one day she might have the courage to play three-handed? Who knows?

[1956]

Rannveig K.G. Sigbjörnsson

Rannveig Kristín Guðmundsdóttir (later Sigbjörnsson) was born in 1880 in Bolungarvík, Ísafjarðarsýsla. She was the daughter of Guðmundur Guðmundsson and Steinunn Bergsdóttir but was raised by foster parents, Jón Sakaríasson and Guðrún Hallgrímsdóttir. In 1901 she entered the Women's Academy (Kvennaskólinn) in Reykjavík, but ill health interrupted her schooling, and the following year she emigrated to Canada. She worked as a maid in Winnipeg for the first two years, when she also took lessons in English. She then entered the Central Business College, where she learned stenography. She worked with The Threshers Company Supply for some time. In 1909 she moved to Leslie, Saskatchewan, where she lived on her homestead with her husband, Sigurður Sigbjörnsson, and their three daughters, Sigríður, Guðrún and Jóhanna. In 1951, she and her husband retired and moved first to Vancouver to live with their daughter Jóhanna and later to Halyk in Foam Lake. She died in 1963.

Rannveig K.G. Sigbjörnsson published articles, reviews, short stories and translations primarily in *Lögberg*, but also in *Eimreiðin*, *Heimilisblaðið* and in the Lutheran women's magazine, *Árdís*. Collections of some of her short stories were published under the titles *Pebbles on the Beach* (Treherne, 1936), *Þráðarspottar* (Reykjavík, 1937), and *In Days Gone By* (Ilfracombe, 1956).

"Hávamál at Vöð" is translated from "Hávamál á Vöðum" in *Þráðarspottar* (188-194); "In the Morning of Life," which was originally written in Icelandic and published under the title "Á vormorgni lífsins" in *Lögberg* (26 June 1947, 7), is a revised and edited version of the author's translation in *In Days Gone By* (23-35).

Hávamál at Vöð

Vöð was a remarkable farm. It was one of the most prosperous homes in the district. Peace, harmony, proficiency, and orderliness in all things reigned there. Of all the homes in the district, Vöð enjoyed the most respect.

The farm at Vöð was situated by a highway. Yet, the hospitality was generally not above average, although the minister often stayed there. Occasionally other wayfarers lodged there as well.

The lord and lady of Vöð were well liked, even though the general public considered them to be on a much higher plane than themselves; such was the radiance that shone from them.

The mistress of the farm came from a noble family, and she was determined to retain the dignity of her family both inside and outside of the home. She had succeeded so far, although the household at Vöð was a large one. People's honour and welfare were guarded with extraordinary attention. If, for example, the daughters sank so low as to arrange a meeting with one of the farm employees in the shed or the storehouse, the master of the house would instantly appear on the scene. He spoke but a few words, quietly and bluntly, but it was enough to send the labourer crestfallen toward the seashore and the daughter even more ashamed home to her mother. But the master of the house went out into the courtyard, gazed toward the sea, and helped himself to a pinch of snuff. With that the adventure ended, as if one had stepped on a spark of fire.

In this way people at Vöð were watched over, and they took this well, because it was done with Nordic dignity and calmness. The daily demeanour of the couple of Vöð was in this spirit: we are people who know how to conduct ourselves, and only gentlefolk will be tolerated here. And it was a fact that no matter how mediocre a person went to Vöð, then he or she became more accomplished.

But then one day Elrún had labour pains. Nothing more nor less. Elrún was the niece of the mistress of Vöð, and was unquestionably the most beautiful and the most majestic woman at Vöð. She was also quiet in her daily behaviour. She hardly ever gave more than a slight smile. It was not considered proper at Vöð to engage in laughter and noise.

Elrún gave birth to a boy. She declared Marjas Jónsson to be the child's father. Marjas worked for Jens at Vöð; he was not exactly a member of the household but worked on his ships at one of the branches of the farm.

What a surprise! Marjas! Foul-mouthed, given to drinking, and useless at most things. But that was how it was. Marjas acknowledged the child, but the matter proceeded no farther, and he gave no indications that he wanted to marry Elrún. The master of Vöð did not hire Marjas again. A man who had brought such disgrace and grief upon the people at Vöð was not to be seen there any more.

Yes, and how could Elrún have done this? Elrún hung her head and hardly dared look at her son except furtively. She resumed her duties, and it made her more cheerful, but it also made the newcomer lose his mother's attention. He often cried for want of this care. He was placed in a hay rack in "the empty bed" so that he would not soil the bed linen at Vöð. Like everything else, the linen at Vöð was of the highest quality. To let the helpless little child soil it was unacceptable. And there Gestur cried, sometimes continuously throughout the day and night. The people were in the fields, meadows, or on the farm haymaking, milking, and doing other useful things. There was little time to care for Gestur.

Then one day at Vöð it happened that little Gestur stopped crying. He had died.

Yet another day had dawned at Vöð. It was an autumn day with a nip of frost in the air. Nonetheless, everything was in a state of confusion. People were streaming to and from the farm at Vöð, especially to, because Vöð was being auctioned. Everything had to be sold, stock, utensils, including bed linen, and even the estate itself. Many years had passed since the death of little Gestur until this day came. During these years the children of the house had died, and now the master of the house had passed away.

People had always thought that the family line would not be broken on this farm and that Vöð would remain an ancestral farm for many generations to come. The land had been in the property of the family for many generations before them. But now it had come to this.

Old Sesselja from Klúka came wading across the ford outside the farm clearly in the direction of Vöð.

Sesselja looked quite ridiculous. She was skinny and tall. Her eyes were red and her face distorted. She had long been mentally disturbed. She scuttled about in the district, her skirt clutched up in front, and spoke and laughed with everyone she met, sometimes sensibly, sometimes not. Most people found it nonsense, because it was a long time since Sesselja had lost her wits. She had been the mistress of her farm for many years and had borne many children in poverty and difficulty. She had raised them and given them a good start in life, despite her husband's drinking and abuse. Then apathy and confusion descended on her. But she was harmless. It happened that Sesselja hit the nail on the head when she spoke with people, and then she would laugh a lot and say: "That's it, Setta remembers."

Now Sesselja was heading for Vöð. It was typical of Sesselja to rush off to an auction. No one had ever heard of a woman at an auction. It was sad that the poor wretch should behave in such a way — an old woman and the mother of many children going to an auction, where only men were present. It would really be something to listen to Sesselja Sebedeusardóttir there, and there were those who mocked and poked fun at her. Poor soul.

Sesselja, however, went straight to the farm, her feet wet, and her skirt gathered up in front. She clutched the hem of her skirt at her waist and, rolling her blood-red eyes wildly, stared at the ones she met. She was silent, which was unusual. She paused for a brief moment in front of the farmhouse and listened to what was going on and then went into the kitchen, where the maids were working.

"Where is Madam Þuríður?" she asked.

The girls didn't know. But one of them had seen her walking up Álfahjalli a short while ago. Sesselja did not answer, but staggered out without saying a word. She went straight to Álfahjalli and climbed up to where the mistress of Vöð was sitting looking over the land — the ancestral farm on which she had spent her entire life, as had her parents before her, and her grandparents before them. Þuríður was silent and serious, even more than was usual at Vöð.

Sesselja was silent, too, as she struggled up the hillside. Her eyes became redder with each step; her mouth was working and her lips drooling. Now and then she muttered under her breath, and in this manner she reached the mistress of Vöð.

Þuríður knew Sesselja and didn't move, although she saw her approaching.

Sesselja looked at her with her terrible, almost ghostlike eyes and panted a bit.

Finally the mistress said: "How do you do, Sesselja."

"How do you do, Þuríður of Vöð."

Sesselja said no more and shuffled her feet.

"Do you bring any news, Sesselja?" she asked.

"Gestur has died," Sesselja said.

The mistress gave a bit of a start, but then asked calmly: "Which Gestur?"

"Little Gestur, the son of Marjas and Elrún."

"That's a long time ago," Þuríður said.

"A long, long time! Don't you know that a thousand years is like one day and one day like a thousand years? It's all the same."

"Do you have no other news than that?" the mistress asked, and it was as if she wanted to steer the conversation in a different direction.

"Yes. Vöð has been sold. Torfi in Eiður bought it for a mere song, a price he'll never pay, for Torfi never pays anything because he never owns anything. He never gives anything. Torfi has no sense of honour." At this Sesselja roared with laughter.

The mistress made a move to get up.

"Wait a minute," Sesselja said and pointed a long, skinny, and crooked finger at the mistress. "I want to tell you something."

The mistress sat still.

Sesselja waved her gnarled finger in front of her, and through her broken teeth and scarred lips she hissed out the words:

"There is no point in playing host to the minister if the door is barred against the Lord," she said.

Then she sauntered down the hill again.

[1937]

In the Morning of Life

Morning air breathed softly over the earth, the sun shone in a blue sky, the colours of the earth and ocean were so many, soft, and beautiful that they filled the air with purple mist. The ground was green, and the forest covered large areas with its emerald foliage waving gently in the soft breeze. The flowers grew in groups, clusters or singly, and crowned themselves as it were with the beauty of the air. One tiny flower, blue and charming, grew humbly in the deep grass, wrapping itself in the green mantle of its community. It seemed happy in its shelter and smiled at the soil. Its fragrance was very delicate, but it created an enchanting picture to the eye, and in its wee, drooping but beautiful petals it kept a ray of life which remained a secret for untold ages. The sun had told it to carry this greeting in its tiny wing. It did that, although it was a long time until man could read that greeting, for the flowers had not even been named yet, nor had their relation to the sun's rays been read.

A red, beautiful bloom grew strong and aggressive, pregnant with its own blood. Its form was wondrously made, its fragrance was lovely and strong. But on it grew thorns that stung all life that came near to it. Still, its fragrance was so sweet, its colours so lovely, its form so beautiful, that it drew life towards itself, even though life was aware of the thorns.

A white flower, dignified and tenderly beautiful, with yellow pollen carriers, grew towards the sky in a rather large shape, like a goblet. In a smaller form it bent its head meekly towards earth. The sun, air, earth, and sea, painted endless versions of flowers from these foundations in colours, to exist while the earth lasts.

In the early morning, the dumb creatures rose from their sleep. Tunes from many voices floated around in the air of the early and glorious morning. Birds, dressed in the beauty of colours, also painted by light, air, earth, and sea, flew around in the forest, flashing through the network of foliage or soaring above all other earthly creation, coming down again, building their nests, flying up and above again, singing their gloria of life.

The lion thundered for its prey; the sheep disappeared into its mouth. The tiger came out into the open, caught the hare on the run, and swallowed him. When the tiger and the lion had got their fill, they laid themselves down and gave their young ones a drink from their breasts and fell asleep in all the glory around them.

When the dusk fell on the forest, soft and soothing, the mouse came forth. The cat awoke from its daytime sleep, caught the mouse, and ate it. The gopher had to fetch its daily nourishment, too, but the cat saw it and caught it. The gopher was bigger and more difficult to deal with than the mouse, but the cat just reared on its hind legs and did not heed how the gopher moaned, while he tore it to pieces alive and ate it at leisure.

Adam and Eve came forth in the morning. They were both beautiful in the extreme. He was bigger and stronger, she was softer of limb and moved with still more grace. They ate the fruit from the trees and drank the clear, cold water that trickled in the brooks down the hillsides. They found satisfaction in looking around at the birds, flowers, and whatever else met their eyes. Still, the true, deep beauty was hidden from them. They looked at everything like children. When the cat was eating the screaming gopher, they clapped their hands with enjoyment or screamed with some wild joy, as when the crow cawed loudly, the birds sang, or when some other prey than the gopher screamed from the torture it was subjected to. Peace, heavy, sleepful, unapproachable peace, seemed to rest so deeply in the souls of these humans that nothing could disturb it. Their plays were the plays of little children that are still unconscious of any reality of life. They possessed a good deal of shallow joy, but no depth of understanding. They swam in the lakes, they climbed the trees, ran in the open glens, slept in the shelter of the trees or out on the open prairie.

Eve preferred to be in the forest and eat of the fruit she found there. Adam liked best to run around with the animals, which did not hurt them. A shallow consciousness of the things around them and some physical pain of their own constituted their understanding of life. When Eve saw the big animals tear the smaller ones to pieces and when the screams and moans of the suffering creatures, which rent the air, came to her ears, she laughed and waved her hands. She liked to run after butterflies, catch them, and tear them to pieces like she did with the flowers she picked.

Eve swam in the lakes and rivers like Adam, but she became tired sooner than he. She climbed the trees even more nimbly than he, however, and sat up there, sometimes for a long time. She might climb out on a branch that was too weak to carry him and did not move from there even if he asked her to come down.

"You're to name the flowers today. I've named the animals," he said to her one day, but she paid no heed to that. She liked to run in the open, roam the woods, pick flowers, and run along with the animals, especially the smaller ones. She had no desire to understand more than what she saw, nor had she any desire for work. She found complete peace and satisfaction in what she had. So she just ran into the forest when Adam spoke of naming the flowers.

Adam enjoyed life in a similar way, only he seemed to desire her presence even more than she did his. He was also less inclined to look for fruit to eat. For long intervals, he could stay in the same place in peace and quiet, especially if she was with him, but also when he was alone and she was roaming about. He frequently ate what she brought him, sometimes lying down under the trees. He also enjoyed eating the fruit that fell from the trees right into his mouth.

"You're to name the flowers today," Adam said again to Eve. But Eve paid no attention and just ran away to play among the flowers and the wild creatures.

Later in the day it was warm. Eve went far into the forest. It was her natural inclination to seek the cooler places but also curiosity for unknown places that took her there. Away in the dark forest she saw a creature she had seldom seen before. It was long in form, green in colour, and it seemed to move along close to the ground by crawling rather than walking like the rest of the creatures she had seen. This creature moved nimbly in between the trees with swift movements, its magic colours flashing between the branches.

Eve stared spellbound at the creature, even though in her mind some fear awoke, which both she and Adam had felt before when coming close to this place. Then she followed the snake as if drawn by a magic power. Its bright colours and agile movements made her forget everything else. At last, the creature began to coil itself around a big tree in the centre of the darkest forest and lifted itself by lithe movements and lightning speed to the top of the tree. The crown of the tree was large and covered with fruits which Eve had never seen before. The shadows of the tall trees of the surrounding forest cast a shadow over the fruits, so that the sun had scarcely reached them to affect their growth. The snake ate the fruit greedily and then circled itself back to the ground.

Eve stood still for a while under the spell of this sight. She was more frightened from this than from anything else she had seen or heard, but the fruit of this tree was so appealing. Among the sun-coloured stripes on it were the hues of the earth, more so than on any other fruit. These unusual earthly shades and the agility as well as the colours of the creature that fetched the fruit and ate it created a wild desire and daring

162

in Eve. The charms of the creature seemed to overpower her soul. It was as if the snake were challenging her to try the fruit.

Eve looked around. Everything was quiet. Everything seemed to be at a standstill. Only this lone, strange creature that had fetched the fruit and was eating it. But suddenly, the snake raised himself and stood halfway up in front of the young woman, staring at her with his spellbinding eyes. Eve forgot everything except those magnetic eyes with their glittering colours, which seemed to charm her into doing just as their owner wished.

Eve climbed swiftly and silently up the dark tree and fetched the beautiful fruit which the sun had not fully ripened. How strangely beautiful it was with its dark, red, and golden stripes. Eve picked some and ate them. She threw some down to Adam, who had come to look for her in the dark forest. Adam quickly ate the fruit.

Adam was writhing in agony. Never had he felt such pain before. Eve, too, was ill. Some terrorizing distress of both body and soul had seized both of them.

"It's all Eve's fault. She gave me this dark forest fruit," he moaned.

"It's the snake's fault. He bewitched me into doing it," Eve said, gasping from pain. "He was so handsome and charming that everything he did captivated me until nothing seemed as lovely as this dark forest fruit, neither in sight nor taste."

Eve wept bitterly and writhed in manifold pain. Their bodies became sore and sick within and without. Something strange and to them hitherto unknown had touched their spirits, too. They became aware that they were naked and were ashamed.

And now the Doom fell on them.

In the breeze, breathing through the foliage of the forest, they heard words of chiding spoken to them. They had never understood the breeze in the foliage before. They made themselves kirtles of leaves to cover their nakedness. But cold and heavy storms came over them, and their kirtles of grass did not suffice. With much effort in thought and deed they made themselves kirtles of skin. This entailed much struggle, even hardship. Now they heard thunder and lightning, something they had scarcely noticed before. Heat, cold, and all the turmoil of the elements touched them so much more keenly than before. They feared the wild animals and didn't feel nearly so much enjoyment in the presence of the harmless ones as before. They were ever imbued with fear, sickness, and anguish. At long last they understood what really was happening: they were being driven out of Eden.

"My suffering is greater than yours," said Eve, when neither she herself nor Adam could help her. "And it's your fault," she always added. "I'm going to leave you, and I don't ever want to see you again."

Just inside the garden gate, the Lord bent down and whispered something in Eve's ear. Then the gate was opened, and they went out. Angels carrying shining swords were placed as guardians of the gate, and the young couple walked feebly away, broken-hearted, poorly dressed, and ill.

"I feel most sorry for the small creatures which the big ones tear to pieces; I'd have liked to stay in the garden if only to help them — help those that suffer in our garden. It's horrible to think about it," said Eve.

"It wasn't given to us to understand what was needed there until it was too late," said Adam.

"Oh, Eden, beautiful Eden," Eve wept in anguish. But then her pains overwhelmed everything else. "It's your fault," she cried and could hardly get out the words because of pain.

"No," he said, "you gave me the fruit."

"The serpent gave it to me," she said.

"Let's turn back and try to get into the garden again," Adam said.

"That's of no use," she moaned. "There are armed angels guarding the entrance."

"Yes," he answered with indescribable sorrow. "We've been driven out of there for good. There's nothing ahead of us but cold and darkness."

"Yes, pain and suffering," she added.

"Eve," he said hesitantly. "What was it the Lord whispered in your ear inside the garden gate?"

She looked at him quickly and shyly, but didn't answer.

Eve went to a glen in the forest and gave birth to a child. She put the child to her breast, for this was what the animals of the forest had done in the Garden of Eden. Then she turned back to Adam.

They continued their sorrowful journey. The thistle stung them, the forest tore them, the wilderness refused them food and drink, the heat burned them, the cold froze them, the wild animals frightened them, the child cried pitifully, and many times they didn't know what to do.

At long last they came to an opening in the forest where there was much vegetation. There was the tiny blue flower growing in thick clusters, and the red flower with the strong fragrance and beautiful form which grew among its heavily thorned shrubbery. There was also the white flower breathing dignity and peace as in the Garden of Eden, the white flower with the gleaming yellow star inside that reminded them how beautifully the stars had twinkled into their eyes in the nights when they lived in hallowed peace in the Garden of Eden.

Eve laid her crying child on the blue flowers. It soothed the baby to feel the cool softness under its head.

"You shall be named Viola," Eve said. "You are beautiful, humble, and soothing. On your lovely petals my child receives consolation."

Eve walked to the thorn bush. She picked the red flower and didn't care though the thorns stung her till she bled. She picked the thorns from the stalk and gave her child the flower. The child smiled when the lovely fragrance came to his nostrils.

Then Eve went back to the thorn bush and said to the flower: "Your name shall be Rose. You have no equal in charm, beauty, and fragrance."

Later, when they had drifted over far places and long distances, they again came to a large meadow richly endowed in vegetation, and there Eve gave birth to another child. They stayed there for a long time and their daily needs were fulfilled through their efforts at tilling the land. Then Death came and took one of their children away. The parents sorrowed in desolate anguish for the lost one. When they had carried their son from the scene of death and laid him out at home, Eve walked once again to a glen in the forest. There she found the white flower with the golden star in the centre. She picked the flower and placed it on the forehead of her deceased son.

"You shall be named Lily," she said to the flower. "Your innocence and dignity are to be found in Paradise only."

"What are you talking about?" Adam asked.

"It's my son's crown," she answered.

Adam looked carefully at the flower. The glowing centre shone into his eyes.

"Star. Paradise. This is how the stars looked in Eden. Still, one of them seemed to me more beautiful than the others, but I saw it only once."

"When was that?" she asked.

Adam looked still more sorrowful. He put the lily back on the head of the boy. "Paradise, you say. The star of hope. For one moment, when the words of Doom thundered over us, the star shone into my eyes," he whispered. "I saw it, but it disappeared from my sight."

Eve touched the head of her son.

"I saw it," he went on, lifting his head a little. "It sparkled so beautifully in the night's heaven. Its rays shone so wonderfully, something like the star in the flower there, only much more brightly. Now you tell me that its dignity and beauty can be found in Paradise only, and from there we've been driven."

"Yes, its dignity and beauty are to be found there, but it's also true that we've been driven out of there," she answered despairingly.

He pondered this for a while, but then said more cheerfully: "Since it exists, even though only in Paradise, perhaps there's hope for us, Eve. Eternal hope. We'll enter the garden again, the garden of heavenly bliss."

"Don't deceive yourself, Adam." Eve shook her head dejectedly. Her face was swollen from crying, but she was still defiant.

"The hope you speak of was connected with me and my descendants. My lovely son is dead now, and there's no hope of help from a brother who's a slayer. I'm not going to bear more children, because that entails more suffering than I can bear to even think about."

Adam was discouraged by her words. He went over to the dead boy, touched his forehead, and said: "The seed of the woman shall crush your head, and you shall crush its heel. That is how it was spoken to the enemy. My son, you have been caught under the heel. Still, can it be that you are dead? You who were destined to crush the serpent? She says that everything is over."

Adam looked at the lily on the head of the deceased boy. "Innocence. Dignity. Paradise. The star. I believe there's still something left for us."

The couple continued their journey over strange and difficult roads. Roads of thorns and thistle, hunger and cold. Sometimes across deserts in blinding sandstorms and under a burning sun, deserts which had no nourishment to offer to life. Eve was exhausted.

"Adam," she whispered at last, with pale lips touched by death. "I

166

love you better than life itself. That was the gift the Lord gave me within the garden gate."

Adam fell on his knees and implored the master of life and death for mercy for Eve.

The blood streamed into her lips again and strength into her whole being, and Eve became the ever youthful and most beautiful of all women.

[1956]

Jakobína Johnson

Jakobína Sigurbjörnsdóttir (later Johnson) was born in 1883 at Hólmavað in Aðaldalur, Suður-Þingeyjarsýsla, the daughter of the poet Sigurbjörn Jóhannesson and María Jónsdóttir. She emigrated to Canada with her family in 1889, settling in the Argyle district in Manitoba, where she grew up. After graduating from the Collegiate Institute in Winnipeg, she was for some years a public-school teacher in Manitoba. Soon after her marriage, in 1904, to Ísak Jónsson (Johnson), a builder by profession and the brother of the poets Gísli and Einar P. Jónsson, the couple moved first to Victoria and, in 1908, to Seattle, Washington. There they raised seven children: Kári, Ingólfur, Konráð Ari, Haraldur Björn, María Guðrún, Jóhann Ísak and Stephan Jón. They lived in Seattle until their deaths, Ísak in 1949 and Jakobína in 1977.

Jakobína Johnson published her first poems in 1913, and from then on her poetry appeared regularly in Icelandic and North American Icelandic newspapers and magazines, notably *Tímarit Þjóðræknisfélags Íslendinga*, but also *Lögberg, Heimskringla, Eimreiðin, Dvöl* and *Lesbók Morgunblaðsins*. A selection of her poems was published in *Kertaljós: Úrvalsljóð* (Reykjavík, 1938), *Sá ég svani* (Reykjavík, 1942), a children's book, and *Kertaljós: Ljóðasafn* (Reykjavík, 1956). In addition, she translated into English a large number of poems by leading Icelandic poets. These have appeared in various North American literary magazines including *The Icelandic Canadian*, *American-Scandinavian Review*, and *The Literary Digest*; a considerable number of them are contained in the collections *Icelandic Lyrics* (Reykjavík, 1930) and *Icelandic Poems and Stories* (New York, 1943), both edited by Richard Beck, in Thorstína Jackson Walters's *Modern Sagas* (Fargo, 1953), and in her own *Northern Lights* (Reykjavík, 1959). She also translated into English the dramas *Lénharður fógeti* by Einar H. Kvaran, *Galdra-Loftur* by Jóhann Sigurjónsson, and *Nýársnóttin* by Indriði Einarsson, as well as a number of short stories by Elinborg Lárusdóttir, Svanhildur Þorsteinsdóttir, and Ólafur Jóhann Sigurðsson.

Jakobína Johnson was active in cultural and literary societies and lectured extensively on Iceland and Icelandic literature and culture. In 1933 she was awarded the Icelandic Order of the Falcon, and in 1935 she visited Iceland as the special guest of the Young People's League (Ungmennafélag Íslands) and the Women's Society (Kvenfélagasamband Íslands).

"Dawn" and "Candlelight" are translated from "Morgunróði" and "Kertaljós" in *Kertaljós: Úrvalsljóð* (10-11 and 48); "I Know of a Bird" and "Like Seeds" (the latter originally delivered in 1940 at the Íslendingadagur, the Western Icelanders' annual festival) are translated from "Ég veit um fugl" and "Sem frækorn" in *Kertaljós: Ljóðasafn* (90-91 and 96).

Dawn

You rosy morning with red-gold sky
And sun in the crowns of the forest high,
Like smoke the tiredness fades as I wake,
For ample reward the sight of you does make.

Of toil, hurry, and grumbling I am free,
For in advance I am paid my day's fee;
Morning, I have fixed your image in my mind,
Where the darkest shadow I was wont to find.

[1922]

Candlelight

You great power, you broad-winged emotion,
Carry me over the deep blue ocean!
For early I heard the beat of your wings
When at the end of day with joy one sings.

I was not born in a tough stirring age,
Nor have I the strength or heroic courage
To force my way through the rocks so grim.
—All I hold is a candle, small and thin.

170

Though the candle lights up but a short way
My search for beauty could brook no delay.
—Little poems along life's path I found
Like elves and flowers strewn all around.

You strong inner yearning, you great powers,
Oh, show me rare and hidden flowers;
Let beautiful words be ne'er far from my lips
Till the candle burns into my fingertips.

[1938]

I Know of a Bird

I know of a bird that never flies south
Although the leaves fade in the fall,
But winter long of spring and delight
With the voice of spring does call.

I know the origin of the open fire
That lasts the whole day through
And makes a poor home a palace
Till the sun sinks down from view.

[1938]

Like Seeds

Like seeds from far distant strands,
Which with the ocean's currents flowed,
Upon the shores of the western lands
A powerful race was bestowed.

The country took from older nations
The vigorous pioneers and their claims.

In concord they ploughed new plantations
And set themselves the highest aims.
With the new land's precious bounty
The old yearning bore fruit at last,
Which from history's bonds would flee
To fly the flag of progress on its mast.

For the settler's dream can be understood,
Though long silent has been his voice,
To show the way to a new brotherhood
—A noble nation of freedom and choice.

[1940]

Helen Sveinbjörnsson

Helen Sveinbjörnsson (the pen name of Helen Swinburne Lloyd) was born in 1892 in Edinburgh, Scotland, the daughter of the well-known composer Sveinbjörn Sveinbjörnsson, who was a teacher of music in Edinburgh, and his Scottish wife, Eleanor (née Christie). Helen Sveinbjörnsson was educated at two private schools, Strathearn College and Craigmount, after which she entered the College of Fine Arts in Edinburgh. In 1915 she received her diploma in design, secured a position teaching art in a private school in Edinburgh for a time, then taught for a year at the Academy in Forfar, Scotland, where she also supervised the art instruction in four public schools. From there she went to Kilwinning, where she continued teaching art. In 1919 she emigrated with her family to Canada, settling first in Winnipeg, where she taught at Earl Gray Junior High School and at Kelvin High School. In 1921 she married Ralph E.A. Lloyd. The couple made their home on a farm near Calgary, Alberta, where they raised their four children: Benjamin, Francis, Eleanor and Jon. Eleanor is now a well-known painter and writer in Alberta. After her husband's death in 1943, Helen Swinburne Lloyd moved to Calgary where she died in 1979.

Helen Swinburne Lloyd began writing poetry about 1930, and her poetry has appeared in a number of papers and magazines, including *Lögberg*, *Heimskringla*, *Árdís*, *Tímarit Þjóðræknisfélags Íslendinga*, *Farm and Ranch Review* and *Country Guide*. She also had poems accepted for the *Alberta Poetry Yearbook* and the *Nova Scotia Yearbook* sponsored by the Canadian Authors' Association. A collection of her poetry was published under the title *Cloth of Gold and Other Poems* (Devon, 1973).

"Cloth of Gold," "The Cabinet of Curios" and "Dream World" are reprinted from *Cloth of Gold and Other Poems* (21, 68 and 114-115).

Cloth of Gold

My loom was rough and shaped by hand, my thread
Was only flax which round my feet lay spread;
I wept a bitter tear.
I longed to handle silken thread and fine,
To weave a pattern of my own design
That to my heart was dear,
To work in harmony with colours gay;
I wept in vain, yet longed to have my way.

I wove my piece of cloth and, in the weaving,
I learned to weep no more, to cease my grieving,
And taught my lips to smile;
Long since I looked upon my work then proven,
The warp and weft so closely interwoven,
I paused to muse awhile,
When lo . . . like finest silk, fold upon fold . . .
It lay before me changed to cloth of gold.

[1973]

The Cabinet of Curios

Arrayed on shelves of polished wood, they stand
Inside glass doors, each quaint and curious thing
Wrought by the artifice of human hand,
And to the mind some far-off memory bring,
Or thought of olden times long passed away.
Within this little world apart, I see
A Maltese cross of silver filigree—
An inlaid box—a gaily-painted tray.

Two little Chelsea cats with friendly faces
Beside a fragment of handwoven shawl,
A pair of Spanish castanets, with laces
Of gold, that hang above the mirrored wall,

174

A panel sewn in silk by patient fingers,
Mellowed with age, a faded Valentine—
And many a treasure formed in strange design—
Whilst over all an air of mystery lingers.

We yet may dream of some gay fantasy
From a carved fan with roses painted red,
Or hear a merry lilting melody
The click of castanets, and overhead
See the lights gleaming with a warm glow.
We yet may drift with fancy in her flight
And through the rolling mists of time alight
Into the wondrous world of long ago.

[1973]

Dream World

Beyond the hold of stern reality
The unending regions of a dream-world lie:
'Tis but a step
To fare; untrammelled I
Rove therein with Nanna, daughter of Nep;
Upon her carpet shining buttercups
Pour their golden thanks unto the sky;
And here and there a jewelled butterfly
Alights and sups
On blossom-laden bough;
The rose, the lily, one with another vie,
But fairer far than these
Blooms Baldur's brow.

Now like a passing cloud rent in twain
And changing form, my fleeting phantasm fades
And shapes again;
I pass down green by-ways, through mossy glades,
Where vibrant notes in wild crescendos rise
From feathered throats; where dove coos to dove;

And Iðunn, spirit of eternal spring
Listens to the voice of Bragi sing
A song of love.

No swifter wings could beat the air than these
Dream-wings which bear me on their powerful flight
And poise where I can hear the restless sea's
Unceasing song;
There Ægir's helmet riseth dark as night;
And Rán moves nigh, icy-lipped and wan,
Guarding her secrets, sheltering her hosts,
Flinging her molten silver to the dawn.

And far above the seething waves that lash
And fret against the lonely rocks, I see
The mighty boughs of the Yggdrasill tree,
Life-giving ash
Nurtured by the sacred well of Urð;
And I behold the flash
Of shining shuttles where the Norns are weaving
Men's destinies; the pattern of the Past,
Age-mellowed, fades into obscurity;
The Present, weaving fast,
And faster still,
Brings forth a pattern lit with lurid flame
At Örlög's will;
But, lying unwoven in the Future's hold,
Gleams thread of Gold.

O dream-world, with thy fountains ever-flowing,
Thy boundless realms, thy blossoms ever-blowing,
Thy wealth untold,
Give back to us our fairest thoughts and longings
Forged in finest mould.

[1973]

Laura Goodman Salverson

Laura Goodman (later Salverson) was born in Winnipeg in 1890, the daughter of Lárus Guðmundsson and Ingibjörg Guðmundsdóttir, who had both emigrated from Iceland in 1887. Following her father's *wanderlust*, the family had by 1912 travelled in search of stability and financial security to Minnesota, North Dakota, back to Winnipeg, to Selkirk, back to Winnipeg, to Duluth in Minnesota, to Mississippi, to Duluth again, and finally back to Winnipeg. Although sickly, she managed to acquire some high-school education prior to her marriage, in 1913, to George Salverson, with whom she had one son, George. George Salverson was employed by a railway company, and the couple was consequently moved from place to place. Laura Goodman Salverson was a member of the Leif Erikson Society of America and actively involved in the establishment of *The Icelandic Canadian*, a Winnipeg quarterly, of which she was editor-in-chief in 1942-1943. She died in Toronto in 1970.

In 1922, Laura Goodman Salverson won a prize for the best short story describing life in western Canada in a contest held under the auspices of The Women's Canadian Club in Regina, Saskatchewan. It was entitled "Hidden Fire" and was her first short story; it appeared simultaneously in *Maclean's* and *Maple Leaf.* A year later, she published her first novel, *The Viking Heart* (Toronto, 1923), which won her instant recognition as an author. The book was followed by short stories, plays, radio sketches, a volume of poetry entitled *Wayside Gleams* (Toronto, 1925), an autobiography entitled *Confessions of an Immigrant's Daughter* (Toronto, 1939), and the following novels: *When Sparrows Fall* (Toronto, 1925), *Lord of the Silver Dragon* (Toronto, 1927), *The Dove* (Toronto, 1933), *The Dark Weaver* (Toronto, 1937), *Black Lace* (Toronto, 1938) and *Immortal Rock: The Saga of the Kensington Stone* (Toronto, 1954). Some of the novels were originally published in serial form in magazines and newspapers. *Lord of the Silver Dragon* and *The Dove*, for example, appeared in *The Canadian Home Journal* and *The Western Home Monthly* respectively; one of the novels, *Johann Lind*, appeared only in *The Western Home Monthly*.

Laura Goodman Salverson was the first Canadian author to win the Governor-General's Award in two literary divisions. She received her first award in 1937 for *The Dark Weaver*, a chronicle of Scandinavian settlement on the Canadian prairies; the second award came two years later for *Confessions of an Immigrant's Daughter*. In 1938 she won a gold medal from the Paris Institute of Arts and Sciences, and in 1955 she received the Ryerson Fiction Award for *Immortal Rock*, an historical novel based on Norse explorations in America. These awards are particularly remarkable because she knew no English before the age of ten.

"Hidden Fire" is reprinted from *Maclean's* 15 February 1923, 14, 50-51; "The Greater Gift" from *The Western Home Monthly* December 1924, 11, 63; "When Blind Guides Lead" from *Maclean's* 1 February 1925, 13, 50-52; and "The Alabaster Box" from *Maclean's* 15 December 1927, 3-4, 41-42.

Hidden Fire

The most humble of mankind are not without their quota of ennobling sorrows and heartening joys. Neither are they lacking in those significant moments which are impregnated with the desires and hopes of better things.

It may be that such experiences are but the fragments of that first "divine discontent" which drove mankind from an Eden of irresponsible existence to the rugged paths of painful thought; a reversion to that hazy, unformulated desire that forced the first reptile from his cosy bed.

But whatever the psychological explanation may be, this clear, indisputable fact remains, that regardless of how great our self-satisfaction is today, discontent, even misery, may rule our lot tomorrow; and this without any definite or apparent change of circumstance.

Such, at least, was the experience of Martha Croyer, "Old Martha," as the villagers of Neah familiarly called her. Not that she was actually so old in years, but rather because through toil and suffering she had acquired a garb of age. For thirty years she had been the faithful wife of John Croyer, drudging uncomplainingly upon his farm. She had so long been a silent, unobtrusive toiler, that the rising generation remembered her only as a somewhat heavy-featured old lady, entirely commonplace and said to be under her husband's thumb.

On a certain spring morning, however, Old Martha arose from her bed with unusual alacrity, threw a faded shawl over her flannelette nightgown, and hurried to the window. The newly risen sun had lifted the morning vapours, leaving the meadow fresh and beautiful, like some fairy island lately emerged from the sea. The arbour to the east of the house was sheathed in that delicate green seen only in springtime, and from an adjacent birch a cardinal darted, challenging the world with his rapturous song.

But all this had transpired upon many another bygone day, kindling usually no deeper sentiment than this that here again was opportunity for fruitful labour at field or wash tub.

Not the beauty of the spring, then, nor yet the call of mating birds had drawn her to the window. No, the lure was a rollicking, old-fashioned song, borne in all its buoyant gaiety upon the fragrant morning air. Somewhere beyond the farm fences were carefree campers making for the distant hills, leaving behind them the echo of their song to re-awaken yet other echoes for Old Martha.

Suddenly, she was overwhelmed at the sense of her misery, appalled at the price she had paid for her dull, peaceful life. Yet she could not but marvel at the foolishness of the human heart. Was the resignation bought by the persistent patience of a lifetime to be undone by the spell of the simple lyric? Yet how wide it has swung the fettered gates of memory and emotion!

One by one they rushed upon her, these memories, jostling one another in their swift approach. Old hopes, old dreams, old desires! Hurriedly, with trembling fingers, she finished dressing, for she had caught the sound of noisily clanging barn doors, denoting that John had finished the morning "feeding" and, in accordance with all sensible habit, a hot and plentiful breakfast should await his return to the house.

On opening the kitchen door, admitting a flood of sunlight, Old Martha heard with relief the voice of some neighbour hailing her husband. It would give her grace to get things well under way, this early morning gossip, whatever its import. But though she worked swiftly and efficiently, to all outward appearances the same placid housewife, yet her thoughts were alien to the tasks in hand and were very strange thoughts indeed.

While carefully measuring the coffee to the desired strength, and beating the eggs for an omelette, she pondered, later coming to the astounding conclusion that since these emotions, so long and conscientiously subdued, now again broke forth in fierce new strength, it was right and desirable they should do so. That now, at last, she could be free to heed them, to snatch from life at least a semblance of joys long missed, before it be forever too late.

For the first time it dawned upon her habit-shackled mind that she could put to some tangible use the little hoard of money, which, to her frugal eyes, had in the last few years grown to a considerable sum. With that quickness of decision which sometimes comes to conservative natures, she formulated her plans. She would go to Elizabeth, her brother's widow, who still dwelt in the little mountain village where their youth had been spent. Yes, with Elizabeth she would live again in dreams and come at last to a knowledge of the fullness of life. John, she argued with herself, was hardly aware of her except in such tasks as were hers to perform. These, she knew, could equally well be done by another, and John could now easily afford the expense such help would incur.

For the last few years affairs had been going well at the farm; the stock had increased and the crops had been abundant. Yet, apparently, it made little difference. Fortune had smiled so late upon them that the Croyers, in their deep-rooted, poverty-ridden ways, derived about as much satisfaction from her gifts as an infant would from a saddle horse. The only discernible change lay in the new barn buildings, the sleek stock, and in that little hoard of Martha's — money earned from poultry products, a source of income which always had been hers and out of which she procured all household staples. Back in the hard, lean years when each succeeding failure wrung something of joy and life from both of them, she had, with ever increasing resourcefulness and self-denial, met many a minor debt with this slender revenue. With a grim smile she thought of the simple pleasures and the long-deferred hopes lying in the grave of those debts.

John Croyer entered the house much after his usual manner. Yet, to Martha, surreptitiously watching him at his morning ablutions, it was plain that something was amiss. It was, however, not his way to talk on an empty stomach, so she held her peace. Over his fourth muffin and second cup of coffee, he suddenly burst forth as she knew he eventually must:

"Matt's having a tough time again. Tilly's downright sick — powerful fever!"

"Seems as I'd call it Tilly's tough time if I had my say," his wife replied.

John glared at her. "This is no joking matter, old lady. Matt says Dr. Bonn thinks she'll not pull through, and little Carey's only eight and the baby just six months. Fine mess for a man to be in!"

"So 'tis, so 'tis, John Croyer, and a fine cheap servant he'll lose too, in Tilly. Fine worker Tilly was till the last two little ones came. Matt's grey mare, I've noticed, has been browsing round quite some time with her little colt, but then, horses is horses, and wimmin's only wimmin! Lucky she'll be, I'm thinkin', poor Tilly, to get her rest!"

John Croyer was not only surprised by this tirade, but stricken dumb. With his mouth full of muffin and his eyes popping, he stared at the sarcastic stranger sitting in the seat of his commonly self-effacing wife. Then he blared out:

"You talk like a crazy woman and a sinner, making light of the trials sent by the Almighty! Better hustle through your work. I'll harness Ginger along towards noon. You'd best be doin' what you can at Matt's and save your tongue. Gabbin' never done no good!"

"No, gabbin' never done me any good, John Croyer, but at least I don't lay it against the Almighty. I'll be ready when Ginger is harnessed and I'll lay out a bit of lunch so's you needn't want till I get back." With which remark she left the table and went upstairs, leaving behind a sorely troubled spouse to brood on the general cussedness of women.

But if it was a perverted old woman who presided at John's breakfast table, it was, nevertheless, an angel of mercy who stepped into Tilly's bedroom. One look at the sorely tried woman and Martha knew affairs were even worse than she had believed. Another besides Dr. Bonn was in attendance — that Oldest Healer of the universe who brought relief at the first sickbed, and who will attend the last, and laid his insignia upon Tilly's red face.

Matt was standing stupidly beside the bed, while the six-months-old Joseph crawled about his mother's feet. In the window close at her head a great, grey cat sat preening itself in the sunshine. Martha shooed it away.

In the kitchen little Carey was feeding the other two children bread and milk, while a neighbour woman was frying pork and potatoes. The odour of the food hung heavily about the sickroom — an accusation to the dying woman, who had no business to be dying in a world where so much pork was yet unfried, so many babies yet unreared.

Dr. Bonn drove up in the midst of this, breezed into the sickroom in his customary dapper way, took the patient's temperature, listened to her heart, administered a stimulant in a tumbler of water, then beckoned for Matt to come outside. Martha sent the baby away with him.

After their departure, Tilly clutched at Martha's hand.

"Martha, Martha, I'm dying — and I'm glad. Only — there's little Carey — already she's a slave, and she's never had nothing."

Tilly's grip tightened, and Martha patted her cheek in silent sympathy, fighting back her own tears. With difficulty the sick woman went on:

"Matt'll get another woman — housekeepers is hard to keep. But my Carey — seems as if I can't bear her to be a-slavin' for another woman. Martha, you and John's fixed well with no little ones — take my Carey — and let her play, Martha — till life gets her like the rest of us!"

At one time Martha would have felt it incumbent upon her to consult John, but in the strength of her new rebellion she hesitated not at all.

"Yes, yes, Tilly, I'll do what I can. Your little Carey'll play — I promise you good and plenty."

The exhausted woman, falling back upon the pillows, lay with closed eyes. Life seemed to ebb out quickly now that the mind had relaxed its tenacious hold upon the great desire. Freedom, happiness, beauty! These things denied her, could they be won by the little daughter then all were well.

In Tilly's humble world, the men were lords, and though they toiled yet were they free. Hence she worried less about the little boys. Yet now and again she aroused herself from the enveloping stupor, bemoaning little Joseph so young, so helpless.

Eventually she fell asleep, and Martha returned to the kitchen where the dinner, now cold, waited untasted upon the table. The neighbour woman had taken the children out. Martha saw her walking to and fro in the pasture, little Joseph in her arms and beside her Carey — miniature mother — watching with serious eyes her little brothers as they gleefully chased the chickens about the field.

Martha heard subdued voices and, recognizing one as that of her husband, she stepped out upon the porch.

Matt and John were seated, their broad backs toward her. Matt's body sagged dejectedly and she caught his rough, broken speech.

"All along I've been that mean and stingy — saving, saving, so's some day I could bring Tilly the bank book and say: 'See here, Tilly, now we can ease up a little and maybe do something fine for the kids too.' Now I know what an ass I've been. Hard work, the doctor says, killed her. My Tilly that was so beautiful! You should have seen her, John, her blue eyes full of mischief! — That granary last year could have waited, the money gone for help. Now it's too late. John, John," the poor man groaned, "why are men such fools?"

To Martha's wonderment her practical and unemotional husband muttered: "Just naturally born so, I reckon, not allowin' of it for conceit. Buck up, man, buck up! You can make good to the children!"

"But my Tilly, my Tilly . . ."

Martha stepped down from the porch confronting the men. "Matt," she said, "do this for Tilly, tell her what you just said — not that you're a fool, she knows that, I reckon, but that you love her — that she's still beautiful. No woman ever lived but would stop outside paradise to hear her lad say that."

Like a priestess of some strange religion she continued, her voice vibrant with emotion: "You think I'm a crazy old woman, but for twenty years I've been what your Tilly was for ten. Tell her of the old days, and Matt, promise me this — say that Carey shall get what her mother never had, and" — whimsically — "tell her you'll buy Carey a new dress — a silk dress, Matt — tell her that. It sounds so foolish, I know, but that's just what makes misery, Matt, what's so little to some, is a tragedy to others. I know what I say, I've seen your Tilly in her shabby dress standing out in yonder field, a tiger lily pressed against her poor white cheek, lookin' off into nowhere with such eyes as it hurt to see. Oh, yes, Tilly will know what you mean better'n you yourself ever will, when you tell her Carey gets a silk dress."

Having said this to the stupefied men, she hurried off to relieve the other woman of Joseph's care. Later, between them, they hustled the little ones off to the next farm, leaving at home only Carey, who was old enough to understand the calamity which was about to engulf them.

Two hours later, when Martha tiptoed into the sickroom, she beheld one of life's miracles. Tilly lay propped up in her husband's arms, on her face a look of rapture defying expression. Toil and pain were painted out by the artistry of love. Slow, heart-wrung tears were stealing down Matt's brown, unshaven face, while with that tenderness which lies dormant in most big men, he caressed his wife's head, stroking her corn-coloured hair, the one attribute of beauty which neither toil nor time had touched.

Tilly smiling — Tilly with flying hair! Old Martha had a vision of her as she must have been long before coming to this valley farm. Like one gazing into a secret place and feeling ashamed, she crept away, her eyes dim, and made ready to go home to the evening milking.

For the angel of death may visit us, yet the homely tasks rise up and claim us. Only momentarily, on the wings of joy or grief, are we lifted out of ourselves, realizing vaguely the majesty of life. Then we descend into the commonplace, and for our common selves this is well.

A week after Tilly's funeral, Old Martha was rummaging up in the attic looking for odds and ends with which to furnish Carey's room, for John was willing the child should come and Matt was eagerly grateful, promising to provide well for her needs.

John had driven off to the village early in the day, so his wife decided that the opportunity for making certain changes in the household, a thing abhorrent to her husband, was unusually good. Moreover, being still decided upon her trip, she wanted to ascertain whether certain old trunks were suitable for the journey. Now, however, because of little Carey, the adventure was to be only a holiday, and the child, of course, was to go with her. These various tasks had used up the day, and it was already growing dusk when as she dusted out the last hide-covered trunk, an eager voice shouted:

"Mattie, Mattie!"

Something long buried arose within the old lady's breast. Her heart beat rapidly, sending the blood to her head. How long the years since she had heard that call! Agitated, she dropped weakly down upon the trunk, just managing to answer:

"Here, Johnny, here in the attic."

Sheepishly, like a small boy caught giving his lady an apple or a tadpole or some such token of love, John Croyer entered the attic carrying a paper box. Not only was he freshly shaven in the best Sabbath style, but arrayed from top to toe in new and expensive garments.

The eternal coyness of woman raised its long-silent voice:

"My, but you're handsome, Johnny!"

But, John, flushing painfully, seated himself on a neighbouring box and thrust the package into his wife's lap.

"I'm hoping you'll do some more understanding, Mattie," he said, then falling silent sat twisting his new hat around in his hands.

From folds of tissue paper, clouds of grey silk, with here and there a touch of rose, peeped forth. With trembling fingers Martha held aloft the treasure. It was a dress, so delicate and beautiful that she knew her husband must have ordered it from the distant city. No country village had its equal.

Then, in spite of the difficulties she was having with her throat, a desire to laugh assailed her. John's line of reasoning was so obvious. A dress for Carey — a dress for her! From the dim recesses of memory came a recollection. Once on the far blue hills, where they had dreamed their little dream, she had voiced a longing for a white, bell-shaped blossom growing near a certain bluff. Thence on, the fragrant bells were hers whenever procurable, but — never a different flower.

A premonition of the useless silk dresses which would now be hers for all future time burst upon her, and she broke into a cheery laugh.

"Oh, Johnny, Johnny," she cried, "you've not changed a bit! I see it now, I see it now!" And half fearful that this merry mood might pass: "Johnny, do you remember the Ryans' ball — when Freddie broke his fiddle string?"

"Because I danced so long with the belle of the ball?" he finished for her.

"Mattie," he shouted, "the schottische, the schottische."

And with, it must be confessed, a stiff and awkward bow, he said:

"Come, give me your hand. We'll just try the step!"

[1923]

185

The Greater Gift

Little Magnús considered the weather gravely. It looked as though it were going to snow. Above the shacks opposite, the sky seemed singularly low. He had an idea that if he could ascend a house-top he might run his finger along the woolly clouds.

Out in the street he saw where a small hungry-looking dog sniffed at the hard earth as he loped along disconsolately. It reminded Magnús that he was not so *very* full himself.

Slowly he turned round to watch his mother busy with her ironing. She was a small, vigorous woman, and the perspiration of her face curled the fine hair about her temples instead of dampening it — perhaps this was nature's way of flying undaunting colours. Now she was flushed and hot and very tired. Beside her on a chair was a large basket of clothes. They were all to be ironed so she might deliver them that afternoon to the grocer's wife.

"Mama, I think I'm just a little, *little* hungry."

She set the iron down sharply, wiped her forehead, and smiled.

"It's good that, isn't it, my lamb? Then it'll be such fun to have your porridge. If you'll just wait till I finish this blouse, then we'll waken María and have our dinner."

"Mama, is it true that God loves children?"

"What else could he do, beloved?"

"And, mama, isn't this Christmas?"

"In the old land we would say that Christmas begins this midnight. You'll see, the stars will shine with a twinkle, for the angels shine them anew in their joy."

"Mama, Samuel told me there'll be a tree at the church. Couldn't I go? A tree with lights on it! He said so. Oh, mama! I never saw one — it isn't so cold — please couldn't I go?"

His mother had finished the blouse. She hung it carefully over the back of a chair, set aside her ironing board and went to the small stove. Perhaps it was to hide her emotions that she peered so carefully and so low over the porridge pot.

From the next and only other room came a weak voice asking the time of day.

"It's half past twelve, Pétur," said his wife.

"Mama, couldn't I go?"

"Won't you be frightened going alone, dear? And with papa so ill I couldn't take you."

Little Magnús's face lit up with joy. "No, no. Oh, mama, it'll be Christmas! And I'll hear the singing and see the stars, too — papa, papa! I'm going to see the tree at the church," he called shrilly, running to the door of the bedroom.

White and very worn from his long illness, the poor father regarded the child, saw his big shining eyes so full of expectation, and he groaned.

"You'll freeze, Magnús, and become sick like papa."

"But no! I'll run — and see, I'll stick my hands into my coat-sleeves — and mama puts paper in my shoes — it isn't so cold then if you run fast."

Over the meagre dinner, his mother tried to make plain many things without revealing too much.

"There'll perhaps be gifts, Magnús, for the little children whose fathers are well. You must not let it grieve you if there aren't presents for you."

But little Magnús had another belief. Hadn't his friend told him of a mysterious person who brought gifts to good little boys, and hadn't he been a good little boy, carrying wood and water and helping his mother with the heavy baskets of clothes? And did he not mind María while their mother was away? And had not his mother said God loved small children? So, of course, there would be something wonderful for him on that tree! The tree in God's house — he was sure of it. He had even hinted a little to God in his prayers.

Shortly after seven he began to wash himself. He was very careful about his ears, even asking his mother to look into them; and he brushed his stiff close-cropped hair long and painstakingly. Then his mother helped him into a clean shirt, brushed his old coat, lined his worn boots with paper, and watched him with a heavy heart.

But little Magnús sang with delight. It made his father clench his hands in the darkness to listen to the shrill sweet voice. How the child sang! Like a bird in the morning.

"Oh, Lord," he prayed, "fill with compassion some heart — poor little child, poor little child."

When Magnús was ready he flung himself upon his father and kissed him. He squeezed his little sister till she cried out in pain, then he flew to his mother's arms. She smiled into his eyes, kissing them one after the other.

"Be a good child and remember if it weren't for papa's illness you'd have a gift too. Be a little man and be brave."

He turned back to wave at her, hunched in the shoulders through habit in fighting the wind, and called gaily, "You'll see, mama, something will happen, just you wait."

When he was gone she sat down heavily. María picked at her sleeve but she did not heed her. The child sighed and then slipped off into a corner where she sat down and talked to the people behind the wall.

"My dear, wasn't it unwise to let him go?" Pétur called tonelessly.

"No doubt, but he wouldn't have understood or forgotten that we denied him so little a thing. Oh Pétur, but that it should be Christmas Eve!"

Then they said no more. After a time María fell asleep weary with her make-believe and her mother put her to bed. From time to time she glanced at the clock. She tried to knit but the stitch was irritating. She wiped off the stove, swept the floor again, putting away the papers María had scattered about.

But Magnús ran on gaily. He gritted his teeth and refused to believe that he was cold. The long streets were white, and the dim light of the street lamps cast a ghostly glimmer over them. Now and again someone passed him, or rather he fled by them unseeingly.

When at last he saw the big grey church, tremendously big to him, all alight with its Christmas candles, his little heart swelled to bursting. He thought how beautiful the yellow patches of light were that flung themselves from the church windows out upon the snow. And up aloft over the church steeple gleamed the white cross, silvered in the moonlight. He was so happy to see all this that he wanted to cry. And when shivering with cold and nervous excitement he slipped into a far back pew, he was even more delighted.

At first he was just a little confused. It was so warm and there was such a wonderful odour of spruce in the air, and such a buzz of voices. With stiffened fingers he tugged at his comforter and at last unwound it. He hung it carefully behind himself so as not to get it in anyone's way. Then he sank back against the seat and just looked and looked.

The arches of the church were garlanded in green, and everywhere were candles twinkling down at one like tiny golden spirits. But wonder of wonders — beside the altar was a tree! Great and tall and all a-glitter! It was like a wonderful dream. It was unbelievable and yet it was true. High above the altar was a flaming message done in golden tinsel; "Glory to God in the Highest." He could read it quite well; he had read it so often for his mother. But now it dazzled him. He felt its glory enveloping him in a hot flame.

He did not hear so much of the sermon, but he wished he dared sing. The singing was so lovely. And when, after a bit, a band of little children dressed in white marched around the aisles singing "Oh Little Babe of Bethlehem," he had to blink hard and fast for somehow his eyes would not behave.

But all the while he was so still and so quiet that no one observed him. A gaunt woman had settled down on one side of him and a fussy red-faced man on the other. They looked at him with some annoyance and surprise at first — and then forgot him.

When the programme ended, a big man with a smiling face began calling out names. And every time he called, some child hurried up the aisle and came back from the wonder tree with something hugged close. Little Magnús sat up, very stiff and very patient. When a child passed him he longed so to say how glad he was and perhaps to see the present. And the man called on and on. It was very peculiar, Magnús thought, how long the man was calling the children. And now the tree seemed to be stripped of so many, many bundles that had swung there so gaily before.

Then suddenly he came to himself with a shock. The man had stopped calling. There were no more children passing up the aisle. Then in one movement the congregation rose. It seemed to him the people all became one huge moving mass. And it rose, this mass of living people, and sang very loudly and discordantly, and then began pushing past him.

The thin woman wrapped her fur around her, picked up her purse, and left the seat beside him. The fussy little man found his overshoes, grunted in putting them on, sighed, and went also. But little Magnús sat on like stone — this was God's house and he had been good, but God had forgotten him. He bit his lips hard, fumbled for his muffler, and stumbled out.

With the passing of each slow hour his mother had become increasingly disturbed. Something urged her to action. She darted to the cupboard. There was little enough there, but she decided to make a few pancakes. She had grown very clever at making pancakes without eggs and they were not bad at all. When they were made, she rolled them carefully, cut them in two, and piled them in curious formations round the big plate. From an old trunk she drew an old tablecloth and spread it on the pine table. Then she removed the lamp chimney, shined it anew, and set the lamp in the centre of the table. Not knowing why, she hunted feverishly again in that old trunk and, miracle of miracles, found a little white candle and a bit of ribbon. She fastened a smart bow around the candle and then put it under the plate, waiting for Magnús. This done she sat down again listening for every sound.

A little past ten she caught at her breast as if to silence the beating of her heart. She flew to the door and flung it wide. It had begun to snow. Heavy gusts of wind carried the flakes in sweeping eddies. She was almost blinded as she ran out into the path. And there like a stray, black flake, he came, the little disillusioned one, sobbing aloud and fighting the wind. He almost fell at her feet.

"Oh mama, oh mama! And I was so good!"

She lifted him up high in her arms and carried him in. She hurried to the chair by the stove, and there with him on her lap drew off his shoes and his wet clothes; saying nothing, letting him cry his pitiful little cry; saying nothing, but thinking fast.

When he was wrapped warmly in a shawl, she took his face in her hands smiling at him brightly and said:

"So, my precious, you *did* get the best gift of all!"

His eyes widened, and he fought his tears. He was an imaginative child. Perhaps it had come to the house. How silly he had been!

"What, mama?"

She cuddled him close again and swung him around so that his feet might get the warmth from the fire.

"You remember the little Christ-child. You remember that when

He came to earth there was no room for Him. Only a little stall near the sheep."

"Yes, mama."

"And think, perhaps His mother, the blessed Mary, wept a little for sadness; it was not much for her baby, this stall. And then you remember how the king would have killed Him, the most blessed one. And they had to flee, those good parents. This, too, was sad, little Magnús, don't you think?"

"Yes, mama."

"And perhaps there were few joys for the little Jesus in the days to come in Galilee, and you remember all the sadness that followed this again. You remember the lonely Jesus in that garden one dark night, and that day before Pilate, and you remember the cross."

"Yes, mama."

Little Magnús was now ready to weep for the abused Jesus.

"And this Christmas, it is first a time of remembrance and then a time of joy, you know that, little one? And every year at Christmas time, the most blessed Lord comes down to earth again in the likeness of the child He once was, and He comes and stands behind the child He has found most worthy that year. And while He stands so, the shadow of His cross falls upon Him again as it did in the manger, and falls, too, upon His little chosen one. This is the *real* Christmas gift — this is God's favour."

"Oh, mama!" Magnús's eyes were bright with amazement. His mother swallowed painfully, smoothed the shawl about him, then holding him close, smiled her beautiful smile.

"And *this* is the gift you received, little Magnús."

"But, mama . . ."

"Think — weren't you unobserved? Did anyone see you. Did anyone speak to you? Or seek to detain you?"

"No, mama, but . . ."

"There then! Can't you see? It wasn't possible! It wasn't possible — they didn't see you, these people. You were over-shadowed. And it's ever so. Those that are favoured by the cross, they go alone walking with their Lord. Little joys aren't for them — they have the stars for company and the friendship of the angels. Come, my sweet, smile again. Aren't you proud to be so loved of your God?"

"Oh, mama!" Suddenly little Magnús flung his arms around her neck, kissing her passionately. "Oh, it's so beautiful! But how *did* you know it?"

She laughed happily, now much relieved, got up, and carried him to the table.

"Oh, perhaps it was whispered to me, who knows? And look! Here we have a party — isn't it gay?"

She stepped about briskly, pouring him out a little coffee and milk, then sat down beside him.

When Magnús lifted his plate and found the candle, tied so smartly with its red ribbon, he clapped his hands.

"Oh, let's light it, mama, and watch it burn while we eat."

"No, my precious, we'll light it when you're in bed, and it shall burn beside you till you're asleep. It's the Christmas candle, such as the children burned for the Christ-child in my dear country. And as you sleep I've no doubt that you'll dream — you, the little chosen one."

After he was in bed, watching the tiny flickering candle drowsily, he called his mother. She came toward him, tired-looking but satisfied, and bent above him. He wound his arms around her neck.

"Mama," he whispered, "do you think He was sorry I should have cried — that I didn't understand?"

She smiled down at him mistily.

"No, my beloved. I think above all else He would understand."

Just a little while the child gazed up at her earnestly, then he smiled contentedly.

"I guess the shadow fell on you too, mama, when you were little. That's why you always understand."

[1924]

When Blind Guides Lead

Springtime, with its throbbing bird-notes and shining showers, seemed destined to bring mental turmoil and distress to Martha Croyer — "Old Martha," as the villagers of Neah called her. Last year, this turmoil had amounted almost to anarchy; at any rate, she had awakened one fine morning vibrantly alive to the dullness of her lot, resentful and rebellious against every heretofore defended habit of a lifetime.

As banked fires burst into flame at the wind's fanning, so had the long hidden fires of ambition, hope, and little tender dreams leaped into riotous blaze before the storm of her mysteriously awakened discontent. She had looked back along the dull years and in the light of this inner blaze had found them meaningless and futile. In that terrifying moment she had realized the pathos of bartering the soul's birthright for daily bread.

Firm in her newborn independence, she had decided then and there to leave her self-satisfied husband to his well-filled barns and sleek cattle, to go her own way at last in search of the more satisfying things of the spirit. But no sooner was her mind adjusted to the intoxicating thought of freedom than a new and sombre development presented itself.

Her nearest neighbour and friend sickened and died, and in dying had enjoined upon Martha to take charge of her little daughter Carey. So, in one flash of springtime glory, Martha caught the long-lost gleam of youthful ardour and poignant desire, only to lose it again in the shadow of this overwhelming responsibility — yet in this very responsibility she was indeed to find a renewal of happiness.

Now another spring was pouring out its wine upon the dried old world, and once again Martha had awakened, disturbed and critical, doubtful this time of her right to the past year's happiness. Throughout the morning this distressing doubt pursued her; agitated and cross, she at last resorted to her knitting, a soothing occupation generally.

Old Martha knitted furiously, frowning above the half-turned sock; and the faster the needles flew, the deeper grew her frowning. When the bright blue ball of yarn slipped from the safety of her lap and rolled into the dusty stove corner, she did not trouble to reclaim it — other and more weighty matters preyed upon her mind.

"I declare, Carey's thinner if anything; seems to me her dresses hang more loosely round her little waist each mortal day. Land sakes, 'taint natural! Here it's another spring since the poor mite's mother up and died, and she still moping. 'Pears to me, Martha Croyer, you're just about a complete failure at this adoption business."

In the midst of this unpleasant soliloquy, Martha discovered she had dropped a stitch, which added to her disapproval of things in general and herself in particular. "A complete failure, that's what. . . . There was that poor dying woman with just one awful worry on her mind. 'Martha,' says she, 'take my Carey, you've no little ones and are well fixed. Take my little Carey and let her play — until life gets her like the rest of us. Make her happy, Martha, let her be young.' Sakes alive," groaned the good woman, "if these spirit worshippers are right, what's poor Tilly thinking of me now?"

These reflections proved too much for her; angrily she flung aside her knitting, glanced at the clock, and seeing how close upon noon it was, began to hurry up her dinner. Never had she banged the stove-lids more wrathfully nor stirred a boiled dinner with greater fury. Martha was not one to brook defeat easily, and she derived, therefore, a sort of pleasure from this abusive method; it was her way of proclaiming that strength still was hers and that she intended to make good use of it.

The old seven-day clock upon the wall chimed the half-hour and Martha, calmer now, stepped to the doorway facing out upon the lane. Yes, there she came, a small, desolate figure, treading carefully, avoiding the jolly brown pools that dotted the path. Somehow this extreme care irritated Martha. "Poor mite, she's afraid to dirty her boots," she thought. Disquieting visions came to her of wind-blown, marshy places where the dog-eared violets and the great golden cowslips beckoned to erring little feet; came also the companion memory of muddy boots before a glowing hearth and an exasperated mother. Still, somehow, the perfume of violet and wind-blown earth lingered uppermost. "Poor little mite," she whispered, and her eyes grew very soft. What was there for little Carey to remember? Greasy dishes, wailing babies, and Tilly's plaintively fretful voice — ah yes, and the endless ache of her tiny, young arms.

The little girl looked up, saw her benefactress, and waved a thin, white hand. "It's kind o' wet yet, Mis' Croyer," she announced gravely in her soft treble voice, as she wiped her feet carefully on the rag mat outside the door.

Knowledge of her own helplessness made Martha's voice some-what sharp: "Sakes alive, child, ain't I told you to stop 'misissing' me. 'Aunt Martha', that's what I ought to be if anything. There, there, that'll do, you're clean as a cat now; run in and sit by the fire. You'll find a picture paper on the kitchen shelf; your Uncle John's been to the post office this morning."

Quietly, obediently, the little girl did as she was bidden; but her fingers were listless as they moved from page to page of the rustling paper; and old Martha, who was watching her from the corner of her eyes, though she seemed intent upon other things, saw how her gaze idled away, straying to the sunny window. "If I could only see the insides of her head," thought old Martha, and with a sigh she asked:

"See anyone on the way from school?"

"No'm, leastwise no one particular."

"Your Uncle John met your pa to town this morning. 'Pears like his new wife has persuaded him to move down river."

Carey heard this in meek silence, but her eyes were more eloquent than words.

"The boys are going along," Martha resumed, "but Mrs. Parks at the feed store is going to keep the baby."

Then a smile, poignant and sweet, illuminated the listless pallor of Carey's delicate face. "Oh, Mis' Croyer, mayn't I go for the mail Saturday?"

Martha was dishing up suet pudding and fussily making room for it in the warming closet, thinking crossly that man's affection and memory were even less reliable than harvest weather, and hoping unsympathetically that this new wife of Matt's would make him toe the mark; so the beautiful eagerness in Carey's face escaped her.

"I don't calculate your Uncle John will be going to town, Saturday, leastwise not if it's good weather for seeding."

"Oh, Mis' Croyer, I meant could I walk? Really, truly, I used to when I was . . . I mean truly I can walk easy."

"Land sakes! You don't expect me to let a little mite like you traipse three miles to the post office? Why, what would people say?"

The little girl accepted this with her customary resignation, but the light went out of her little face, leaving it drooping and pale. Later, when Martha stepped out from her immaculate pantry with dishes and cups in hand, Carey offered timidly to help set the table.

"Now, child, sit where you are and enjoy yourself, time enough to help when you're older, or when I'm taken with a spell of something."

"But I'd *like* to do it," insisted the child desperately. "I'd like to do *something*, Mis' Croyer."

"Well, you can ring the bell for your Uncle John. Dinner's about done to a turn."

John was not the taciturn man he had been before what he termed his "awakening" — the death of Carey's mother had brought about his awakening. Yes, Tilly, that pathetic household drudge, who welcomed death rather than life if only little Carey might be spared a fate such as hers, had, with her dying, shaken all John's self-complacency and uprooted his life-long habits. Why, Tilly's husband was an upright man, an honest, hardworking man, careful of his animals and foresworn against intemperance and borrowing; yet such things were evidently of little worth to women.

To be sure, Tilly had been going downhill considerably the last few years, but wasn't that natural? Those had been her bad years with babies coming fast, each one adding to the already heavy burden. But thus it had ever been with women and doubtless ever would be. When he came to think of it, his own mother had shown similar signs of decay before the youngest children found their "weatherlegs," so to speak. Yet she had lived to wave him and Martha a gay farewell when they set off to that first far cabin in the hills.

That memory had made him smile then, and more often of late — powerful glib with her jokes she had been, that bent, old mother of his. What was it she had hurled after the newly wedded pair, that long-gone day? "Mind you keep a loose hand on the lines, Johnny. Horses love a bit of fling to their heads and so do women." Martha had laughed and cuddled close . . . strange how he had forgotten what a girl she was for laughter in those days. "A loose hand on the lines"! Would he ever be done marvelling that this jocund command should have come echoing down the years on that grief-stricken day of Tilly's death?

Tilly dying . . . the laughter gone from those twinkling eyes of Martha's . . . himself a dour, old man. What a morning of revelation that had been! Had anything more been needed to open his stubborn, old eyes — that is, anything more after Martha, the obedient wife of years, had openly rebelled and threatened to leave him — that more was added by Tilly's distraught husband. With all a reticent man's horror of emotional display, he had been forced to look upon Matt's helpless sorrow. Tilly, the buoyant, the beautiful — Tilly, the utterly beloved — so had he been forced to see the bedraggled woman whom he had known as only a dull and commonplace neighbour.

That day, John made up his mind to loosen the reins and give Martha her head. The thought that she had to all intents and purposes already taken the bit in her teeth never occurred to him nor dulled the ardour of his good intent. Yet, undoubtedly, this high resolve might have come to nothing had it not been for little Carey. Planting their old feet once again upon the high road of happiness might have been work to despair of, an effort doomed to perish of its own ludicrousness; but to nurse this wee sprig of femininity into happy adolescence appeared good and hopeful. In their desperate resolve to make the orphaned child happy, they themselves grew happy, so happy, in fact, that the incredulous truth of Carey's own depression was only now becoming apparent to them.

John, man-like, left the interpretation of childish vagaries to his wife. Such mysteries belong to a woman's sphere. How should he reflect that an old, childless woman had forfeited the key to ready understanding? He was pleased with himself, pleased with Martha, pleased with the child; this pleasure consumed his every thought. Had he not learned the ways of appreciation? Was he not become expert at ordering bonnets and gowns for his Martha and that even from catalogues? Yes, and did he not see to it that each feast-day found her freshly arrayed though she chided him for extravagance; and were there not shining new pots and pans in her pantry and a bright checkered linoleum on all the floors? Yes, and was he not all but decided upon buying an organ for his little adopted daughter, such a carved and shining organ as the minister had in his parlour? Upon some such reverie as this fell the sound of the dinner bell. Mellow and at peace with the world, John beamed at little Carey when he drew near the house.

"Well, well, little mouse, getting so you order my comings and goings, eh?"

She smiled a little flickering smile at his joke.

"Dinner's about done, Mis' Croyer says."

Despite his satisfaction, the child's listlessness disturbed him. She looked a bit peaked, did Carey. Well, young ones often contracted something or other . . . he remembered having the measles himself.

Over the meal both anxious guardians watched the child closely.

"'Pears to me she's not so pert as she might be," remarked John.

"I've been thinking to make a mess of sulphur and molasses," responded his wife. "I recollect how my own mother always had it on hand each spring. . . . You ain't feeling weakish nor hot, Carey?"

"No'm, Mis' Croyer, I'm right smart."

Nonetheless, she scarcely touched the pudding, at which Martha cast a significant glance toward her husband, who shook a sympathetic but mystified head.

When the decorous little girl had set off again to school and John was seated comfortably upon the doorstep to smoke a leisurely pipe before returning to the fields, they fell to talking.

"You don't calculate she's coming down sick, do you?"

"Well, no, but she's uncommon quiet. It's not natural for a child just turned nine to grieve this way."

"You think she's still taking on about her ma?"

"John Croyer! What else? The little mite just mopes and mopes. Does she ever play with them dolls we bought her? No. Does she ever skip and jump like a child at all, I ask?"

"She was always an uncommon quiet little thing, Mattie, shy as a whiffet."

"Shucks! Shy do you call it? Was she ever anything but a little old woman, trailing round them babies of Tilly's, and herself but a little one at best?"

This was unanswerable; yet something, a vague enough notion, stirred the depths of John's slow mind. . . . Carey never had known real childhood . . . why, that was it! She didn't know how to play!

"Mattie," he announced triumphantly. "I have it! She's got to be taught to play."

"Humph! You're right smart this day, John Croyer. Taught how, may I ask? Isn't the whole live-long day hers to play in? Aren't there books a-plenty with coloured pictures and such cluttering up her room, and dolls and dishes a-setting by like in a store window? What does she do with them? *Dust* them, John Croyer, and set them back in a neat row against the wall."

John scratched his unruly thatch, a sign of uncommon mental activity in him.

"I've noticed she sort of hankers after helping round. Perhaps she'd enjoy doing a little something."

"John Croyer! Are you insinuating for me to put that poor wee thing to work — me, who promised a dying woman to save her from just that! 'Already my Carey's a slave,' she said to me. John Croyer, 'already a slave and has had nothing . . .'."

"Now, now, woman, don't rile yourself. I reckon it was happiness Tilly wanted for her little girl, no matter how it's come by. And if sitting round idle don't make her happy, 'pears to me it's as plain as the nose on your face that you've taken the wrong way with her."

"Shucks!" said Martha. "I've a good mind to get right to town and buy that organ we talked of. But if you think any woman-child just naturally hankers to be messing round the house, you've got a lot to learn."

But John clung to his own ideas, vague though they were; this much at least was clear: Carey, possessed of her new freedom, seemed more miserable than formerly. Out of this astounding fact must come his enlightenment and solution. Throughout the day he sifted and weighed with diplomatic care each and every thought, with the result that he became even further estranged from Martha's point of view.

That night his confirmations were strengthened through a simple enough incident. Dusk had fallen; he was settled down for a comfortable doze by the fire with Carey, quiet as a mouse, sitting nearby reading her Cinderella, one of her few new favourites, when Martha, very much wrought up, dashed in from the chicken yard carrying something in her apron.

"Sakes alive! That crazy hen has up and stepped on this poor chick — after me paying two dollars a setting at that!"

"Oh, Mis' Croyer, let me have him, let me mind him! Please, please, Mis' Croyer. I can wrap him in wool, I'll make him a bed in my shoe-box."

Martha was fussily intent upon the chicken, feeling of its wings, its tiny chest, holding it over the warm stove; absently, somewhat shortly, as was her way, she answered:

"You don't want to be messing with the thing. Like as not it'll die anyhow."

But John had caught the quick gleam which for the moment lighted up the child's eyes; had noted, too, the swift and painful disappointment that followed.

"Let her have it, Martha."

Something in his tone brought Martha out of her absorption, and, glancing around in surprise, she, too, caught the quiver of those childish lips; consternation overwhelmed her. Why, Carey was fighting tears, and it was her doing! Hers, who desired laughter above all else from little Carey.

"Mercy me! Here, child, take it. After all, I've no time to putter around with it."

The little girl bounced to her feet, caught the tiny chicken to her lonely little heart, and flew up the stairs.

"Oh, I've such a nice piece of cotton wool that came with my bracelet, and I've got my shoe-box all empty. I'll be down in a minute!"

"Well, don't that beat all!" exclaimed Martha helplessly.

"Mmm, I'm thinking," said John, "thinking."

Next morning, Carey actually skipped down the stairs. Martha had never seen her so pretty; the stiff blue frills of her frock cascaded about her; she lent them grace despite their heavy starch. A little airy thing she seemed, a little happy elfin, dancing down the old stairway in a burst of morning gladness.

"Oh, how is he, how is he this morning?" she shrilled before her eager feet had reached the bottom step.

"He who? Oh, the chicken. He's dead, as I expected," said Martha and hurried to fix Carey's porridge just right.

All that airy grace oozed away from little Carey, leaving her an ordinary pale little girl in a much too frilly frock. According to habit, she made no outcry, one thin little hand fluttering up to her lips, her one betraying sign of pained emotion.

To John, who from his seat at the breakfast table had observed this little scene, that action was somehow more pitiful than tears. His old heart ached for her, so pathetic she was, so resignedly brave, so small; his eyes were not quite clear as he followed her saddened progress to the table. Why, by all the shining stars, he had it at last! Carey was pining away for want of something to love, to fuss over, bless her dear little heart. What blind idiots they had been!

So much a bolt from the blue was this happy thought that he could scarcely restrain himself from shouting, but guile, which is surely an inheritance from Eden, came to his rescue.

"Carey, my little mouse," he cried, "I'm real ashamed to ask it, but you see I'm in a heap of trouble, and I can't imagine who's to help me if not you."

Those patient brown eyes of hers opened wide and into their dullness leapt that ready gleam of hope; her small spiritual face turned toward him in its expectancy like a thirsty flower.

"Yes, miss," he ran on with unaccustomed glibness, "a heap of trouble, that's what. Why, that old sow, Maggie, has up and deserted one of the finest little pigs I ever saw."

"Why John . . ." Martha began, but something fierce in his encountering glance silenced her.

"That little pig is about as lonesome and bad off as can be — shouldn't wonder but what he'd up and die on my hands unless you can tend him."

Carey shot from her chair like a bolt. "Uncle John!" she cried, flying to his side, "where is he? Just you give him to me. I can feed him with a string and a bottle . . . I know how to do . . . Oh, be quick . . . and Uncle John, couldn't you get a nipple next time you're in town?"

He did some rapid planning on the way to the barn with Carey hard at his heels. Once there, he whispered cautiously:

"You just wait outside a bit, Carey. Maggie's in a bad mood. She's liable to desert the whole family if she gets excited."

Carey found it easy to obey, and with a sigh of relief John skipped into the barn, robbed a contented and conscientious mother of her very contented offspring, and returned with it to Carey.

The pig was a lusty little pig and voiced its displeasure at this indignity vociferously.

"Oh, oh, the poor little dear. Listen how he cries, uncle! He must be about starved. Oh, hurry, hurry! Get a bottle. I'll just ask Mis' — Aunt Martha for some warm milk."

John watched the flying little figure ahead of him through a mist of tears. Wee tender one, wee tender little woman-thing! Here he brushed the veil of an age-old mystery, not yet discerning even so much as poor mortal may. But that bottle — he must be on hand with that bottle!

Fussing with her fractious charge made Carey late for school, but Martha, having drawn closer to realities, decided that this day, being Friday, might with little loss be crossed from the calendar of school days.

"I'm so glad," sighed Carey, with shining eyes. "He'll get used to me by Monday, and he's so restless now. Oh Aunt Martha, I think he's just the sweetest pig!"

A little later John made some excuse to go to the house. There was an air of victory about him as he entered, and his eyes twinkled as he looked at Martha.

"Well, old lady," said he.

Then he heard a piping little voice singing, and his banter faded into tenderness. Together they stole to the window at the sunny side of the house. Just without sat little Carey, the sunlight making ripples of gold in her auburn hair and sheer beauty of her radiant little face; her arms cradled the now resigned little pig, and she was singing in that sweet treble voice from a full heart, singing as she had so often sung to her little brothers.

Down Martha's kind old face the tears slid unheeded. John cleared his throat huskily; and both of them learned in this pregnant moment a great and eternal truth: Love, once having found its usefulness, may not live idle.

For a moment Martha's hand found her husband's and their fingers interlocked. Then she chuckled softly. "Well, Johnny, I'll have to admit that it's your score this time."

[1925]

202

The Alabaster Box

Bianca counted her blessings before the Lord: a hundred-weight of flour, sugar, salt, tea, ten gills of blackstrap, potatoes in a barrel, and a flitch of fat bacon. Enough and more to last throughout the winter.

So many blessings! And still no mention made of the Manitoba spruce piled roof high in the crippled shed that clung to the sagging shoulder of her tar-papered shanty. Or, best of all, the alabaster box hidden at the feet of the little dust-covered Madonna that through the trying years had smiled upon her devotions.

"Hail Mary; full of grace! The Lord is with thee — "Think of it, potatoes and bacon and wood enough for the winter. . . . "Blessed art thou among women — " No need to trouble about felt boots. . . . Praise God she had gone down the river, folks welcomed a pedlar there — "Holy Mary . . . full of grace — "No, no, so many blessings were confusing the order of her prayers! What was she saying, the Salutation or the Angelus? "And the word was made flesh." . . . Something wrong there. Well, no matter, her heart beat high and true with gratitude.

Her devotions ended, Bianca rose from her stiff old knees in luxurious slowness, grunting and blowing to her soul's comfort. Ah, it was good, this leisurely lifting of a worn, old body! Twenty years with the pack took the spring from the knees and pride from the back, but never on any account must an old pedlar groan like a camel before the good customers! Now, however, thanks to the alabaster box, she might wheeze and sigh and rise as slowly as she pleased.

"*Sì, sì,* Garibaldi, you shall have your suet and a crust," she consoled the grey cat mewing round her feet. "Patience, patience!"

Later, while she sipped black tea, rocking peacefully before the frugal fire, and Garibaldi resumed his meditations, Bianca gave way to the luxury of dreams.

All her life she had wanted leisure to dream — as a girl in the olive orchards of her lovely Italy where soft, blue skies and warm suns tempted, but there was bread to be got and a mother always ailing. . . . "The getting of bread, Garibaldi, gives little time for dreams." Still, with the coming of Piedro — Piedro, the persuasive lover — bread had mattered less and dreams more than all. Bianca shrugged, baring broken teeth in a rueful smile. "Never doubt it, Garibaldi, lovers make short work of dreams. Poof! Bang! Like the slamming of a shutter on a sunlit window. *Si*, but not for that we weep, but for the little ones all passing like the roses with never a day to give to their remembering."

Bianca refilled her cup absently, a thousand long-forgotten things flooding to confusion her tired mind and heart. What was lost in Italy she had thought to see reborn in America. *Si*, at sight of those broad, yellow Canadian prairies she had dared to dwell again on dreams. . . . Alas, twenty years with the pack through the rains of summer and the snows of winter lay between that day and this.

Twenty years of toilsome tramping and slavish pleasantry to contemptuous people. "The pedlar? The pedlar? Send her away, we'll have none of her truck!" Smiling, scraping, making pretty speeches to impertinent children (never a one like her wee, dead Mercedes), for to live one must eat. "Ten cents for a roll of tape? You old thief, it's worth no more than five! Five eh? I thought so! Well, I'll take it for five!" Day in, day out, the same soul-wearing procedure. Bowing, scraping, the pack edged forward temptingly. "The pedlar again? Oh, slam the door, it's much too cold for argument!"

Bianca ran fond eyes over the old, red pack still lying in the corner. Ah, she could smile now, could Bianca. Come sleet tomorrow, thaw, cold wind, or driving snow, it mattered little. Like the ladies in the houses at whose back steps she had been scraping these many years she'd sit and watch the weather in vast, unruffled content.

"*Si*, Garibaldi, with two hundred and thirty-seven dollars and fifty cents in the alabaster box no need to fear the weather."

Just the same she hoped tomorrow would be fine. There was her dear *bambino* Mary-bell Jetta to visit. Mother of Goodness, hold her heart in keeping! How long was it now since that blessed child had entered into her barren life to make it sweet with human love once more? Five years? Six years? "Garibaldi, can you believe, it is eight years! Eight years come springtime! *Si*, *penseroso* that you are, Garibaldi, you can understand the joy of getting a friend."

It was very wet that day, eight years ago, when at dusk she had entered the shop of Olse Jetta, the shoemaker, a cold, wet day with a hard wind blowing from the sullen waters of the Red River — a black day. Black, too, and very still, and smelling of much leather, the shop of Olse Jetta, the shoemaker. A pit of darkness, save where, by the boot lasts, a tall child, grave-eyed, stood bravely smiling. "Come in madam. Oh, you're wet! You're cold! Quick, you must dry yourself by the fire! This chair, please, madam, it's not so hard to rise from as the other." True, for that other had no seat and but three legs to stand on.

"The shoemaker?"

"He'll be back soon. Grandfather needs the air. A little walk in the evening does him good."

"My shoes, *bambino*."

"Let me see them, lady. Soaked through and through! Oh, how lucky Grandfather is away; now you can dry them while you wait."

That wait! Would she ever forget it? Mary-bell Jetta, smiling her sad, brave smile as she fed the fire stick by stick from a meagre pile in the corner, talking of ships and the sea where they had once lived, and the dear mother who had died on the passage to Canada. Meanwhile the shadows deepened, and the grey eyes of Mary-bell deepened too, and a strange expression, half dread, half pity, gave a look of age to her pale little face.

Bianca knew men. "He's late, the grandfather? Perhaps it's better that I should come again tomorrow?"

"Dear madam, kind madam! It's warm here, and you're tired. Oh, I know, we'll make tea!"

"God's pity! Garibaldi, do you hear what I tell you? 'We'll make tea,' and the little can empty of all but a few sweepings. The bread-box worse and the wood fast vanishing."

"Listen, now." Bianca struck an attitude, pitching her voice to a masculine growl: "'Grow old with me' . . . fool, fool, who does not! 'the best is yet to be!' . . . Olse Jetta enters, bowing, smiling, drunk as a lord and with a lordly manner: 'A thousand pardons, madam, to keep you waiting. A thousand more to keep you yet awhile.'"

Ah, Bianca had not known a Piedro for nothing! That once, the pennies went their proper channel. . . . Olse Jetta slept and Bianca had earned a friend.

The morrow was kind. Cold, it is true, but bright, as only a prairie day can be bright, with a shine and a glitter and a leap of joy about it. But at the shop of Olse Jetta no joyous voice cried greetings, no light step sped to meet her.

"Mary-bell, *bambino*! What's this? You're sick? You're suffering, my child? Mary-bell Jetta! What has befallen you, jewel of my heart?"

Close, close to the bereaved breast of Bianca, the young girl, slim as a reed, fair as the Holy Madonna, burrowed her tear-stained face. "That little pain we laughed at in the foot, you remember? It grew and grew and grew. . . ."

Shudders, anguished and terrible, rent the young frame, and entered like a dart in the soul of Bianca. "There is something wrong with the foot? A doctor has seen it? A good doctor from the hospital?"

"Yesterday, Mother Bianca. That's why you find me such a coward. Ah, how shall I bear it! Something is wrong with the ligaments. I cannot walk. . . . I shall never walk again."

Never walk? Mary-bell Jetta, at the dawn of womanhood, the mother-heart like a warm bird in her bosom, never to walk again? No, no, God were not in his heaven if feet so eager to serve might run no longer on missions of mercy!

Unbelievably tender, the voice of Bianca: "My foolish *bambino*, one doctor is not all! There is a way. *Sí*, you'll yet teach that school in the country, where the green runs out to meet the big sky. *Sí, sí*, and play at tag with a dozen grandchildren. Not walk? To say it is a blasphemy!"

Three hundred *Aves* Bianca said to the good Saint Anne for the healing of Mary-bell Jetta, the Protestant. And still the weeks dragged on with never a sign of improvement. Then Bianca decided to take matters into her own hands. Bundled in her old mackintosh, last year's felts on her tired feet, she trudged through the December snow to interview that doctor who, she suspected, never told Mary-bell the half of truth.

But Dr. Finn was brusque and honest. "Of course, she may get better, but it requires skilful surgery."

Bianca's shrewd eyes narrowed just a little, and a look Piedro once had feared swept across her weather-beaten countenance: "That skill, it comes not by charity? It takes money?"

"I'm afraid it does, my good woman. Though, of course, in a case like this we'd do our best . . ."

"How much?"

Ah, Bianca could snap that query effectively! "How much, Mr. Doctor? *Sí*, that best, how much?"

"Covering precious time only, time that another patient might be needing, you understand, I should say not over two hundred dollars."

Bianca sat stunned. It must be very terrible that foot of Mary-bell Jetta's to take so much mending. Two hundred dollars! . . . Two hundred dollars! . . . Hard earned — heart wrung. . . . Two hundred . . .

"Mother of Sorrows! It'll take long? Be very dreadful, that two-hundred-dollar doctoring?"

The question, scarcely more than a whisper, annoyed the celebrated surgeon. The pity of it, he had really made a generous offer. "Not at all. Skill, not time, my good woman, that's the thing. An hour, scarcely more, and your young friend walks again as well as ever."

All the way home the strangeness of it droned in her consciousness like an angry wasp. An hour! One little hour! Not enough time to sell ten shoe strings. Just one hour for two hundred dollars! Five years, six years — hands crooked like claws with the cold, feet like lead, and the back one ache of protest, *that* made two hundred dollars for Bianca the pedlar. Skill, not time . . . Mercy of God! Who gave that skill? . . . But the blessed *bambino*, Mary-bell Jetta, *might* walk again.

That night Bianca took down the pack from its roost in the shed, a very ingenious pack, made from a round piece of red oilcloth with brass curtain rings tacked round the top. "Old one," she said, pulling the string sharply, setting the rings jingling together, "tomorrow, give good weather, tinsel, and red paper, and holly ribbon sells without haggling."

A week later, on the twentieth of December to be exact, Bianca knocked at the door of the Padre Taddeo's little house just behind the humble church precariously perched in the crook of the river. The Padre was very old, not so sharp of hearing; and his soutane quite as rusty and mud-spattered round the hem as Bianca's shabby garments. They peered at each other, those two, grown old in service, through the gloom of late twilight. The good Padre shook his head slowly as he smiled his recognition.

"Daughter, wasn't it you who prayed to be delivered from the pack? And here you are again, tempting the weak and the foolish!"

"*Sí, sí*, Padre Taddeo. But that pack he cries for the road. Like a lover who cries. To deny is impossible."

"Daughter, there is something else, something real. Bianca Corella, what are you up to now?"

Like a child confessing fault, Bianca told her story in tumbled, incoherent sentences. Quick tears and passionate prayers at first rendered much of it unintelligible and utterly confusing to the old Padre. But at last he understood the whole of it.

"This money, which is your all, you intend for the doctor? I'm to keep it, while you go down river to catch a death of rheumatism? I'm to pay the great doctor the whole of your savings?"

"*Sí, sí*, Padre. So the little Mary-bell wakes on Christmas finding the foot like the good God made it."

"It's madness. Bianca *mio*, you're much too old for the pack this weather. You say there is food and fuel till springtime. You said nothing of rent. A roof costs something?"

Bianca shrugged. "Ten dollars the month since the new shingles. But down river folks welcome a pedlar . . ."

"Think carefully," the priest counselled. "It's not money alone you're giving, but rest and freedom, the much needed peace for the body's healing."

Bianca forbore to answer. He would understand by and by, the old Padre, understand and approve.

Up from the depths of the pack came the alabaster box never before out of the keeping of good Saint Anne. Clumsily, with a nervous clatter, she laid the precious thing on the stand between them, a mist of happy tears dimming her sharp, old eyes. Gnarled, age-withered, unspeakably weary, but with the light of ineffable joy, soft as a lover's caress, on her wrinkled face, she stood there gazing down upon it. Her precious alabaster box of sweet offering! Her gift, *per conto. Sí, con amore*!

Prudent words, prompted by pity for this waste of needed substance, sprang to the Padre's lips never to be uttered. Bianca the pedlar, renouncing with joy her last fond dream, was lifted high above his pity. Humbled before the glory in her face, Padre Taddeo himself saw a great light: "There came unto Him a woman having an alabaster box of very precious ointment and poured it on His head as He sat at meat . . . and they had indignation saying, to what purpose is this waste . . ."

"My dear daughter," he said at last, too wise, now, for other counsel, "what you wish shall be done. Mary-bell Jetta, God willing, wakes with joy on Christmas morning."

Aye, joy ineffable, the joy of Christmas angels! So thought the Padre when, the miracle over, Mary-bell smiled into his face, her eyes clear wells of love and happy dreams.

"Bianca? My Bianca? Why is she not here? She must come. Unless it's too cold. She must come, my mother Bianca, to see me laugh and hear me tell about the little school we shall keep together."

But down by the old Red River, where a small tar-papered shack crouches before the wind, a little group of women stood gathered. Some whispered. Some wept. Some talked indifferently. The old Padre, walking slowly, grey head bent, heard, before he saw them:

"Dead! And not a soul with her. No, just a cat curled against her breast."

"Yes, for several hours. It's heart failure they say."

"What? At the feet of her patron saint? Ah, poor deluded woman!"

"Oh, very old. Eighty, if a day."

"Well, she should have known better than try the roads this weather. What was she, Italian?"

"Heart failure, eh?"

"Yes, through exhaustion."

"Exhaustion? Bianca? Why, only last week she sold me Christmas candles as shrewdly as you please!"

Old Age! Exhaustion! Heart failure! Ah, no! Padre Taddeo, entering humbly that house of high devotion, knew better. The good God had called Bianca from loneliness and toil to that exceeding peace awaiting the bearers of alabaster boxes spilled for love's sake.

[1927]